MOONSHINE!

MOONSHINE!

**Recipes • Tall Tales • Drinking Songs • Historical Stuff
Knee Slappers • How to Make It • How to Drink It
Pleasin' the Law • Recoverin' the Next Day**

by Matthew B. Rowley

LARK BOOKS

A Division of
Sterling Publishing Co., Inc.
New York

EDITOR:
Terry Krautwurst

ART DIRECTOR:
Kristi Pfeffer

COVER DESIGNER:
Suzie Millions

EDITORIAL ASSISTANCE:
Delores Gosnell
Rebecca Guthrie
Rosemary Kast
Nathalie Mornu

ASSOCIATE ART DIRECTOR:
Shannon Yokeley

ART PRODUCTION ASSISTANCE:
Jeff Hamilton
Bradley Norris
Lance Wille

ILLUSTRATORS:
Jason Krekel (humorous illustrations)
Orrin Lundgren (technical drawings)
Olivier Rollin (how-to illustrations)

EDITORIAL INTERN:
Sue Stigleman

PHOTOGRAPHY:
Steve Mann

Publisher's Note

This book is intended as an informational source on the subject of distilling alcohol, a practice that, without proper compliance with national and local government regulations, is against the law in many countries, including the United States and Canada. The author and publishers of this book urge you to determine and follow the letter of your nation's laws in this regard. The author and publishers will not be held responsible for any claims, damages, or losses that may result from using information in this book in any way that is noncompliant with any and all applicable regulations.

Library of Congress Cataloging-in-Publication Data

Rowley, Matthew B.
  Moonshine! : recipes, tall tales, drinking songs, historical stuff, knee slappers, how to make it, how to drink it, pleasin' the law, recoverin' the next day / by Matthew B. Rowley.-- 1st ed.
    p. cm.
  Includes bibliographical references and index.
  ISBN-13: 978-1-57990-648-1 (pbk.)
  ISBN-10: 1-57990-648-6 (pbk.)
 1. Liquors. 2. Whiskey. 3. Distilling, Illicit--Anecdotes. I. Title.
TP597.R69 2006
641.8'74--dc22

                        2005034042

10 9 8 7 6 5 4 3 2 1

First Edition

Published by Lark Books, A Division of
Sterling Publishing Co., Inc.
387 Park Avenue South, New York, N.Y. 10016

Distributed in Canada by Sterling Publishing,
c/o Canadian Manda Group, 165 Dufferin Street
Toronto, Ontario, Canada M6K 3H6

Distributed in the United Kingdom by GMC Distribution Services,
Castle Place, 166 High Street, Lewes, East Sussex, England BN7 1XU

Distributed in Australia by Capricorn Link (Australia) Pty Ltd.,
P.O. Box 704, Windsor, NSW 2756 Australia

If you have questions or comments about this book, please contact:
Lark Books
67 Broadway
Asheville, NC 28801
(828) 253-0467

Manufactured in China

ISBN 13: 978-1-57990-648-1
ISBN 10: 1-57990-648-6

For information about custom editions, special sales, premium and corporate purchases, please contact Sterling Special Sales Department at 800-805-5489 or specialsales@sterlingpub.com.

Table of Contents

Introduction

Wine, I can understand, and brewing one's own beer has long been the purview of reasonable people —but you? You want to make *whiskey*? A wellspring of refined spirits from the world's larder awaits you in any halfway decent liquor store. Why bring on the consternation of making your own?

If answers flood your mind almost as soon as you ask yourself that question, rest assured that you are not alone in your mad notions. Home-made whiskeys and brandies are making a come-back. Some new distillers want to get in touch with their heritage. Others thrive on the technical challenges of making better whiskeys and more efficient stills. A good number derive deep satisfaction from making spirits unlikely to show up on local liquor store shelves, or live nowhere near such stores. A lot simply can't stomach the high cost of drinking; they make to save money. Occasionally, a lateral-thinking tinkerer with a glut of fruit just gets to musing.

Is whiskey-making hard? Not really. If you can make cornbread, you can make corn beer. Corn beer is halfway—some wags might say *kissin' cousin*—to corn whiskey. Now, admittedly, not everyone's cornbread is good; some is burnt, some doesn't rise, some is so dry you choke it down only as an exercise in good manners. It takes practice and, likely, some failures before you come up with something you'd want to share. Liquor's no different. Making whiskey or brandy is not the least bit difficult: making something you'd want to drink ... well, that may take some practice. Don't despair if you flub a few batches. Keep careful notes and try again: you will get it right.

This book is for the utter novice distiller, for the curious first-timer who maybe has never made even beer before—or who, having made beer and wine for years, wants to push an old hobby in new directions. The solid yet flexible instructions and recipes are specifically adapted for beginners. If you already brew beer, many of the ingredients, techniques, and equipment here are old friends. If not, don't worry; the descriptions and explanations are simple and straightforward. Small-batch distilling is a fantastic hobby. Here, you'll learn the basics of doing it safely.

For experienced distillers, whom I hope will find some new tidbits to supplement their existing expertise, I've dug up some history, a look at current trends, some new recipes, and an adaptable basic still design. Finally, for those of you who are drawn to the subject and culture of moonshining but aren't interested in making your own, I hope you will enjoy the stories—and I encourage you to try some of the mixed drinks, macerations, and other nondistilling recipes in this book (see pages 128-153). Don't worry if you don't have any genuine moonshine; for those recipes, commercial liquors make reasonable substitutes when none of the hand-cranked variety is around.

Distillers may want to call me to task for gaps they notice, things I don't mention or that are essential to how they themselves make liquor. I know, I know. An exhaustive treatise on moonshining and small-batch distilling would run into a dozen volumes—see the bibliography for a taste. No, this is a comprehensive beginner's introduction. I am not presenting *the* way to distill small-batch spirits, because there is no one way. The methods, materials and equipment here are what work for some distillers as they pursue their craft. They may or may not be the perfect match for you, but they will form a solid framework upon which to build your personal distilling style.

Bottoms up! It's time to get started.

Be Legal!

I'm not going to come at you with a disingenuous wink-wink approach of instructing you how to make moonshine, and then turn around and claim that such information is strictly educational and that you would *never* make your own liquor because that would be illegal. I *want* you to make liquor—imagine the day when small distilleries are as common as brewpubs, churning out regional recipes and forgotten favorites—but just as important, it's up to you to make sure you do it legally. Right now, the United States government strictly controls distilling, but it has procedures in place for applying for permits. State and local government regulations also must be met. Although time and expense certainly are involved, it is possible for you to distill alcohol legally. See the "Moonshine and the Law" section starting on page 51 for more details.

CHAPTER 1

A Wet Goods PRIMER

There was a time not long ago when a person interested in learning the craft of distilling spirits usually did so at the side of an established moonshiner, clandestinely helping to tote bags of sugar or sprouted corn to the still site, minding boiler fires, or filling jugs with the potent product. A working knowledge of the basics and the actual process of making liquor were acquired hands-on.

These days, such opportunities are fewer and further between, and probably not advisable. This book is intended to be the next best thing to an on-the-job apprenticeship. The bulk of it is devoted to the step-by-step how-to of making moonshine. But first, it's important to establish some fundamentals. What exactly is moonshine? How, in general, is it made? Where is it made? And, no less important, how do you drink it?

What Is Moonshine?

White lightning, popskull, mountain dew, wet goods—call it what you will, it's all *moonshine*. But what exactly does that word describe?

The word moonshine can encompass a wide range of meanings, depending on who's talking. Some people—economists, mostly—label any illegally or illicitly produced or sold alcoholic beverage as moonshine. This intellectual construct includes not only illegal whiskey but also beer, wine, ale, cordials, and basically every other kind of homemade hooch the world over.

In the American idiom, the term is not quite so all-encompassing. *Moonshine* refers to illicitly distilled liquor—illicit because the distilleries are unregistered, contrary to the law, and the liquor untaxed, also contrary to the law. Moonshine, typically, is whiskey made illicitly for sale, but few begrudge illicit gin, vodka, rum, or brandies the title, too—and in fact, that's the broad sense in which we use the term in this book. If it's liquor made in secret and outside the law, it's moonshine. And it's the *moonshiner*, of course, who does the making.

Although spoken usage is undoubtedly older, the earliest written reference to moonshine is in Grose's 1785 *Dictionary of the Vulgar Tongue*, an English publication describing it as "white brandy

"Moonshine" or "Artisan Liquor"?

Among modern distillers, "moonshine" conjures ghosts from distilling's tarnished past that suggest, at best, a crude sugar-bred stepcousin to the handcrafted liquors made from wholesome ingredients by skilled do-it-yourself distillers.

Well. There's no denying that distilled spirits can and do run the gamut from toxic to ambrosial (see "Drinking Moonshine," page 15). Likewise, there is no denying that many of today's talented distillers, and the extraordinary spirits they produce, embody the very concept of "artisan."

Regardless of where they lie on the hooch-to-honeysuckle spectrum, in these pages the word "moonshine" respectfully represents all homemade spirits.

> **He is called moonshiner because it is supposed that he engages in his illicit traffic on moonlight nights when there is enough light to make work easy and enough darkness to make him secure.**
>
> John C. Campbell,
> *The Southern Highlander and His Homeland*, 1921

They call them moonshiners. An engraving from an 1867 edition of *Harper's Weekly* reflects the historical meaning of moonshining: illicit alcohol production carried out under cover of night.

smuggled on the coasts of Kent and Sussex, and the gin in the north of Yorkshire" at night to avoid detection. The term found fertile ground in America, where patriotic smugglers eluded British naval blockades to transfer valuable goods into and out of the fledgling American colonies. In some areas, non-tax-paid liquor is still known as *blockade whiskey.*

Bootlegging, a related endeavor, refers to *selling* rather than making spirits illegally. A bootlegger may sell moonshine or legal spirits under illegal circumstances, say in "dry" communities where liquor of any kind is prohibited or on days when it is not permitted. Some moonshiners operating in small, local markets may also bootleg, but the two terms are generally considered separate activities.

Later in this book, I'll explain how to distill spirits in detail, step by step. But for now, let's just take a look at the basics.

Oh, they call it that old mountain dew,

And them that refuse it are few,

I'll hush up my mug,

If you'll fill up my jug,

With that good old mountain dew.

"Mountain Dew," lyrics and
music by Bascom Lamar Lunsford/Lulu Belle
and Scott Wiseman, 1973

Moonshine Slang

Over the centuries, humankind has invented a lengthy lexicon of circumlocutions that reflect moonshine's unique effects, animal-like attributes, origins, economics, mode of manufacture, and other properties. Here's a sampling, arranged by likely etymological category.

EFFECTS

Block and tackle
Busthead
Bustskull
Conversation fluid
Forty rods
Popskull
Rotgut
Skull cracker
Skullbender
 'splo (short for explosion)
Stagger soup
Stingo
Tangleleg
Thump whiskey
Tongue oil
Tonsil varnish

CRITTERS

Bug juice
Bumblebee whiskey
Cat daddy
Monkey rum (made with molasses)
Mule
Mule kick
Old horsey
Panther's breath
Snakehead whiskey
Squirrel whiskey
Sweet spirit of cats-a-fighting
Tarantula juice
Tiger's milk
Tiger's sweat
White mare's milk
Wildcat

ORIGINS

Alley bourbon
Brigham Young whiskey
Deep shaft
Field whiskey
Hillbilly pop
Stump
Stump hole whiskey
Taos lightning

INGREDIENTS

Buckeye whiskey
Corn
Corn liquor (or likker)
Corn squeezin's
Sugar whiskey
Sugarhead whiskey

METHODS

Blockade whiskey
Bootleg
Radiator whiskey
Split brandy

WATERS

Cool water
Firewater
Mountain dew

LIGHTS AND COLORS

Blue John
Moonshine
Red dynamite
Red essence
Red eye
'shine
White lightning
White liquor

JUICE

Joy juice
Jungle juice
Kickapoo joy juice
Ruckus juice
Scamper juice
Tantrum juice

HOUSEHOLD SUPPLIES

Lamp oil
Wet goods

How Moonshine Is Made (The Short Version)

Making moonshine is surprisingly simple—and also surprisingly complex, depending on how far you decide to take the journey from basic craft cookery to artistic alchemy, the other end of the spectrum.

ESSENTIAL INGREDIENTS

To make moonshine, you need 1) water, 2) yeast, and 3) some sort of sugar-yielding organic material: grain (such as corn or barley) for whiskeys, fruit for brandies, and/or sugar itself (such as molasses or refined sugar).

In the case of grains for making whiskey, you'll also need malt, which is grain that first has been partially sprouted to make its starches available for conversion to sugars, and then ground. You can buy malt, or make your own.

The classic American moonshine is pure corn liquor, made from maize. But throughout the colonial era, nearly every native grain and fruit could be—and frequently was—purified in a still's belly. Farmers and householders considered whiskey making a God-given right, as pragmatic as curing hams, putting up preserves, or growing corn. Whether one ground that corn or distilled it was a matter of personal choice and local economics.

These days, the most common moonshine contains little corn. For those who make sellin' whiskey, plain white table sugar is the lifeblood of the industry. Sugar is cheap; plentiful; and available coast to coast by the pound, pallet, or railcar. It yields more alcohol per pound than corn, and ferments faster and more completely. Some distillers add corn in small portions to flavor the rough product. This is the standard, quick moonshine a casual buyer is likely to find. As one moonshiner put it, "You add the sugar to make your alcohol, and you add your corn to make it taste good."

Home distillers, along with the occasional traditionalist moonshiner making for a small local market of friends and neighbors, are more likely to make corn whiskey with nothing but corn, water, malt, and yeast. Rather than the cattle feed or straight sugar used by organized moonshine syndicates, they are also more likely to use wholesome grains as well as fresh fruits, such as apples and peaches. Because home distillers tend to drink their own product rather than sell it, they care deeply about what goes into the pot.

> **Let me tell you, suh, there's only one likker that's properly qualified to caress a gentleman's palette in the way a gentleman's palette deserves to be caressed; and that's red likker—the true and uncontaminated fruitage of the perfect corn ...**
>
> Irvin S. Cobb, *Red Likker*

THE PROCESS

Using these basic ingredients (as well as any additional elements a particular recipe may call for), you make spirits via a two-step procedure: first you *ferment* the ingredients, and then you *distill* the alcohol produced by those fermented ingredients.

Fermentation is a natural chemical process that breaks down organic compounds. If you've ever enjoyed yogurt, sauerkraut, Korean kimchee, sourdough bread, Scotch whisky, champagne vinegar, pickle relish, or aged cheese, you've wallowed in the pleasures of a vigorous ferment of one sort or another. In this book, we're interested only in one kind: alcoholic fermentation, in which yeast converts sugars into carbon dioxide gas (CO_2) and, more important for our purposes, alcohol—specifically, ethyl alcohol, or *ethanol* (C_2H_5OH).

Distillation is the process of extracting that alcohol by heating the fermented ingredients (known as the *mash*, wash, or *beer*) until the alcohol, which boils at a lower temperature than water does, evaporates, rises as steam, and wafts to a separate, cooled container where it condenses back to a liquid, leaving behind much of the water.

Logically enough, you distill alcohol in a *still*. There are several different types and many variations thereof, as explained in chapter 5. For our purposes here, we're showing a traditional pot still setup. Here's a simplified version of how it works:

1. The fermented mash is placed in the still's primary *boiler* and is gradually heated to a temperature of about 174°F (79°C).

2. The alcohol evaporates and rises as steam to the *head*, *helm*, or *cap* of the still.

3. The vapors waft through the still's *arm* and into a condenser, in this case a *worm*, a coiled pipe that spirals around inside the *flake stand*, or *worm box*. The flake stand is a container—usually a bucket, box, or barrel—through which cold water is constantly circulated.

4. The circulating water cools the ethanol vapors inside the worm, causing them to condense back to a liquid. The distilled spirits flow from the flake stand out the end of the worm and are collected in containers.

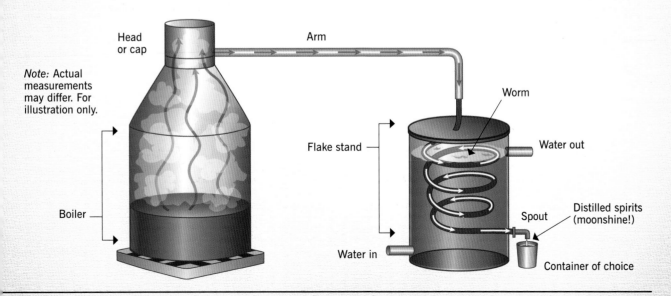

Head or cap

Arm

Note: Actual measurements may differ. For illustration only.

Worm

Flake stand

Water out

Boiler

Water in

Spout

Distilled spirits (moonshine!)

Container of choice

Bare-bones still. This confiscated still, photographed in the 1920s at the U.S. Treasury Department, is minus its flake stand and is unlikely to have been fired in actual use by a Bunsen burner, but the basic components of a traditional pot still are there: boiler, head, arm, and worm.

That's the short and considerably simplified version, intended only to demonstrate the basic principles of distillation. The actual process of producing potable moonshine is more complex and relies as much on the distiller's skill, judgment, and instinct as on the equipment itself.

For instance, because the spirits exiting from the first *run* through a pot still also contain varying amounts of disagreeable (harsh, hangover-causing, or even dangerous) impurities, depending on the stage of the distillation, a distiller must be able to discern which portions to draw off and discard, and which to keep. Then, too, even the "good" spirits produced by the first run, called *low wines*, usually benefit from a second run, to further re-

move impurities and increase the ethanol content. A third distillation can produce even smoother spirits. On the other hand, too many distillations can diminish or completely destroy an earlier run's flavor and character.

What goes into the mash, and how long to let it "cook"? What sort of still to use? When to start drawing off a run, and when to stop? Single, double-, or triple-distilled? Aged? Filtered? Flavored? These are matters for each distiller to determine; they're the stuff of learning and experience and—ultimately, at some impalpable higher level—art. In part two of this book, we'll look at them all in more detail.

XXX Marks the Spot

◐●●○○◑●◐

Look at any cartoon or comic-strip moonshiner, and chances are he'll be holding a jug or jar scored with three black Xs. Why?

Some say it all began because illiterate moonshiners couldn't write "whiskey" on barrels and jugs so instead scrawled "XXX"—but that hardly seems a satisfying explanation. Closer to the mark, I think, are those who say the Xs simply indicated a grade: more Xs meant a finer product. Some further suggest that each X indicated a run of whiskey. The first run was marked with a single X. Some distillers would stop there and ship their low-grade product to *rectifiers*, who distilled it into more palatable spirits. That second run, higher-proof whiskey, was labeled XX. If a third run was called for—high quality stuff indeed—it would be tagged XXX.

Be aware, however, that those potent Xs were not necessarily exclusive to moonshine: some say they were used to point to any powerful contents—not just whiskey, but also poison (which is still indicated by the familiar single X of crossbones and a skull). If you should come across an old pottery jug marked with Xs, do NOT use it to store liquor. It could just as easily have held farmyard poisons as whiskey.

Drinking Moonshine

My Uncle Henry is allergic to moonshine; whenever he drinks it, he breaks out in handcuffs.

Anonymous

One of my earliest run-ins with drinking moonshine came during my college years near the Missouri/Iowa border. Late one evening, as the beer supply diminished, my friend Bob asked if I cared for a shot of 'shine. Beer-blurred and game, I allowed that I did. He laid out a glass jug and two jelly glasses on his kitchen table. Bob sloshed a little on the table as he poured, and continued his late-night filibuster. My attention wandered from his story about Vincent Price to the glasses before us. I noticed that in its meandering across the table toward the low end of the kitchen, the spilled whiskey had seared an unwholesome trail of pink into the white tabletop. We both decided that perhaps it was time to call it a night.

My next shot of homegrown hooch had to wait until some months later, the following spring. When Derby Day and the beginnings of julep season rolled around, another friend brought out a flask of his family's applejack and gave me the barest capful, an amount no more generous than that afforded by a thimble. David was not being stingy, as I first thought. He knew the power of the drink. The warming glow of apples was so unexpected that I closed my eyes and was—just for a moment—transported somewhere else. The elixir he poured that day was the work of tenth-generation Appalachians, true artisan mash-cookers. That was the drink that made me realize that—properly made—moonshine can be sublime.

ADVICE FOR THE UNINITIATED

Ever since that first sip of applejack, I've been sniffing out locally made sub rosa liquors, and the lessons I learned in early encounters with moonshine have held true: some are very good, some are not. My advice? As you search for the sublime, exercise reasonable and due caution.

Irvin S. Cobb, the American humorist and bourbon aficionado, once thundered against sketchy likker like a brimstone prairie preacher: "It smells like gangrene starting in a mildewed silo, it tastes like the wrath to come, and if you absorb a deep swig of it you have all the sensations of having swallowed a lighted kerosene lamp. A sudden, violent jolt of it has been known to stop the victim's watch, snap his suspenders, and crack his glass eye right across ... If you must drink it, always do so while sitting flat on the floor. Then you don't have so far to fall."

If you get a hold of some homemade spirits, smell and taste it—just don't guzzle. It might be ambrosia. Or it might just crack your eye across.

> **It was a brutal cold Monday, the kind of day when ditching in an open field in half-frozen ground makes hell seem almost inviting... The liquid they offered me was crystal clear, of course, which further assured me, falsely, that it must be mild and harmless.**
>
> *Good Spirits*, Gene Logsdon

Judging 'Shine

Remember that, in a wholly unregulated cottage industry, on top of risking some bad-tasting liquor, you're also risking some bad-for-you liquor when you get it from covert sources. Few people expect you to gulp down buckets of 'shine, so it's not bad form to sample just a sip's worth if you feel it's warranted.

Here are some rules of thumb to keep in mind as you judge a spirit's drinkworthiness.

First, look at it. Good liquor may be amber-hued, much as is barrel-aged bourbon, Armagnac, or tequila; or it may be uncolored like vodka or kirschwasser. Either way, it should be crystal clear with no sediment, dark specks, or insects. It should never be cloudy. The old trick of gauging the proof by shaking the container and eyeballing the resulting beads, or bubbles, works (larger, longer-lasting beads indicate higher proof; see page 113), but beading oils lend substandard whiskey a false veil of credibility, so beads alone should never be taken as prima facie evidence of "the good stuff." Infused spirits may, of course, contain spices, herbs, fruit pieces, or even, in the rare bottle of homemade goldwasser, flecks of real gold leaf.

Above the nose-wrinkling ethanol punch, home-distilled hooch often smells slightly and agreeably sweet. You may take a snoot from the container or rub a little into the back or palm of your hand and smell; warming the spirit releases compounds for a more revealing on-the-fly analysis. Brandies especially carry strong notes of their base fruits. Sulfurous or medicinal smells suggest poorly made and possibly dangerous liquor. Liquors stored in plastic often take on a chemically aroma; avoid them.

Okay, so you've examined it and smelled it. If you're satisfied that all is well, go on and taste it. A small sip—about a teaspoon—is enough to tell you whether the taste is sound. Drink a small amount because you want to evaluate it, not to get knee-walking drunk in a half-hour. Pause and really evaluate what you're tasting. Does it feel oily on your tongue? No good. Is it hot and solvent-like? Don't drink it.

Of course, none of these techniques replaces laboratory analysis that can reveal the presence of lead salts, mercury, arsenic, or other heavy metals from the source water or faulty production—a good argument for making spirits yourself, or at least knowing your maker.

Although it's often too long between excellent homemade whiskeys, first-rate brandies crop up wherever I travel. In the hands of even an amateur distiller, a batch of peaches, apples, pears, or cherries can be transformed into sheer liquid joy. Because distillers across the nation have long made peach and apple brandies, these two in particular are venerable benchmarks in American foodways, and excellent examples know no regional boundaries. Apple brandies and cherry bounce are among my absolute favorites. Find and support someone in your community making them right (maybe you become that person). Lesser-known brandy varieties such as scuppernong, persimmon, or banana are easy and inexpensive to make, but a shallower pool of living distillers familiar with them means that you're more likely to find great ones only in areas known for those styles.

Respect the Power

The primary complaint against moonshine (or argument for, depending on which side of the aisle you sit on) is, in fact, its potency. Because it is so strong, moonshine can produce a quicker and more profound effect than the same volume of legally made alcohol. Even for accomplished boozers, moonshine can make off with your dignity before you understand what's happening.

Well a city slicker came and he said I'm tough

I think I want to taste that powerful stuff

He took one slug and he drank it right down

I heard him moanin' as he hit the ground

Mighty mighty pleasing, my pappy's corn squeezing

Whew! White lightning!

"White Lightning," lyrics and music by J.P. Richardson, 1959

Compared to commercial whiskey's usual 80 proof (40 percent alcohol by volume), white lightning is traditionally poured at 100 proof and can exceed 120 proof. Some rustic specimens creep up to a volatile 160 proof, or 80 percent alcohol. A pint of bourbon simply does not have the kick its country cousin does.

In 1885, a journalist writing for *Dixie* magazine related his take on incendiary moonshine: "The instant he has swallowed the stuff he feels as if he were sunburned all over, his head begins to buzz as if a hive of bees had swarmed there, when he closes his eyes, he sees six hundred million torchlight processions all charging at him, ten abreast, and when he opens his eyes the light blinds him and everything seems dancing about." In 120 years, the product has not changed much. A Northeast bookie compared drinking moonshine to a gullet sunburn: "The only way to make it better is to drink more."

DRINKING METHODS

When you've got a hold of moonshine you feel is safe, there are a few schools of thought on how best to approach it. An old-style trick is to drink it at room temperature straight from a ceramic or glass jug by hooking one finger through the handle and raising the container in the crook of your arm to take a sip. Old-time jugs are less common these days, so drinkers are more likely to sip their spirits from bottles or glasses at room temperature, or blood-warm from hip flasks.

Just swallow and grin.

Anonymous distiller, when asked how best to drink moonshine

You'll always find those who prefer liquor straight, but soft drinks, especially Mountain Dew (I can't help but smile), Dr. Pepper, RC Cola, and various orange sodas are favored mixers. Don't be surprised to see folks taking a swig of 'shine, then a sip of cola, then more 'shine and more cola. Shots are popular, too, but they easily lead to overdrinking. Besides, really excellent spirits deserve closer appreciation.

Warm, iced, or neutral, it's your call; any home-distilled spirits ought to be enjoyed in the same fashion as their commercial equivalents. As always, pacing is key: too much moonshine is significantly less than too much vodka.

The Overdrinker's Thesaurus

DRUNK:

Annihilated

Bent
Besotted
Blitzed
Blitzkrieged
Blotto
Bombed
Booze-blind
Borracho
Bottle fever
Brined

Corned
Crippled

Demolished
Dizzy
Drenched

Faced
Flat-faced
Floored or floor-hammered

Gathered a talking load
Getting your drink on
Getting your swerve on
Glazed
Greased
Guttered

Hammered

In your cups
Inebriated
Intoxicated

Jiggered
Jimjams
Jugged

Knee-walking drunk

Leathered
Liquored up
Lit
Lit up
Loaded
Looped
Loose

Mangled
Mashed

Numb

Obliterated
On a bender
On autopilot
Ossified

Pickled
Pie-eyed
Piqued
Plastered
Plowed
Potted
Pottzed
Pot-valiant
Pounded
Put a load on

Reeling
Riotous

Sauced
Senseless
Shattered
Shellacked
Skewered
Skunked
Slagged
Slammed
Slaughtered

Slopped
Sloshed
Smashed
Soaked
Soused
Spins, the
Staggers, the
Staying afloat
Stewed
Stinking

Tangle-footed
Tanked
Tied one on
Tight
Tipsy
Torn up
Tossed
Trashed
Trousered
Trucked
Tub-thumped
Tweaked

Under the influence

Wasted
Well-oiled
Wheelchaired
Whacked
Wiggity whacked

Zoned

HUNG OVER:

Barrel fever
Cotton-mouthed
DTs
Irish flu
Katzenjammered
Kittens in your mouth
Parrot-mouthed
Pulling socks off your teeth
Shakes, the
Sheep in your mouth
Trembles, the

The Morning After

So, despite common sense and the warnings of reasonable people, you hauled off and drank yourself stupid. Now? A jittery palsy finds you slow, aching, dehydrated, and nauseated. Congratulations. If you'd paced your drinks, this would have been avoidable. I can't vouch for hangover prevention shortcuts such as eating lots of bread, taking vitamin B_{12}, or having a shot of olive oil before drinking. Nor, once blessed with post-debauchery shakes, am I courageous enough to mainline a saline drip as some of my medically inclined friends have done. But my personal research has turned up a few things that help me.

If you need to hurl, do it. Get that poison out of your system. You may be surprised ("Lima beans? When did I eat lima beans?"), but you will feel better.

Rehydrate; some swear by sweet colas for the sugar and caffeine. Others dote on strong coffee. I stick with water and lots of it, often with Peychaud bitters. Sleep as time permits. Slough off the night's excesses with a long shower.

I'm not a fan of the hair-of-the-dog technique, but I have friends who drink alcohol on waking at the crack of noon to stop a hangover in its tracks. Eat the foods your stomach can handle. Some hangovers allow carne asada or green chile burritos; others refuse anything more solid than Gatorade. Gently cooked eggs on buttered toast provide a safe middle ground.

Last, review your mobile phone log and the contents of your pockets to determine what, if any, restitution is in order.

Water of Life … or Jugged Death?

Is drinking moonshine good for what ails you … or a sure road to oblivion … or both?

WATER OF LIFE

Whiskey's medical authority is of ancient origin. Arab physicians reputedly used spirits of wine as medicine in the ninth and tenth centuries. In medieval Europe, aqua vitae and other "strong waters" were the province of alchemists and monks. The latter kept extensive herbal gardens full of medicinal plants with which they made cures, some effective, some unfortunately less so. These herbal infusions, decoctions, and distillations were the progenitors of monastic liqueurs and, later, patent medicines. Wholly ineffective whiskey-based cures continued even in the professional medical field well into the nineteenth century. One manual, for instance, declared spirits most effective for ridding a body of "taints acquired in the school of Venus." Going on a three-day bender might take one's mind off such maladies, but it wasn't likely to clear them up.

On the American frontier, the same remoteness that allowed families to distill largely unmolested also meant that they endured a meager scattering of doctors. Illness and trauma were family matters handled at home. For the frontier family, whiskey was one of the "good creatures of the Lord" that

> **Here's to corn whiskey!**
> **It whitens the teeth,**
> **Perfumes the breath**
> **And makes childbirth a pleasure**
>
> Anonymous

maintained good health. It kept them warm when biting winds howled, and lightened their hearts in lonely hours. As an anesthetic it was crude, but whiskey was a potent antibacterial and disinfectant. Many who might have died in infancy owed their lives to midwives who anointed their hands in whiskey before getting down to brass tacks.

Even today, in dry counties or where a public preference for moonshine prevails, some doctors still prescribe medicinal whiskey. One rural doctor from Georgia I interviewed told me that he always stocks moonshine confiscated by the local sheriff for certain patients who hold high regard for moonshine as a tonic and restorer but don't put much stock in pills and pharmacies. "If I prescribe pills and a shot of moonshine, then they know they're getting real medical treatment. Otherwise, they just don't take the medicine."

JUGGED DEATH

In the early 1930s, a mysterious paralysis left many Southerners and Midwesterners barely able to control their legs or feet. Those who could walk at all flapped and flopped into doctors' offices where, at first, nobody could explain their ailment. The thread that bound them turned out to be a high-proof alcoholic extract of Jamaican ginger known as *jake*, widely and falsely marketed in pharmacies as a low-proof patent medicine, that they drank to sidestep prohibition laws. Their characteristic gait quickly became known as *jake leg*.

But it wasn't the ginger itself that was hurting these men. Makers of jake routinely added not only more alcohol than government regulations of patent medicines allowed, but also adulterants to disguise the fact—most of them harmless, such as glycerin or molasses, but some not. Jake leg was traced to two Boston brothers-in-law who adulterated jake with tri-ortho-cresyl-phosphate, a chemical plasticizer used in lacquer and airplane finishes, and a potent neurotoxin. Those they poisoned—tens of thousands of people—were crippled for life, and their shambling walk lives on in blues songs such as "Jake Walk Papa" and "The Jake Walk Blues."

That illicit liquor manufactured beyond the watchful eyes of government inspectors can contain unsafe or otherwise nasty ingredients is undeniable. For commercial moonshiners, getting caught red-handed at the still never makes for a good day, so in the name of speeding fermentation some have made a pungent contribution to the mash with shovelfuls of high-nitrogen, yeast-boosting bird droppings. Reaching for a harder kick, bootleggers have added lye, methanol, carbide, bleach, and various acids to whiskey, especially when making wildcat sales to chance buyers rather than to established clientele.

In addition to the health consequences to heavy drinkers regardless of their beverage of choice, chronic moonshine drinkers are notoriously prone to lead poisoning because of the not-uncommon use of lead solder and piping in stills. Although most distillers understand that the solder in automotive radiators contains dangerously high levels of lead, radiators still are pressed into service occasionally as ready-made condensers. In the

WARNING

DEADLY POISON
Moonshine Liquor
Being Distributed Locally

DO NOT DRINK ANY Type of BOOTLEG LIQUOR regardl of source. **DEADLY POISONOUS** Lead Salts are be found in WHITE LIQUOR. This poison can cause **DEATH** serious illness as much as a year after drinking.

The next SMALL DRINK May Bring the amount c Salts in the Body to the concentration point necessary t **DEATH!**

DR. J. W. R. NORT
State Health Director

Fair warning. There is no denying that spirits manufactured beyond the watchful eyes of government inspectors can contain undesirable if not outright toxic ingredients, as proclaimed in this 1960s North Carolina state health department poster.

I can't eat, I can't talk,
Been drinking mean Jake, Lord, now can't walk
Ain't got nothin' to lose,
For I'm a Jake walkin' papa with the Jake walk blues.

"The Jake Walk Blues" by the Allen Brothers, 1930

Pig Squeezin's

To discourage sampling unbranded liquor, anti-moonshining literature by the government and the legal distilling industry often cites unsanitary—if not outright filthy—conditions at illicit stills. Originally and fatally attracted by the warmth and sweetness of a fermenting mash, insects, birds, dead 'possums, and pig carcasses regularly bob to the surface in antimoonshine tales.

The stories are not altogether untrue; mashed-in critters have a long history in distillation. But not all of the immersions have been accidental. In *The Accomplisht Cook* (1678), Robert May proffers this recipe:

To Distill a Pig Good Against Consumption:

Take a pig, slay it, and cast away the guts; then take the liver, lungs, and all the entrails, and wipe all with a clean cloth; then put it into a Still with a pound of dates, the stones taken out, and sliced into thin slices, a pound of sugar, and an ounce of large mace. If the party be hot in the stomach, then take these cool herbs, as violet leaves, strawberry leaves, and half a handful of bugloss, still them with a soft fire as you do roses, and let the party take of it every morning & evening, in any drink or broth he pleases.
You may sometimes add raisins and cloves.

Whiskey Adulterants

FOR KICK	FOR COLOR
Carbide	Burnt sugar
Chlorine bleach	Charred oak
Embalming fluid	Charred peach bunkers (pits)
Lye	Iodine
Rubbing alcohol	Poke root berries
Wood alcohol	Tobacco or tobacco spit

mid-twentieth century when the practice began, it wasn't long before the effects of the lead that leached into distillates began manifesting in the drinking public: tremors, convulsions, nausea, hallucinations, apathy, and blindness.

The truth is, even the sweetest, smoothest, purest, and most traditionally made alcohol, free of contaminants, pigs, and raisins, is by its nature a toxin when taken in high doses. Don't believe me? Drink a liter bottle of the most expensive "tasteless" vodka in one sitting, and you'll become all too well acquainted with the poisonous nature of alcohol—any alcohol. Some home distillers claim that pure spirits cannot poison an individual; if drinkers are poisoned, they say, the spirit wasn't pure. This bit of circular logic might convince someone already in her cups, but "pure" ethanol must be treated with the respect and common sense one would accord any strong drink.

> **It is a paradox of the times that a man who might scream out at the possibility of a shipment of poisoned tuna fish or recoil at the thought of eating cranberries with an excess of insect spray will drink moonshine by the gallon.**
>
> Jess Carr, *The Second Oldest Profession*

A Belt of 'Shine

Moonshine's heritage may be rooted in the South, but today the stuff itself flows from stills in every state, in cities and small towns as well as backwoods hollows.

The American moonshine belt is a swath of southeastern states with deeply rooted mercantile and folk traditions of clandestine distilling. These states, in no particular order, include North and South Carolina, Tennessee, Alabama, Georgia, Virginia, West Virginia, Mississippi, Alabama, and Kentucky. In the last 130 years, the staggering number of still seizures among them has bolstered popular images of these lands as the stomping grounds of backward-looking people who, through some perversion of logic, make their own liquor rather than buy it in stores.

Such wide publicity do these Southern states garnish for moonshining in the popular imagination that a body might be forgiven for regarding it as a uniquely Southern practice. Actually, since splashing ashore in the seventeenth century,

moonshine has filtered throughout the continent.

This past autumn, I was offered a snoot of "corn from down South" in a Mid-Atlantic home-brew shop. Any alcoholist with a working tongue could tell the high-octane distillate was not corn liquor. It was poorly filtered *'splo*—a sugar "whiskey" with a surprisingly venerable heritage. I nearly gagged. As to its Southern pedigree? Hmpf. Go pull the other one.

Homemade whiskey is so strongly identified with "the South" that distillers across the East and Midwest use the region as an undeserved badge of quality and authenticity when pawning local stuff on gullible customers: "This is the good stuff; pure Southern corn likker. I wouldn't lie to you, honest." I suppose the deception may also be intended to throw overly curious Yankees off the scent of illicit and quite local neighborhood distilleries.

Where do you find moonshine outside the South? Try New Jersey applejack, or hausgemacht rye whiskey from Pennsylvania. Touring the West

> **And as for Mormon Whiskey, Wh~e~u~w! … I mind Old Mike Gardner drunk a pint of it, and went home and stole one of his own plows and hid it in the woods, and didn't know where it was when he was sober, and had to git drunk agin to find it.**
>
> Mark Twain, *Roughing It*

Not just whistlin' Dixie. America's long history of making and consuming moonshine reaches far beyond the rural South. Here, revenue agents dismantle a still in San Francisco, California.

Okolehao, okolehao

There's a man-made moonshine in Hawaii now

Okolehao hip-hip hooray

After two sips your hips want to swing and sway.

When the gals begin to beg for just one more keg

The boys know what it means and they send for the marines.

Okolehao, I'm telling you

After one drink you'll think you're Hawaiian too.

"Okolehao," Lyrics and music by Leo Robin, Ralph Rainger,
and Don Martin for the 1937 movie *Waikiki Wedding*

Coast? Inquire discretely about Oregon *eaux de vie* and grappa, or the new California small-batch whiskeys that are even creeping into legitimate production. New Orleans, traditionally a moonshine market rather than a big producer, is home to a growing number of aficionados of absinthe, the famous *fée verte* that is not only high-proof but actually banned in much of the Western world because of its alleged mind-shimmying thujone content. For more than 200 years, native Hawaiians have distilled their cherished okolehao, and sour cherries give up the ghost in ways Michigan tax rolls do not suggest. Even abstemious Utah Mormons developed Valley Tan, an early Western whiskey that could match New Mexico's Taos lightning in a bare-knuckled wallop contest.

Moonshine consumption is widely regarded as a backwoods "hillbilly" practice, but it is in fact both a rural and an urban phenomenon; it has been since North America could boast cities at all. A recent study at an Atlanta hospital concluded that moonshine consumption was common enough in urban settings that doctors ought to ask about moonshine habits while taking histories from patients who drink, in order to red-flag potential poisoning from lead solder in stills. (Of course, dis-tillers who eschew lead in their distillation equipment and use potable water eliminate the possibility of lead poisoning from the alcohol they produce.)

Whether annual output is measured in thousands of gallons or just a few liters, there probably isn't a settled patch of America that isn't host to unregistered distilleries and regional favorites.

South of the South

◐ ● ● ○ ○ ◐ ● ◐ ●

Clandestine distilling is common throughout the Americas. Regional names vary, but aguardiente (a contraction of *agua ardiente*, "strong water") is commonly understood from the Southwestern United States through Mexico and beyond as potent spirits, whether illicit or not. Examples are made from sugar, sugarcane juice, corn, and even the roasted hearts of Mexican agaves for mezcal (of which tequila is one variety).

Especially around Christmas and Three Kings Day, immigrants from the south of Mexico may toast the holidays with mistela, a maceration of fruits in homemade spirits (see page 148).

CHAPTER 2

A Long and Storied
HISTORY

If you make your own spirits, you're following a path blazed by independent-minded folk that trails back to the dimmest reaches of civilization. The history of moonshine is as much about human spirits as it is about alcoholic spirits; it is about conflict and violence, regulation and rebellion, and—maybe most of all—independence and ingenuity.

Moonshine Comes to America

In North America, diverse hands have tended still fires since the early seventeenth century; Dutch, English, French, Spanish, Scots-Irish, and German farmers, artisans, and householders fermented and distilled anything and nearly everything growing in their new land.

About 1620—around the time the *Mayflower* alighted at Plymouth—English colonist George Thorpe began distilling the New World's first corn whiskey in Virginia. At the time, English settlers referred to grains generally as "corn," but it was the native grain maize *(Zea mays)* that we know today as corn that Thorpe coaxed into spirits and that grew eventually to form the spine of Southern distilling.

The first commercial American distillation centered in Dutch Manhattan, where Willem Kieft, the director general of New Netherland, caused a still to be erected around 1640 to produce and sell a grain-based distillate. This is about the time when the Dutch were perfecting techniques of large-scale distillation, especially of a juniper-flavored whiskey called *jenever* that the Dutch still hold in high esteem (think of it as the Dutch bourbon—an old man's drink enjoying resurgent popularity). When the English later took possession of the territory, they converted the still to the production of rum from Caribbean molasses.

Although it was English and Dutch colonists who introduced distilling to North America, with contributions to the art in the early seventeenth century by the Germans and French, moonshining as a way of life didn't really get started until the Scots-Irish began arriving around 1717.

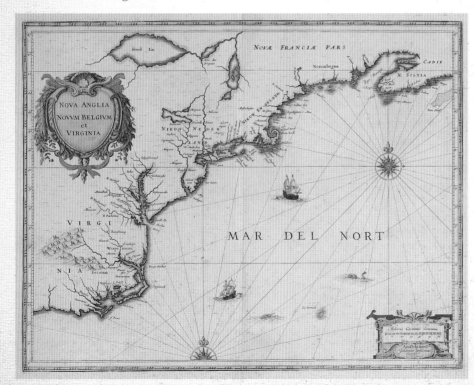

Maybe even more American than apple pie. By the time this map of the New World was published in 1639, nearly 20 years had passed since the first Virginia corn whiskey had been distilled.

LONG FUSES, SHORT TEMPERS

Whiskey had been known in Ireland since at least the twelfth century, when English invaders commented on the strength and authority of the native drink. In the sixteenth century, England's Queen Elizabeth I launched a particularly brutal campaign in Ireland to subjugate the largely Catholic Irish, who for over 300 years had resisted English attempts to rule the island. By the time Elizabeth died childless in 1603 and the throne consequently passed to her nearest relative, James Stuart, Ireland had been subdued—but was hardly under the crown's firm control.

Old-World Origins

Distillation is undeniably an ancient pursuit: some historians credit Mesopotamian artisans with having a working knowledge of distilling around 3500 B.C. More than four thousand years later, Arab alchemists and doctors were coaxing the essence, or "spirit," from wine by heating it and collecting the condensed vapors. By the twelfth century A.D., North Africans introduced the practice to Moor-occupied Spain. From there, distillation spread to France, Italy, Germany, and the British Isles. The Dutch in particular gained early renown as mad commercial distillers.

Al kohl, the Arab word for this spirit of wine, should ring a bell. Europeans gave it other names: Dutch physicians referred to this new medicine as *brandewijn* ("burned wine"), which came into English as *brandywine* or just *brandy*. Others found this new medicine so remarkable that they dubbed it *aqua vitae*, Latin for "water of life." The Irish adapted the name to the Gaelic, *uisqe breatha* or *uisqebaugh*, whence came *whisk(e)y*, but whether it was the Irish or the Scots who actually invented whiskey still raises voices in certain quarters.

The biblically famous King James had a solution to quelling the wild Irish: plant Presbyterian settlers from Scottish lowlands in the north of Ireland, an area known as Ulster. In 1610, Scots settlers began displacing the native Irish and settling in the new frontier, where they were free to worship as they wished, to own guns, and to distill if they so desired. In the space of thirty years, more than 40,000 Scots had relocated to Ulster. Combining their knowledge of distilling with that of the native Irish, the Ulstermen —as these Scots-Irish settlers came to be called—soon came to produce renowned whiskeys.

Unfortunately for the Ulstermen, Charles I, successor to James I, nursed deep conflicts with Parliament that spawned civil war in England in 1642. To finance the war, Parliament passed an excise tax on whiskey, shocking the Ulstermen into riot. Nevertheless, the tax held. By the end of the decade, Richard Collins had published a pocket-sized tome of tables called *The Country Gaugers Vade Mecum* that allowed roving gaugers (tax assessors and collectors) to measure the contents of "Small Brewing Vessels, either of a Circular, Elliptical, or Rectilineal Base … either full or part empty." The relocated Scots also were subjected to restrictions on worship and trade, putting a philosophical and an economic stranglehold on the north of Ireland. Landlords jacked rents to outrageous levels.

So it was that in the beginning of the eighteenth century, after barely a hundred years in Ulster, the industrious Scots began abandoning Ireland for the siren call of America. By 1776, as many as 400,000 had settled along its eastern rim, while many others moved from there to the frontier in the western portions of the colonies.

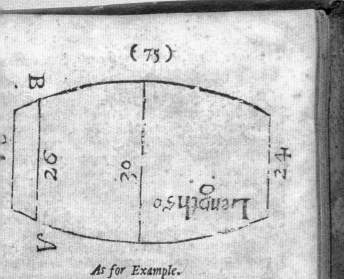

(75)

As for Example.

Let there be a Cask (as the annexed Diagram) hole length is 50 Inches, Boung Diameter 30 ches, Head Diameter 24 Inches, the difference 6 Inches, againſt 6 in the precedent Table you ave 4.2, which being added to the leſſer Dia- eter 24 Inches, makes 28.2 Inches: Seek 28.2 the top of the Table of *Cylinders*, and under eath that againſt 25 (half the Casks Length)

You have 55.37
Vhich being ſet down again thus 55.37
——————
And added together makes 110.74 Ale Gall. the Content of the ſaid Cask.

Note, that when the Length of your Cask is ſs than 31 Inches, you have the Content by in- ſpection in the Table ; but if your Length be ſove 31, then you muſt divide your Length into wo parts, and add the Contents together, as in is laſt Example.

G 2   *To*

When the call for revolution came, the Scots-Irish were only too willing to discuss their long grievances with Mother England down their musket barrels.

It was these stubborn and will-ful people, with their distaste for central government and outside dominion, and who had fought valiantly for the colonies against the British, whom Alexander Hamilton would incite fifteen years later with a particularly odious tax.

Tax man's guide. A page from *The Country Gaugers Vade Mecum* showed tax assessors how to measure a cask of whiskey to determine the amount of tax the distiller owed the King.

To E or Not to E?

The Scots spell *whisky* without an e, but the Irish add one for their *whiskey*. Americans tend to side with the Irish, Canadi-ans with the Scots. Either spell-ing is correct in North America.

Taxes and Rebellion

Tax? Did you say government tax? Them's fightin' words to free-thinking distillers.

Until 1791 in what would become the United States, anyone could distill spirits legally for any reason. Governments showed no more interest in those who chose to distill alcohol than in those who raised pigs or grew vegetables. Rural communities even pooled their resources to construct stillhouses where citizens could engage their local distiller to transform crops into more manageable "value added" products.

In that year, Alexander Hamilton, as secretary of the treasury, inaugurated an enormously unpopular excise on whiskey to help retire debts generated during the Revolutionary War. The tax inflamed already tense relations with independent-minded farmers in the western reaches of the states.

The farmers who protested the new republic's tax were not incorrigible drunks who merely wanted to make their own booze. They were practical-minded men trying to eke out livings in remote territories. The majority of Western farms stood well away from any neighbor and far removed from markets for their goods. In the wilderness frontier, which had no roads in today's meaning, long, infrequent, and often arduous trips over rugged terrain were the only way farmers could get goods to market. Just how much one could bring to sell was predicated upon draft animals' carrying capacities.

If a packhorse could carry 240 pounds of grain (four bushels) to market, it was at little, if any, profit to the farmer. When he converted that grain to whiskey, however, the horse's payload increased substantially because it could carry the equivalent of eight to nearly eleven bushels in eight- or ten-gallon kegs. The farmer who shrewdly concentrated his acres of cumbersome grains to more portable whiskey transformed the journey to market from a bust to a profitable venture.

Tarred, feathered, and riding a rail. Pennsylvania farmers didn't take kindly to revenuers, as you can see from this portrayal of the Whiskey Rebellion, included in 1876's *Our First Century: Being a Popular Descriptive Portraiture of the One Hundred Great and Memorable Events in the History of Our Country*.

Liquid crop concentrate. By converting his grain crop to liquid libation, a farmer could transport his harvest to market more efficiently pound for pound and earn a higher profit.

Hamilton's provision infuriated the farmers not only by requiring a tax to be paid, but also by demanding that they pay the tax in cash at the still site. What cash? The hard currency they made in the cities tended to stay in the cities because settlers immediately used their whiskey profits to purchase other products. Where goods and services were bartered, personally made whiskeys and brandies became currency. There was little cash on the frontier.

What's more, the law taxed stills based on their capacity, regardless of whether or how much whiskey they actually made. Various provisions favored Eastern over Western producers. Small Western farmers realized that the government for which they'd fought to overthrow the British was putting the screws to them over similar taxation issues.

Opposition sparked by enforcement of the new law was so ardent and widespread that in 1794 thousands of western Pennsylvania farmers rose up in arms. They were dispersed only when an army personally headed by then-President George Washington (himself a distillery owner in later years) rode west to quash this so-called Whiskey Rebellion. The conflict convinced thousands to pick up stakes, pack their stills, and strike out with their families to the less-governed backcountry of Virginia, Kentucky, and the Carolinas.

The introduction of the Whiskey Tax and the subsequent Mid-Atlantic uprising set a tone for relations between independent distillers and

Lead Poisoning of a Different Sort

Debilitating and lethal poisoning from lead solder improperly used to build stills is a recurring complaint of chronic moonshine drinkers. As the heavy metal accumulates in the human body over the course of years, it slowly ruins the nervous system. It is not without irony that Alexander Hamilton, architect of the Whiskey Tax, was himself done in by a sudden and fatal exposure to lead. In 1804, Aaron Burr challenged Hamilton to a pistol duel and killed his political adversary with one of the more famous lead overdoses in American history.

government regulators that persists to this day. Farmers fled the region and migrated south, taking their stills and their profound mistrust of the federal government with them. Whiskey went underground, and distillers who refused to pay taxes became criminals.

RESPITE, THEN MORE TAXES

When the anti-Federalist Thomas Jefferson was sworn in as president in 1801, he made an early commitment to do away with the tax that had caused so much grief. On June 30, 1802, the "infernal" excise was repealed. The repeal was as much about repairing relations as it was about fiscal management. But the irreparable rent of trust between the Scots-Irish farmers and government remained. Stills continued to be located in remote and lonely spots to avoid prying eyes. The Irish have long memories, and hard feelings persist through the course of generations to this day.

Except for a brief period (1814–1817) following the War of 1812, liquor was once more untaxed in the United States until the Civil War. In 1862, the Department of the Treasury established an array of new taxes, including those on whiskey and tobacco, as an emergency measure to cover the costs of the American Civil War.

During that conflict, although their copper rigs were in danger of confiscation and conversion to munitions, Southern distillers did not offend any uniform Confederate sense of justice. To their unspeakable indignation, farmers who shouldered packs for the Confederacy found themselves subject to alien taxes on their return from war. They also found a federal government eager to enforce the new laws. Shortly thereafter, three detectives to aid in the prevention, detection, and punishment of tax evaders were hired to "protect the revenue." The taxes have remained with us, and the officers who enforce them have become the stuff of legends.

Searching high and low. For nearly 150 years, Internal Revenue agents have been assigned the dangerous and sometimes deadly task of seeking out and prosecuting those who distill beverage alcohol outside the law, ignoring regulations and evading taxes.

Revenuers!

When Congress empowered the Office of Internal Revenue to hire agents to enforce tax laws relating to distilled spirits in 1863, it created the tools to seek out, capture, and bring to justice those guilty of violating revenue laws. Before long, revenue agents—also known as revenuers, or revenooers—earned reputations as dogged enforcers of the new laws, with field support from federal marshals, local lawmen, and occasionally the U.S. Army.

In the mountainous South, the tax on whiskey stills didn't receive the full brunt of federal scrutiny until the late 1870s, when revenuers began to enforce whiskey tax laws in earnest. During the national depression of the 1890s, Congress raised the federal liquor tax, and even law-abiding farmers were hard-pressed not to run off whiskey to make ends meet. In some areas, outright guerilla warfare erupted between federal agents and local distillers who had long relied on whiskey income.

Local lawmen ostensibly sided with the revenuers, but often their true sympathies lay with neighbors who may have been friends or kin. A sharp distiller would keep local sheriffs and local politicians so well lubricated, well supplied, or well paid that word of impending raids reached them before the raiders. Consequently, local law seemed largely to have sidestepped the violent conflict that characterized relations between whiskey makers and federal agents.

Tales of revenuer adventures—of hunting stills, chasing moonshiners, and other mountain heroics—flooded Eastern magazines such as *Harper's Weekly* and *The Atlantic Monthly*. The growing conflict between moonshiners and those who hunted them captured the popular imagination. In 1881, revenue agent George Atkinson penned *After the Moonshiners*, a popular memoir about his time chasing down recalcitrant distillers who had no compunctions about killing revenuers. On its heels followed T.P. Crutcher's *Spurrier with the Wildcats and Moonshiners*, with more sensational accounts of revenuer derring-do. In 1892, the same year the book was released, its title character, revenue collector Joseph Spurrier, and two fellow revenuers were shot and killed in an ambush by moonshiners.

Tales of derring-do. Sensational tales of backwoods conflicts between agents and moonshiners thrilled the readers of popular journals such as *Harper's Weekly*. On this 1878 cover, a moonshiner ambush is under way.

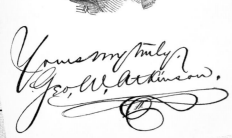

Revenuer writer. Revenue agent George W. Atkinson's 1881 best-seller, *After the Moonshiners*, featured himself literally chasing down offenders of the nation's liquor laws.

Yeah, I'm a revenooer man
I got a badge in my pocket
And a gun on my hip
Damn moonshiners
Better never make a slip
'Cause I'm a revenooer man
Yeah, I'll get 'em if I can.

"Revenooer Man," lyrics and music
by Johnny Paycheck, 1959

Between the 1880s and World War I, rural moonshiners sometimes banded together in "whitecapping" clubs for mutual protection against revenuers and informants. On violent night raids whitecappers intimidated and punished "immoral" characters in their communities, hammering home the message that powerful and united distillers would not be stopped. Those who informed on clandestine distillers or who housed traveling revenuers overnight were beaten, caned, whipped, and driven out of the community by gangs of disguised moonshiners. If additional warning was necessary to anyone tempted by the extra cash offered for turning in distillers, informants' homes were sometimes dynamited. Some were murdered in front of their horrified families.

The law versus supply and demand. After the Volstead Act went into effect in 1920, distillers pumped up production to meet the public's unslakable demand for illicit liquor. When this rig was confiscated in Washington, D.C., in 1922, it was billed as "the largest still in captivity" in the nation's capital.

If any man in the community misbehaves in any way we will take him out and whip him. If he is not satisfied with that we will put him to a limb.

From an 1890s moonshiners' allegiance oath

Distillers who actually paid the federal tax on their spirits were regarded as traitors and could be beaten, their stills destroyed, and their millstones broken. Revenuers and prosecutors helped break these rings by meting out punishment: fines, imprisonment, and forfeiture or destruction of property. By World War I, whitecapping moonshiners were largely history.

THE JOB GETS HARDER

In 1920, when the Volstead Act (officially the National Prohibition Enforcement Act) took effect and ushered in a nationwide ban on alcohol, revenue agents were charged not only with catching moonshiners, but also with enforcing the ban on liquor across the board. This meant seizing and destroying stocks of genuine scotch and Canadian whiskeys coming by car, rail, plane (occasionally), and boat from Canada; whiskeys and rum from Caribbean nations; and tequila and whiskey from Mexico. The task was so enormous that legions of new agents were brought on to handle the volume of violators and informants in a wave of criminality that seemed at times almost overwhelming. America was a liquor vacuum sucking in alcohol from any breech. Bootlegging became a national pastime.

Revenuers stood as best they could against the tide. But the frustrations of such a Herculean charge sometimes proved too much for the revenuers, some of whom had to provide their own weapons and had received no more training than being handed a badge. Outstanding acts of heroism and audacious detective work grabbed headlines, but so did greed, corruption, and incompetence.

In all, more than 120 revenue agents lost their lives to the battle against contraband booze during Prohibition.

LOCAL CELEBRITIES

Not all revenuers came with marching orders from Washington. Many, in fact, were locals who knew the backwoods haunts of moonshiners as well as anyone in the area and were on social terms with the men they hunted, if not actually related by blood or marriage. Many achieved legendary regional status.

In the 1940s and 50s, Kentucky revenue agent William "Big Six" Henderson earned his moniker after a still raid early in his career. When Henderson took after a fleeing moonshiner, he took careful note of the locations of six other stills he came across along the fugitive's flight path. After capturing his prey, Henderson and his cohorts raided the other stills and rounded up what moonshiners and still hands they could. The extra stills became a permanent addendum to his Christian name. In time, Big Six's reputation for relentless pursuit grew so celebrated that when he once commanded a moonshiner to halt his flight from a raid, the man actually obeyed.

If you grew up in the city as a child, you might have played "cops and robbers" or "cowboys and Indians," but "moonshiner and revenuer" was the name of the game in some communities. In a Kentucky twist, children took turns playing Big Six during rounds and wee girls incorporated him into their skip-rope chants: *My* mother *told* me … to watch the *still* … in case Big Six comes … over the *hill* … "

Serious Business

A side room of the New Orleans ATF office holds a small memorial to agents who were killed in the line of duty. The Prohibition-era hunt for moonshine caused many of those deaths. Of the accidents and outright murders, George Droz's case is undoubtedly the most horrific. In a 1929 still raid, the federal agent tumbled into a vat of boiling mash. The burns were so severe that Droz died in hospital a few days later.

One can of worms leads to another.
With luck and a little familiarity with the local area, authorities in moonshining hot spots could sometimes make multiple still busts.

BUSTED!

When local officers confiscated mash and whiskey, they usually poured out the liquids and donated any supplies of sugar to institutions such as hospitals and schools. They destroyed the stills with axes, picks, and sometimes guns. Large stills and mash barrels often were dynamited. Moonshiners captured at the site were sometimes drafted to dismantle their own equipment. Federal officers were also known to burn down buildings in which stills had been operating.

> The guy banging on the door yelled, "Alcohol, Tobacco, and Firearms." I just assumed it was more supplies.
>
> Anonymous

Public pour-out. Confiscated mash and moonshine were sometimes poured out publicly to send clear messages to those thinking of making it ("We'll catch you") and those thinking of drinking it ("Moonshine is for the gutter"). This pour-out was held on the north side of the Leon County, Florida, courthouse in 1958.

Another one bites the dust.
This still, like many before and after it,
meets its demise at the end of a revenuer's axe.

How did revenuers find stills? A lot of the credit for still busts goes to informers, locals who knew or suspected someone was distilling and turned the person in for any of a litany of possible reasons—among them revenge, jealousy, or profit. An informant could be, as Horace Kephart wrote in his 1913 book *Our Southern Highlanders*, "some pizen old bum who's been refused credit," or he might be a stool pigeon who was paid a fee for actionable information, or he could be a landowner who'd discovered a wild-cat still on his property. Often, a wife or mother whose husband or sons came home besotted and belligerent would—if she was brazen enough—demand that the sheriff rid the community of the scourge. In a more reflective moment, she might send her daughters as emissaries to avoid being branded an informer.

Surprisingly, moonshiners themselves went to sheriffs and revenuers with information—not on their own operations, of course, but on competitors in the area. And why not? Knock out the competition, and the local market is a lock.

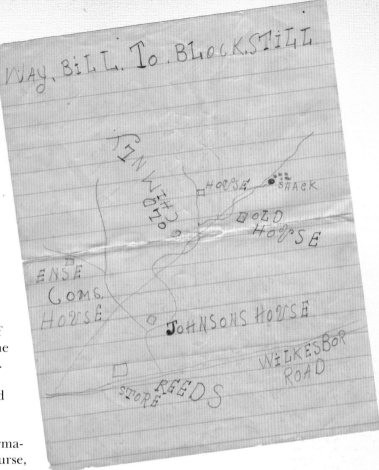

Informer's map. This hand-drawn map showed authorities the way to a still hidden in a North Carolina moonshiner's backroads shack.

I, John Doe, of and for my own self, with my right hand resting on the bung-hole of this keg of "White Mule" and in the presence of this bunch of wild-catters, do hereon solemnly promise that I will never reveal to any person in the world the secret location of a wild-cat still, more especially to a Revenue Officer or Deputy United States Marshall.

The salvo of an imagined moonshiners' allegiance oath by former federal revenue agent Isaac Stapleton

Prohibition:
The Dark Side of the
Moonshine Story

When America officially went dry, high demand and fast profits fueled a boom—and a bad name—for moonshine.

The peak of moonshining in the United States—in terms of both the sheer number of people distilling and the volume of alcohol produced—was early to mid-twentieth century, particularly during Prohibition. The near-total ban on legal beverage alcohol in the 1920s and early 1930s created an unprecedented premium on distilled drinks that outstripped the capacity of traditional farm and home producers.

Of course, alcohol prohibition in one form or another had been the law of the land for much of America. Attempts at prohibiting spirits consumption had met with regional successes in the late nineteenth and early twentieth centuries. The Women's Christian Temperance Union and Anti-Saloon League, in particular, and the hatchet-wielding, barroom-smashing Carrie Nation clamored to eradicate "demon rum" from the hearts, minds, and gullets of Americans. By the start of World War I, 26 states had laws against one form of liquor trafficking or another.

But when a ban on alcohol went nationwide in 1920, financial backers rolled out regional moonshine syndicates to manufacture and distribute huge amounts of illicit alcohol far

All the rage.
The term *bootlegger* is said to date from colonial times, when to evade prohibitions on providing spirits to Native Americans, unscrupulous traders smuggled in flasks of high-proof tangleleg in their boot tops. Here, an early Prohibition-era flapper in Washington, D.C. shows that the practice hardly died out in the eighteenth century.

> On July 22, 1925, federal agents and St. Louis police officers
> nabbed 179 people in a sweep of hidden stills and taverns.
> Jennie Buttee, of 5115 Daggett Street, told officers she knew nothing of
> the 5,000 gallons of mash hidden in a sub-basement of her home.

St. Louis Dispatch
December 14, 2003

beyond what small-time operators once moved. The biggest backers controlled everything from the raw ingredients to the labor and distribution. Without necessarily knowing it, truck drivers, still builders, distillers, chemists, still hands, label counterfeiters, fast-driving haulers, local law officers, and bootleggers sometimes all worked for the same person. Ersatz scotch, so-called corn, "bathtub" gin, and suspect bourbon flooded the market as stocks of legally distilled liquor dwindled.

Clandestine distilling quickly evolved into an agribusiness catering to urban centers often far removed from the distillers' own communities. A division of labor among moonshiners, haulers, wholesalers, and bootleggers meant that distillers' products ended up wetting the throats of unknown strangers far away. If buyers were harmed by their rotgut, who cared? Stills became bigger and ingredients cheaper. In Northern cities such as New York, Chicago, Detroit, and Philadelphia, industrial stills sprang up that dwarfed their Southern cousins.

Drinkers—especially younger ones—put little premium on quality. The market responded. Why labor over real whiskey when quick-fermenting rotgut sold at such high profit and turned around equipment to make more quickly? With a seemingly unending thirst, the United States became a warren of moonshine markets. Bootleggers slaking that thirst did not hesitate to water down the product and boost its kick with added acid, lye, embalming fluid, horse manure, methanol, carbide, or anything else they thought would speed fermentation or impart enough *oomph* to make customers feel they hadn't been cheated.

In 1929, small producers had an even stronger incentive to take up moonshining: the stock market crash brought on a financial depression that lasted until World War II. Moonshining at home allowed tens of thousands of newly poor Americans to feed their families. Here and there, clandestine entrepreneurs made off pretty well. One of my friend's great aunts

Big-city moonshine, big headache. Prohibition moved moonshining from what was once mostly a small, one- or two-person rural enterprise for making ends meet to a major urban industry utilizing complex production and distribution networks. Enforcing liquor laws likewise became a major big-city problem.

made enough well-regarded moonshine during the Depression that she completely paid off a new brick house on her sideline.

Producers at the time, though, were putting out dangerously bad alcohol. Prohibition bankrolled legions of bootleggers, but it spelled disaster for an indigenous American craft by showing that profits could be wrought by mass-producing fantastically substandard moonshine with cheap and even toxic ingredients. That thirteen-year stretch had profound and devastating impacts on what had been essentially an agrarian pursuit for local markets. The demands of a booze-hungry nation brought a chill to high-quality, small-batch whiskeys and brandies made by experienced distillers. So much bad and outright deadly moonshine came on the market

> ## There were places that sold a liquor mixed with liquid camphor, and those that sold a punch composed of whiskey, hot rum, camphor, benzene, and cocaine sweepings, for six cents a glass. Customers most assuredly knew what they were getting into; sometimes the attraction was the low price, more often it was oblivion.
>
> Luc Sante, *Low Life*, 1991

during Prohibition that the reputation of homemade whiskey took a nosedive from which it has never recovered.

The end of Prohibition in 1933 hardly signaled the end of large-scale moonshining. In those thirteen hard years, legions of smaller, legal distilleries that had been unable to diversify had folded tents. Although it was once again legal to drink alcohol in the United States, there wasn't much legal booze to drink. Bourbon and other whiskeys as well as properly mellowed brandies needed years to age in barrels before they were up to standard. Understandably, those first few years after aboveboard production resumed saw some downright skeevy products in the rush to get them to market.

Home distillers and smaller producers slacked off production or stopped it entirely, but bigger moonshine operators filled a demand for alcohol that newly legitimate distillers could not satisfy. Moonshine running continued to be a big business through the 1960s, especially in the rural South and in Northern and Midwestern cities.

Riding the Rails

During Prohibition, moonshining took off in some seemingly unlikely places. By 1920, for instance, an area in southeast Kansas had become home to coal-mining immigrants from more than fifty countries, many of whom transplanted distilling traditions from their various homelands: Ireland, England, Slovenia, Bohemia, France, Poland, and Italy were just a few. This "Little Balkans" region became known during the 1920s and '30s as the source of Deep Shaft, a particularly sought-after whiskey named after the mines in which it was supposedly distilled. Railcars picking up coal distributed Deep Shaft to customers nationwide.

Moonshine on Wheels

Gentlemen or no, liquor-hauling daredevil drivers had started their engines long before auto racing became a national pastime. There were goods to deliver—and revenuers to leave behind in the dust.

With war looming on the horizon, alcohol taxes crept up in the late 1930s. Even though Prohibition was gone and licensed distilleries were up and running again, legitimate, tax-paid liquor just kept getting more expensive. The cost of moonshine whiskey was often less than just the federal tax on the legal stuff, so business boomed—as did the continuing cat-and-mouse games of moonshiners versus revenue agents.

During Prohibition, the automobile had emerged as the moonshiner's method of choice for transporting supplies and distributing the goods to market. To avoid detection, drivers would navigate the back roads at night in cars that had been outfitted to run fast and haul heavy loads while looking like ordinary street jalopies. Heavy-duty springs were added to keep the cars, weighted down with sugar or booze, level. Some runners added an extra fuel tank, or partitioned the existing tank, to hold the 'shine. Tales of bent-for-leather drivers leading revenuers on high-speed chases over curving mountain back roads and through mazelike city alleys became legion.

When the United States went to war in 1942, there was an increased call for moonshine liquor. People enjoy a calming drink or two in wartime, but large amounts of legitimate liquor production had been shifted to wartime necessities, such as medicines and industrial alcohol. Eager to develop the market, ambitious moonshine operations scrambled to secure supplies. Copper was redirected to the war effort; when even pennies in 1943 were made of low-grade steel and zinc, there was little to be spared for stills. The armed forces

Lightning: the load. Without a little mechanical trickery, a car loaded down with sugar or 'shine would ride low on its springs, a dead giveaway to sharp-eyed law officers watching the roads for moonshine runners. Heavy-duty springs were added to jack up this car to disguise its weighty cargo.

Mobile still. The moonshiner who built this still on a flatbed truck must've figured that an operation on the move could elude the law—a mistaken assumption, apparently.

> **The good old boys knew back roads, dirt roads, up people's back lanes and every whichway, and an agent would have to live in the North Carolina hills a lifetime to get to know them.**
>
> Tom Wolfe, "The Last American Hero Is Junior Johnson. Yes!"
> *Esquire,* March 1965

consumed vast amounts of yeast, and buying lots of it became nearly impossible. Sugar, the modern moonshiners' staple, was officially rationed, so honey and molasses were pressed into service instead. Making split brandies—part corn, part fruit—instead of whiskey became plain good business.

Surviving as a domestic moonshiner during the war truly required ingenuity and resourcefulness. Just making the stuff in volume was troublesome enough. Getting it to market was a whole 'nuther headache. New cars were few and expensive. Even though older models

> Roaring out of Harlan; revving up his mill,
>
> He shot the Gap at Cumberland and streamed by Maynardville.
>
> With G-men on his taillight; roadblock up ahead,
>
> The mountain boy took roads that even angels feared to tread.

"The Ballad of Thunder Road,"
Lyrics by Robert Mitchum and Don Raye, Capitol Records, 1958

continued to be pressed into service as whiskey haulers, the parts needed to maintain them became increasingly scarce. The speed-demon haulers, young men who could force swerving, speeding, gravel-spitting cars into revenuer-eluding submission, were away driving tanks and convoys in European and Pacific theaters.

Many of those who returned had earned enough money to purchase their own cars; not just any cars, but big, powerful sedans—Fords, Dodges, Plymouths, Chevrolets—that were built for speed and that took well to lead feet and tight curves. The postwar liquor hauler grew into a legendary, even romantic, figure. Robert Mitchum, fascinated with the cat-and-mouse games of southeastern liquor transporters, cowrote the script and the title song lyrics for the 1958 film *Thunder Road* about liquor hauler Luke Doolin.

START YOUR ENGINES

It has been said that racing a stock car is like dancing with a chain saw. Anyone who does it well is due some bragging rights. So it wasn't long before the haulers and transporters bringing moonshine to market began bragging about themselves and breaking into the occasional spontaneous race. In 1948, Bill France cofounded NASCAR, the National Association for Stock Car Auto Racing, as a nationwide venue for racing aficionados to strut their stuff under strict rules. Stock car racing originally involved "stock" cars from an automobile manufacturer's regular offerings, not specially built racing cars. Any modifications had to be made with parts commonly available to the driving public.

Many of the early drivers were moonshine haulers. In fact, in 1949, Glenn Dunnaway was disqualified as the winner of the first official NASCAR stock car race because the springs in his 1947 Ford had been overhauled to accommodate heavy liquor loads. The liquor hauling didn't seem to be an issue, just the non-stock springs.

Probably no racer's story carries a stronger whiff of 'shine than North Carolina's Junior Johnson. Johnson was a truly gifted racer in those early days of stock car racing; he retired in 1966 at age thirty-four with fifty wins. Most folks attribute his success to his early acquaintance with his father's illicit distilling endeavors. NASCAR was never all moonshiners and bootleggers hell-bent for leather, but the sophisticated business that it has grown into today carries the echoes of old ridge-running origins.

CHAPTER 3

MOONSHINE TODAY

If you think of moonshiners as floppy-hatted, chaw-chewin' mountaineers making gullet-searing firewater in hidden hollers, you're not alone—despite its obvious antiquarian heritage, that outdated image persists, thanks largely to American popular media.

Meanwhile, another widespread moonshining myth has taken root: that real-life distillers practicing their art with skill and care, crafting well-made spirits in small batches, are a dying breed, a remnant of the past akin to cowboys and mule drivers. The truth is, independent distilling is alive and well and enjoying a spirited renaissance in modern America.

Uncle Jesse Doesn't Live Here Anymore

The gun-toting, jug-swilling, bib-overalled back-woods moonshiner with fewer teeth than fingers lives on ... but only in the public's mind.

In his 1876–1877 report, the U.S. Commissioner for Internal Revenue captured the feelings of the day when he referred to illicit still owners as "unlettered men of desperate character, armed and ready to resist the officers of the law."

More than 125 years later, in the popular imagination the moonshiner remains a creature of the backwoods and the mountained South. Never mind that the South's former hinterlands are submitting to suburban sprawl; rough-hewn moonshiners who ply their trade in isolated hollers continue to thrive in the pages of history and folklore, as well as in comics and film.

How ingrained is the public image of moonshiners? In the course of interviewing people for this book, I asked nearly forty nondistillers to describe moonshiners. Virtually everyone came up with the same description: uneducated Southern mountaineers, defiant, fiercely loyal to kin and clan, prone to violence and incest, and spouting a vocabulary riddled with words such as *you'ins*, *vittles*, *commencin'*, and *boughten*. Nearly half men-

Die-hard stereotype.
When this caricature of a jug-swilling mountain moonshiner appeared in *Puck* magazine in 1903, it reflected a stereotype that still persists today, more than a century later.

tioned Curt and Pumpkinhead Martin, two Ozark brothers duped by Bugs Bunny into beating each other senseless during a square dance in the Warner Brothers' 1950 cartoon "Hillbilly Hare." That the brothers Martin never actually swilled any moonshine in the cartoon is beside the point; their barefoot, snaggle-toothed feuding and unlettered bearing were signal enough to generations that they were, in fact, moonshiners.

> " It is impossible to convince these big-boned, semi-barbarian people that the revenue official who comes with an armed posse into their haunts, searching for and destroying their stills, is not an emissary of a tyrannical and unjust government for whom the sly bullet is but too good a welcome. "
>
> *Harper's Weekly*, August 1879

MOONSHINE IN THE MOVIES

Our deeply entrenched cultural image of moonshiners stretches all the way to the mid-1800s, when magazines and novels of the day featured stories of feuds, moonshiners' beautiful daughters, returning Civil War combatants, and star-crossed lovers, all set in the romantic but ever-perilous Southern mountains. Borrowing heavily from the gothic tradition, like many other authors around the turn of the century, Kentucky writer John Fox Jr. wrote widely popular stories, such as *On Hell-Fer-Sartain Creek* (1897) and *A Knight of the Cumberland* (1906), that further fueled the public's interest in mountaineers.

The advent of film gave the public yet another way to guzzle the moonshiner's hootin' and hollerin' image. In the early 1900s, hundreds of thousands of working-class customers—most of whom were recent immigrants unable to speak English—flocked to nickelodeons, where for a nickel admission they were introduced to American life through "flickers" and short silent films. Especially popular were those set in the remote and mysterious mountain South.

1904's *The Moonshiner* was the first such short. Filmed in New Jersey, it ended with the revenge killing of a revenue agent by a moonshiner's wife he had just widowed. Over the next two decades, literally hundreds of similar films followed, most of them featuring stereotyped feuding, revenooer-fighting, moonshine-making Southern mountain people. They had titles such as *A Kentucky Feud* (1905), *The Mountaineer's Revenge* (1908), *A Mountain Maid* (1910), *The Revenue Man and the Girl* (1911), *The Mad Mountaineer* (1914), *Why Kentucky Went Dry* (1914), *The Still on Sunset Mountain* (1915), *The Revenue Agent* (1915), *The Last of the Stills* (1915), *The Feud Girl* (1916), *The Code of the Hills* (1916), and many more (see the sidebar, next page).

By the era of the flappers and zoot suits, "the moonshiner" was a stock American character,

Popular daughter. Melodramas of intrigue and romance featuring a smitten moonshiner's daughter and a big-city federal agent sworn to arrest her father were popular early movies.

> **She was just a moonshiner's daughter, but he loved her still.**
>
> Anonymous

Hollywood Loves "Moonshine"

◗ ◗ ◖ ◖ ◗ ◖ ◗

From the turn of the century to the present day, hundreds of films about moonshiners—most of them featuring stereotyped Southerners—have attracted moviegoers. This list is limited only to titles with the word "moonshine"—apparently, a surefire audience draw.

The Moonshiner (1904), *The Moonshiner's Daughter* (1908), *Moonshine and Love* (1910), *Peggy, the Moonshiner's Daughter* (1911), *The Moonshiner's Trail* (1911), *The Moonshiners* (1911), *The Little Moonshiner* (1912), *A Moonshiner's Heart* (1912), *A Moonshiner's Wife* (1913), *The Moonshiner's Last Stand* (1913), *The Moonshiner's Mistake* (1913), *Red Margaret, Moonshiner* (1913), *The Moonshiner's Daughter* (1914), *Her Moonshine Lover* (1914), *Moonshine Molly* (1914), *The Moonshine Maid and the Man* (1914), *On Moonshine Mountain* (1914), *Moonshines* (1915), *Maybe Moonshine* (1916), *Jerry and the Moonshiners* (1916), *Moonshine Blood* (1916), *Shorty Trails the Moonshiners* (1917), *In the Moonshine Country* (1918), *Moonshine* (1918), *The Moonshine Trail* (1920), *The Moonshine Menace* (1921), *Moonshine Valley* (1922), *The Moonshiner's Daughter* (1933), *Kentucky Moonshine* (1938), *Moonshine Mountain* (1964), *Moonshiner's Woman* (1968), *The Moonshine War* (1970), *Moonshine County Express* (1976)

Be Careful What You Drink:

◗ ◖ ◖ ◯ ◯ ◗ ◖ ◗

Dialogue from *Redneck Zombies* (Troma Entertainment, 1988)

"Look: There were chemicals in this barrel. The chemicals got into the moonshine. You'd think that it would kill them, but my guess is that it would just turn them into horrible maniacs."

"You … you mean that this moonshine … ?"

"That's right: Monster mash."

easily recognized by his unshaven jowls, rough clothing, felt hat, bare feet, and hair-trigger rifle last pressed into service in the War of Northern Aggression. Moonshine was, in fact, the liquid essence of hillbilly culture. That image has persisted in popular culture, as reflected in countless latter-day films such as the Ma and Pa Kettle series, 1958's *Thunder Road*, 1973's *White Lightning*, the 1988 cult classic *Redneck Zombies*, and 2005's *Dukes of Hazzard*, based on the television series of the same name that featured bib-overalled Uncle Jesse as the stereotypical (and ostensibly retired) moonshiner.

NOT DEAD YET

> **We've got news for Hollywood movie makers. They've got to change their old image of the mountaineer. The moonshining era is over.**
>
> "Moonshiner Era Is Over"
> *Asheville Citizen*, January 22, 1975

The *Asheville Citizen* had it half right when it printed the above words three decades back. Modern-day distillers have little in common with the old Hollywood image. Uncle Jesse simply doesn't live here anymore.

But the part about the moonshining era being over? That's a different matter.

When Joe Dabney paid his respects to corn likker in his landmark book, *Mountain Spirits*, thirty years ago, he truthfully claimed that the *craft* of moonshining was dying. Changing customs were putting a stranglehold on a cottage industry that had flourished for centuries. When moonshining became a big business, there just weren't any margins to be made in handmade local spirits. Manufactured ingredients such as yeast, store-bought malt, and especially sugar had proven themselves time and again to be faster, more reliable, less work, and higher profit than the backwoods corn whiskeys people still think of as real moonshine. When distillers who knew better began cutting corners to make better profit margins, the craft all went to the dogs.

At the time when Dabney's book was first published, around the American bicentennial, folklorists and historians turned to fading practices with a genuine feel that as America looked to its future, a good part of its past was destined for the dustbin. So they wrote about it. They wrote about the quaint customs and curious byways of the nation, moonshining included. The almost palpable sense of loss underpinning their documents came to infuse subsequent writing about homemade liquor.

These days, most of what you read, watch, or hear in the media about moonshining still has the ring of an obituary, full of past tense and past glories. Often the subjects of these reports are old men, sketchy bootleg geezers as well as gentle grandfathers putting out Appalachian ambrosia. The assumption is and has been that once they died off, the flow of moonshine—already reduced to a trickle—would stop.

Well, those distillers were old men for a reason: mastering technique can take years. Most of those I interviewed for this book were between thirty and seventy. A few were in their eighties. They are not dying off any more than plumbers, bakers, or cheese makers. And just like those skilled practitioners, they are being replaced by new generations.

Today, the notion that moonshining is a dead, bygone craft is as outmoded and outdated as Hollywood's version of those practicing it.

A dying breed? The media often portray old-timers distilling white lightning as the last practitioners of a vanishing craft. The truth is, those old-timers are being replaced by a new generation, and the craft is enjoying a renaissance.

> **We use what we call 'mule feed' for malt, and we add beading oil to make it bead good. We use a radiator out of a Dodge truck in the flake stand, cleaned out good, of course. I just want to move th' stuff out—get it to th' bootlegger quick as it's made. That's why I use haulers. I admit it's not good liquor.**

Anonymous moonshiner
The Foxfire Book

Renaissance

For nearly 400 years, New World settlers and their descendants have made untaxed whiskey. And for at least half of that stretch, pundits have declared the practice as dead, quashed, dying, or eradicated, in eulogies so convincing that gullible audiences have believed every last word.

Well, certainly the popularity and quality of those spirits have changed from time to time over the years. But the truth is, clandestine distillation is alive and well in nearly every American community. And interest in the craft—not the quick-money moonshine business, but the practice of producing superb, handmade spirits—is surely on the rise.

A NEW BREED

Modern-day commercial moonshiners make their margins by dealing in volume and using ingredients, such as cattle feed and sugar, that are cheaper than corn. Some may sell strictly in regional markets; some may also deal in marijuana or, increasingly in the South and Midwest, meth-amphetamine. Others operate larger syndicates on such a scale that they need massive financial backing and employ strict divisions of labor. These people are in the *business* of illicit alcohol; they are in it for profit alone.

Profit, though, does not drive all distillers. Among these are the traditional whiskey-making moonshiners—the so-called "old-timers" who take great pride in their work, and who may sell their special whiskies or brandies, but seldom make their living that way.

More significantly, a new breed of distillers has been steadily growing over the last quarter-century: distillers whose practice is not rooted in traditional whiskey-making culture so much as grafted onto it, who borrow heavily from beer-making traditions and are often homebrewers themselves. They design and build their own stills, develop their own recipes, and plunder libraries and rare book collections to resurrect bygone spirits using the very best ingredients they can afford. Increasingly, they compare notes online, where a growing number of businesses supply the apparatuses, ingredients, and materials they need.

For these armchair engineers and chemists, profit is almost anathema; they are tinkerers and hobbyists eking out more still efficiency and stubbornly trying to create sublime beverages to share and trade among family and friends. Because of its tatty reputation and the undue legal attention they feel the name might bring, most of these new-school distillers resist calling their hobby "moonshining." Instead, they prefer to be called "home," "small-batch" or "artisan" distillers. Increasingly, they may refer to their products as *hausgemacht* or HG, German for "homemade."

> **Gone forever is the honorable, simple, hard-working, industrious farmer who ran off whiskey in a leisurely fashion for the pleasure of himself and his friends.**
>
> David W. Maurer, *Kentucky Moonshine*, 1974

THE HOMEBREW CONNECTION

This new wave of distillers is something that 1970s historians didn't see coming when they keened over the nearing death of artisanal moonshining. A good part of the home distillers' outlook is tied directly to the 1978 decriminalization of beer and winemaking at home. Unregulated distilling was, and remains, illegal, but the loosening of laws concerning homemade alcohol shifted the way Americans thought of beer. At the time, mainstream American beers captured the best qualities of paleness and lifelessness. Homebrewing grew steadily as a way to put beers on the table that the brewers themselves wanted to drink. In homebrew shops and garages across the nation, small groups gathered to swap and taste beers, compare notes on equipment and techniques, and share recipes for authentic styles of beer not commercially available then.

Nearly thirty years later, homebrewing is a firmly entrenched American hobby. Part of its outlook is based on a 500-year-old throwback. The *Reinheitsgebot*, Bavaria's 1516 brewing purity law, prescribed only barley, hops, and water in beer. The law has evolved (for instance, when the role of yeast was understood, the law was amended to allow it as well), but German brewers still adhere to it. This concern with purity is deeply ingrained in homebrewers' notions of beer, though today it extends to the *quality* of ingredients more than what those ingredients actually are.

Because so many began as homebrewers, it's no surprise that a German-infused mind-set—concern with purity, quality, authenticity, sharing, and openness—characterizes contemporary home distillers, too.

In grafting German techniques to Scots-Irish traditions, amateur distillers are making some of the best local liquor North America has seen in a very long time. Some, especially in Canada, distill to save money on alcohol. Some make their own because they live in dry areas. Most, though, enjoy the challenges and satisfaction of creating

> ## The realization that hobby distilling poses no more problems than beer and wine making and should be afforded the same rights and freedoms is finally taking hold.
>
> John Stone, *American Distiller*, April 2002

excellent schnapps, whiskeys, rums, brandies, and cordials. They rarely sell their product, but will give it away, barter for services, or trade it for raw ingredients such as fresh fruit. Before Katrina's evil visage devastated New Orleans, the green fairy of absinthe beckoned to underground distillers, while Philadelphia winemakers continue to celebrate their Italian roots by learning to create grappa. In their rush to embrace pigs, Moon Pies, grits, and biscuits, graduate students in American Southern studies programs are taking up distillation with an almost belligerent damn-you pride. *Drinking moonshine*, they seem to say, *is tangible evidence that rebellion still flows in our veins*. For all of them, homemade liquor is a shibboleth of authenticity, a tangible link to their pasts.

Meanwhile, small legal distilleries devoted to the art of producing handcrafted spirits are arising from coast to coast—many, not surprisingly, are offshoot businesses of commercial artisan microbreweries. Rum is being made again in several states, and vodka is trickling tastefully from Delaware and Texas. California whiskeys and *eaux de vie* from Washington state are right there if you want them. Traditional corn whiskeys are being produced in Virginia, Alabama, West Virginia, and other states.

In other words, small-scale artisan distilling has begun to reclaim its once-proud image. Whether it's trickling down, percolating up, or simply advancing hand-in-glove, a growing appreciation of well-made spirits is taking hold in legal and extralegal circles.

Moonshine Goes Legit

◐ ◐ ○ ◐ ○ ◐ ◐

In Culpeper, Virginia, distiller Chuck Miller isn't the least bit shy talking about his moonshine whiskey. He'll even show you his still. See, Miller pays his taxes. Like a growing number of other small artisan distilleries emerging across the country, his business is licensed and audited, his equipment is registered, and his production is entirely legal and aboveboard. Miller's products, in fact, are sold to one customer only: the Virginia Department of Alcoholic Beverage Control. His still—a 2,000-gallon copper-pot behemoth—even came to him on a tip from a government agent.

Getting legal was an involved process that took a few years. "When the agent said, 'We're going to wrap this up before Christmas,'" he chuckled, "she didn't say which Christmas!" To get licensed, Miller had to own a still. He told one agent, "You guys go around the country busting up stills, why don't you just save me one?" Turns out the agent knew of an unused still from 1933 in a barn. The owner had been warned that he needed to get rid of it. He was happy to sell it to Miller for scrap.

Miller, a retired airline pilot, began distilling a corn whiskey about fifteen years ago using a barley malt, but soon shifted to an all-corn grain bill for Virginia Lightning, a clear corn whiskey sold in ABC stores throughout the Old Dominion. His Copper Fox is aged like many homemade whiskeys: rather than aging the spirits in barrels, Miller turns the barrel inside out by charring cubes of white oak and suspending them in the liquor, wrapped in cheesecloth, for a few months to impart a foxy hue.

Moonshine and the Law

If you're thinking of distilling your own alcohol, here's step one: separate myth and wishful thinking from legal fact.

A surprising number of American home distillers practice their hobby under the faulty notion that citizens of the United States are allowed to make whiskey, brandy, or other spirits for personal consumption, just as though it were beer or wine. Most moonshiners—the guys selling their makings—know better.

Make no mistake about it:

Distilling alcohol is a very tightly controlled activity in the United States, Canada, and many other countries. Without the proper authorization and without paying taxes, you may not distill beverage alcohol in any amount. Even owning a still can get you in trouble if you haven't done the paperwork to get your operation approved.

The United States did indeed decriminalize the home production of beer and wine in 1978. But distilled spirits remain beyond the pale. Don't let anyone tell you otherwise. I repeat: distilling ethanol without proper permission is illegal in the United States and Canada. Without inspection and the proper approvals, you are not permitted to make any amount for personal use. Not one drop.

Here are the Alcohol and Tobacco Tax and Trade Bureau's (TTB) own discouraging words on the matter, as stated on their "General Alcohol FAQs" Internet site (http://www.ttb.gov/alcohol/info/faq/genalcohol.htm#g1):

Spirits

"You cannot produce spirits for beverage purposes without paying taxes and without prior approval of paperwork to operate a distilled spirits plant. [See 26 U.S.C. 5601 & 5602 for some of the criminal penalties.] There are numerous requirements that must be met that make it impractical to produce spirits for personal or beverage use. Some of these requirements are paying special tax, filing an extensive application, filing a bond, providing adequate equipment to measure spirits, providing suitable tanks and pipelines, providing a separate building (other than a dwelling) and maintaining detailed records, and filing reports. All of these requirements are listed in 27 CFR Part 19. Spirits may be produced for non-beverage purposes for fuel use only without payment of tax, but you also must file an application, receive TTB's approval, and follow requirements, such as construction, use, records, and reports."

"CFR Part 19" refers to the U.S. Code of Federal Regulations, Part 19, "Distilled Spirits Plants"—a dauntingly lengthy and complex legal document detailing all the federal government's many regulatory requirements for starting and operating a distillery. You'll find that document and other useful links, including application forms, on the TTB's Web site, starting at its home page: http://www.ttb.gov/index.htm. (You'll find the full text of Canadian regulations, "Excise Act, 2001," on the Canada Revenue Agency's Web site at http://www.cra-arc.gc.ca/tax/technical/exciseduty-e.html.)

Keep in mind, too, that it's not just the federal government's permission you'll need to get legal. Every state in America also requires distillers to obtain some sort of license or permit, as do many local governments.

WINDS OF CHANGE

Before you become too discouraged over the "impractical" regulatory roadblocks to legal distilling, consider the growing number of new small distilleries that have emerged in recent years (see page 51). It can be, and is being, done. Meanwhile, as public interest in home distillation increases, much as interest in homebrewing took off in the '70s, efforts to relax the federal regulations on small-scale distillation of alcoholic beverages also are gathering momentum. In 2001, a bill was introduced to the 107th Congress (H.R. 3249) that proposed just such a change. Although the legislation died somewhat predictably, the idea's time may be coming—perhaps sooner, perhaps later, but coming nonetheless.

Some say that enforcement attitudes have also changed. Increasingly, they claim, countries with laws against moonshining—including the United States—are turning a blind eye to small, non-commercial producers as their law enforcement resources get diverted to more pressing issues. Small-scale distillers simply aren't on the radar

Get to know the law—but not this way. It's up to you to learn about and comply with all local, regional, and national laws related to the distillation of alcohol.

of enforcement agencies because busting them diverts time, money, and manpower from more pressing matters. One Southern federal agent told me, "I've been in this office 19 years. We haven't had a moonshine case in 18. It's just not an issue."

Presuming that breaking the law, whatever that law may be, is "just not an issue" is dangerous, if not foolhardy—I don't recommend it. However, there is no denying that some have taken that attitude, and that among them are at least some law enforcement personnel with more urgent matters to attend to.

This shouldn't be particularly surprising. United States criminal law divides offenses into two broad categories: *malum in se* offenses, which are considered "naturally evil as adjudged by the sense of a civilized community," and *malum prohibitum* offenses. The former means, literally, evil in itself. American jurisprudence regards *malum in se* crimes such as murder and rape so inherently harmful and destructive that their commission entails grave moral outrage. *Malum prohibitum* crimes, on the other hand, are wrong merely because legislation prohibits them. Parking offenses, for

instance, are *mala prohibita*. So is letting your lawn grow too rangy in some towns. Because moonshining is a tax dodge, it is classed as *malum prohibitum*—not evil, but illegal.

Tether all your notions of moonshine directly to this distinction and drive it into the ground like a spike. No conversation with illicit distillers about their spirits strays far from the idea that distilling is honest labor, regardless of what local or federal laws have to say on the matter. Whether they run off mash regularly as a way to make ends meet or simply enjoy the challenges of producing small batches of artisan spirits, distillers almost universally regard their activities as a harmless pursuit of happiness.

Now, let's be honest. Obviously, some ... most ... hell, nearly all home distillers disregard the law. That doesn't mean you should, too. Homebrewers were able to get the law changed by working with legislators. If you can't abide taxes on homemade spirits, work to change the law, but in the meanwhile, contact the TTB and your state and local authorities (or their counterparts, if you live outside the United States) to learn what the current guidelines are, and begin applying for permits.

> **The golden age of moonshining is now ... The government has quit hunting it. They took their manpower and started using it on firearms and explosives, deciding it was a waste of time to search through the hills for stills. As a result, you can get better moonshine now than you could during the Depression.**
>
> Organizer of Pikeville, Kentucky's Hillbilly Days Festival
> Quoted in *Dubuque Telegraph Herald*, January 18, 2004

CHAPTER 4

MASHING
AND
FERMENTING

In chapter one, you read the short version of how moonshine is made. Now it's time to learn the whole story—or, at least, enough of the basics to get you started.

Getting started, in fact, is what this chapter is all about. Fermenting is the first essential step in the process of making moonshine. You can't distill alcohol until you've coaxed that alcohol from your base ingredients—grains, fruits, and/or sugar—and you do that by fermenting them.

Equipment

Of course, the single most important piece of equipment for making moonshine is a still. We'll cover that subject in the next chapter. Here's what you'll need to get started fermenting and for general all-around stillhouse use.

Many of the items listed here are common kitchen or household implements. Because the fermentation process for distillers is similar to those for beer and wine makers, virtually everything else is available at any well-stocked beer- or wine-making store or wholesale vendor, or from their online equivalents.

Fire extinguisher. I've put this at the top of the list for good reason. Always have a functional, charged fire extinguisher handy whenever you use a flame or heat source. This is a good rule whether you're distilling alcohol, heating mash ingredients, or just cooking a meal. Add to that the notion that distilling alcohol has been likened to boiling a pot of gasoline, and you can see the wisdom of putting this item at the top of *your* list, too. Be sure that your extinguisher is rated Class B, which means that it's suitable for flammable liquids such as alcohol.

Stockpot or boiling kettle. Obtain one that's either stainless steel or, if you're feeling flush, copper. An 8- to 10-gallon pot is about right; it needs to be big enough to hold all of your mash ingredients plus at least 5 gallons of water.

Long-handled stainless steel spoons for mixing your mash and batting away curious cats and errant children, who should never be around a working stillhouse.

Measuring spoons for measuring small amounts of mash ingredients or additives.

Wire-mesh strainer. You'll use this for straining out fruit pulp or grains, and for removing floating foam and residue, called the raft, from fermented mash. A strainer 6 or more inches across works nicely.

Everyday items. You probably already have many of the items you'll need. Shown here (clockwise from left): canning jars, wire-mesh strainer, stockpot, long-handled spoon, pot gripper, measuring spoons. Wine, champagne, and liquor bottles are common modern alternatives.

Bowl gripper. Also known as a pizza pan gripper, this handy device clamps onto the edge of a pan or stainless steel bowl, providing an instant handle, much like a pot handle. It's useful in all sorts of situations, and available in most kitchenware or restaurant supply stores.

Thermometer. You'll need this for monitoring your mash temperature, so that you ensure a proper starch conversion and don't inadvertently kill off your yeast with excessive heat. Any good kitchen thermometer will do, as will a floating thermometer or an instant-read thermometer such as those used by chefs (my personal favorite). Laser point-and-shoot thermometers are not appropriate because you'll want to measure the internal temperature of your mash, not its surface temperature.

Hydrometer. A brewing hydrometer measures the sugar content in a low-alcohol mash by determining its specific gravity (see the sidebar on page 77) and indicates when fermentation has ceased. A spirit or proof hydrometer measures the alcoholic strength of a clear distillate. Some well-stocked homebrew shops carry them, but they are also available from scientific storehouses (see page 112 for more about proof hydrometers).

pH papers or meter. As you may recall from high school chemistry, pH is a measure of the acidity or alkalinity of a solution, based on a scale ranging from 1 (most acidic) to 14 (most alkaline); 7.0 is a completely neutral solution. A mash that is not sufficiently acidic, or too far off the scale in either direction, can discourage the enzyme activity you want for good alcohol production, or cause other problems such as unwanted bacterial growth. Often, recipes suggest a starting pH range; for example, many grain-based mashes need a pH range between 5.2 and 5.5. Strips of chemically sensitive paper called pH papers, available at homebrew shops and druggists, are rough-and-tumble,

Makin's monitors. Left to right: brewing hydrometer, spirit hydrometer, thermometer, floating thermometer.

A Word about Homebrew Shops: Shhhh.

Few homebrew shops carry equipment or ingredients that are specifically intended for small-batch distilling. Nonetheless, homebrew shops are often a distiller's best source for almost everything except stills. Most of the ingredients to make whiskey are stock items. Flaked, whole, and malted grains, malt extracts, and specialty yeasts are there for purchase, as are fermentation vessels, straining bags, pH papers and meters, hoses, airlocks, and more. If the equipment is not directly suitable for the novice, it often can be adapted with only minor adjustments.

Do not assume, however, that these mom and pop owners want anything to do with you or your alcohol—even when you show the proper permits. Many who may be privately sympathetic to hobbyists making alcohol for their own use flat-out refuse to have anything to do with anyone they think may be making—and especially selling—hooch. Yes, they may know who in the community is distilling. They may even have stills themselves. But the prospect of getting busted as a supplier to illicit distillers is enough to make even garrulous homebrewers clam up when it comes to admitting they know anything beyond the most basic distillation principles.

In other words, respect their awkward position. Don't tell them more than they want to know. And don't ask questions they can't comfortably answer.

The Shrimp Boot Method

Smashing grapes with your bare feet is out, but a Louisiana brandy maker of my recent acquaintance puts ripe fruit into a clean child's plastic wading pool, slips on new, clean, white rubber shrimping boots, and stomps the fruit into mush for mash.

cost-efficient tools for measuring and, when necessary, adjusting your mash's acidity. Electronic pH meters are more accurate and easier to use, but can also be pricey.

Fermentation vessel. You'll need one that holds at least 6½ gallons, with no less than 2 inches of headspace to accommodate foam. The vessel also needs an airtight lid. Food-grade plastic fermenters are your best choice; they're inexpensive and have an easy-access wide mouth that won't clog with mash solids. Homebrew shops sell them already fitted out with a hole in the lid's center to accommodate a rubber stopper and air lock (see those items below). Be aware that plastic does have its drawbacks: 1) It can absorb smells and tastes that carry over into subsequent batches, and 2) scratches picked up during normal use can harbor populations of unwanted microorganisms that

can affect taste. If you sterilize the vessel carefully before each use it could last you several years.

Carboy. Carboys are large glass jugs, often between 5 and 7 gallons, that can be plugged with rubber stoppers and airlocks. They are not particularly useful as fermentation vessels in distilling, but if you *rack* (see page 116) your fermented mash into one before distilling it, storing it overnight in the carboy will allow fine particles to settle out.

Pitching vessel. A small glass bowl, a glass flask or beaker, or a medium glass jar is a good choice for rehydrating yeast before adding, or "pitching," it to your mash.

Air locks. Also known as bubblers or fermentation locks, these two- or three-part plastic valves keep outside air from contaminating your mash but allow fermentation gases to escape. Just fill the lock partially with water, cap it, and insert it snugly into the fermentation vessel's opening.

Bubble, sit, and siphon. Left to right: vessel with airlock for fermenting mash, glass carboy for allowing mash to settle, racking cane and hose for siphoning wash.

Racking cane and hose. This is a rigid plastic tube attached to a flexible hose used to siphon clear fermented wash off mash sediment into another container. This process is called *racking*. Whenever possible, use tubing made of alcohol-resistant vinyl rather than acrylic.

Grating, grinding, and crushing tools. Before mashing, whole grains for mash should be ground or cracked to expose the starches inside. Most homebrew stores will do this for you, but if you'd rather do things yourself you'll need a hand-cranked or power *grain mill*. Fruits for brandy mashes also must be crushed, to release their juices. To make a *fruit crusher* for removing the pulp from stone fruits such as peaches, tack clean metal lath screen—the diamond-shaped wire mesh sold in hardware stores and used as a base surface for stucco—to a small wood frame, or stretch some over a 5-gallon plastic bucket. Then just rub the fruit against the screen. A potato masher makes a good tool for crushing small soft fruits such as grapes. Or, use rubber boots (see the sidebar on page 57).

Ingredients

Some folks make whiskey from corn flakes. Honest. It's not a path I'd follow, but if you stick with distilling you'll uncover recipes that call for ingredients far more bizarre than that.

Don't be intimidated by the variety of ingredients you'll find here and in other sources. When all is said and done, there are really just three main ingredients you need to use: 1) water, 2) sugars (in the form of grains, fruit, or concentrated sugars), and 3) yeast.

Let's look at each in turn.

WATER

Good water is essential to whiskey making. Distillers in places with great water such as Kentucky, Ireland, and Scotland have for centuries produced some of the world's truly excellent spirits. Chances are, the water flowing from your tap isn't perfect, but the good news for home distillers is that, by and large, municipal tap water makes a decent mash.

Without question, cheap and plentiful tap water is ideal for utilitarian stuff like cleaning stills and rinsing pots. A degree of common sense does, however, help in deciding whether your water is suitable for distilling something you'd want to drink. If your tap water is particularly "hard" or

The beer won't pay off as good if the water comes from a branch that's got touch-me-nots along its banks...They denote hard water and hard water won't make corn whiskey. For making moonshine, find yourself a branch where red horsemint grows. You can't go wrong.

"Interview with a Moonshiner" by John Parris
Asheville Citizen, September 1, 1989

and others for cutting the distillate (that is, for diluting high-proof, straight-out-of-the-still spirits with water to drinking strength).

In the American mountain south, as in Scotland, clear-running springs grew famous for producing fine whiskeys. Without fancy chemical analyses, mountaineers long ago learned by observation which springs and branches made good whiskeys and brandies. Certain plants growing nearby, for instance, and water that "beaded" when shaken were clues to good still sites.

Okay, so maybe you don't live in Scotland, you can't afford to truck in water from the Kentucky highlands, and there aren't any tell-tale plants growing around your water faucets, but you want to try to use water that's a cut above acceptable. The good news is, in many cases you can mimic prized mountain waters by first contacting your local water department for an analysis of what's flowing from your pipes, and then tweaking that tap water, if necessary.

A water analysis will reveal, for example, whether certain aspects of your source water could be improved to make a mash that converts starches to fermentable sugars more efficiently, or creates an especially hospitable environment for yeasts.

If you decide to analyze and treat your mash water—remember, you may not need or want to when you're starting out—pay particular attention to four measurements that most reports include:

1) **Calcium (Ca) content.** The range should be between 50 and 150 ppm (parts per million). You may need to adjust your mash water with small additions—no more than 1 teaspoon per 5 gallons—of calcium sulfate (powdered gypsum, $CaSO_4$) to get it in this range. Gypsum will lower the mash's pH; see below.

2) **Hardness.** This is often stated as the combined measurement of metallic ions such as calcium, magnesium, iron, and zinc suspended in the water. Ideally, that measurement should not exceed 8 gpg (grains per gallon). Hardness is also sometimes expressed solely as a concentration of

contains dissolved minerals, your final product may well be better off if you use bottled or distilled water instead. What are some other signs of less-than-ideal water? When a rotten-egg smell regularly flows from the tap, when bathwater feels slick even without soap, or when mineral deposits clog your home's plumbing, your water really should not be used straight from the tap for a mash.

For now, you can operate on the basic assumption that if your tap water is fit to drink, it's fit for your mash. With experience, you'll learn the more subtle effects of water on your final product, and may come to prefer particular water profiles—mineral content, hardness, etc.—for your mash, calcium carbonate ($CaCO_3$). Anything over 150 milligrams per liter is considered hard; anything over 250 is very hard. The simplest solution if your water is excessively hard is to use distilled water.

3) **Iron (Fe) content.** Ideally, this reading should be 0. If it's greater than 25 ppm, use distilled water.

4) **pH.** Municipal tap water is often slightly alkaline, between pH 7.5 and 8.5. Although you can, and in many cases should, check and adjust your mash's pH after you've added the basic ingredients (but before adding yeast; see page 130), you may want to adjust your water's pH right from the start if it's significantly too alkaline or acidic. Adding small amounts (no more than 1 teaspoon per 5 gallons) of powdered citric acid or acid blend,

available at homebrew shops, can lower the pH to the proper range. So, too, can adding powdered gypsum ($CaSO_4$) at the same rate. (Note that 95 percent sulfuric acid is also sometimes used drop by drop to lower pH, but can cause severe burns if not used properly; for this reason, many home distillers avoid it.) Calcium carbonate ($CaCO_3$) can be used, if necessary, to raise pH, but be aware that pH over 6.0 slows enzyme activity, can extract some unpleasant tastes from grains, and allows greater opportunity for bacteria to infect the mash. With each small addition of acid or $CaCO_3$, retest the solution and stop adding when it reaches its target pH.

A Little pH Practice Can't Hurt

To measure the acidity of your mash with pH paper, just dip one of the strips into a sample of the solution to be tested. Reagents impregnated in the paper change color according to the solution's pH. Match the resulting color with the manufacturer's pH color chart, and you have the solution's pH. To adjust the solution to be less or more acidic, simply add acid blends or calcium carbonate. Easy, right?

Well, yes. But overadjusting and therefore over- or under-shooting your target pH also is easy. It's worth taking some time to familiarize yourself with these products. Practice taking readings and adjusting pH levels with acid blends or calcium carbonate using small amounts of plain tap water that will *not* go into your mash. Goofing a little bit of water hurts less than ruining a 5-gallon mash of dead-ripe peaches you've stoned by hand.

Dip strips. Inexpensive and easy-to-use pH papers can help you make a mash that's not too acid, not too alkaline— in other words, just right.

GRAINS

Distilled beverages made solely from fermented grain, water, and yeast are known as whiskeys. American whiskeys traditionally have relied on rye, barley, wheat, and most famously, corn. Well-made corn likker is still held in particular esteem, especially when aged in white oak. Though they are less commonly intended for the still, a distiller can also use millet, oats, rice, or practically any other grain. The amount and kinds of grains used in a recipe are called its *grain bill*.

Grains may be bought whole, crushed, flaked, or finely ground into meal. All of the whiskey recipes in this book call for flaked grains, to make things a bit easier for beginners' first forays into distilling. Flaked grains are unmalted grains (see the next subsection, Malting and Mashing Grains) that have been crushed, moistened, cooked, and flaked between rollers. This isn't as strange as you might think; rolled oats are nothing but flaked grains and are a breakfast staple in much of the United States. Brewers and distillers often use flaked grains as an adjunct to their whole-grain ingredients, but many beginners or distillers with limited equipment use only flaked grains simply because they sidestep some of the work and equipment required when using crushed whole grains. They still need to be mashed (see below), but they don't require the other processing involved in using whole crushed grains (also discussed below).

Say No to Seed Grains

Make absolutely certain that you choose dried, food-grade grains. Grains intended for seed are often treated with chemical fertilizers and pesticides and are wholly unfit for consumption. Pesticide-free grains can be purchased readily from health food stores, homebrew shops, and wholesale food distributors.

Always Chew Your Drink

Amylase, the malted-grain enzyme that converts starches to sugar, is also found in fresh ginger, banana peels—and human saliva. Some mash recipes, therefore, actually call for the ingredients to be chewed first. *Kava*, for instance, is a mouth-numbing Fijian drink made by chewing and then fermenting kava (*Piper methysticum*). In the Andes, Peruvian locals brew the ancient corn beer *chica* in a similar manner.

Malting and Mashing Grains

Regardless of whether they're whole, crushed, flaked, or whatever, grains contain unfermentable starches and, without alteration, will not yield much alcohol. That alteration comes by way of two processes, *malting* and *mashing*, that together convert the grains' starches into fermentable sugars. Those sugars, in turn, will easily produce a fairly high-alcohol "beer"—a fermented mash—that can then be distilled into the even more potent elixir we call whiskey.

Malting is the practice of steeping grains in water, allowing them to germinate partially, and then quickly drying them to kill the sprouts. Brewers, distillers, and moonshiners refer to the resulting soaked, sprouted, and dried grains as *malt*.

Why would you want to do all that to perfectly good grains? Because the process produces enzymes (primarily alpha- and beta-amylase) that have the potential of converting unfermentable starches into fermentable sugars. That potential is activated when you heat the grains in water—when you *mash* them—at certain temperatures for certain time periods. The hot-water soak releases the starches in the grains, allowing the enzymes to go forth and do their conversions, making sugars of starches.

All whiskey recipes, therefore, require malt. But not all the grains in a particular recipe need to have been malted. Instead, malt is most often used as an adjunct to a mash made primarily of unmalted grains. Grain bills with 20 to 25 percent malt are sufficient to induce effective conversion of most usable starches.

Malted barley (or "barley malt"), malted corn, and malted rye just refer to the type of grain. Barley malt is the most common commercially available. When you're just starting out, the kind you want is pale barley malt. Once you get the hang of distilling, you may want to experiment with roasted, toasted, or caramel varieties, which can add some truly wonderful aromatics in the finished spirit. You may use six-row barley (so-called because it bears six rows of grain on each ear) for its big enzymatic punch, but the common two-row imparts less tannin. The malt should be ground before adding it to a mash of unmalted grains.

Mashing

Because they've already been partially processed, mashing flaked grains is easy enough: You simply add the flaked grains to mash water heated to the temperature indicated in the particular recipe you're making and proceed from there, adding

Make Your Own Malt?

Make no mistake: most distillers buy their malt, and with good reason. Excellent barley malt is universally available wherever big bearded men gather to swap stories about hops, sparging, and understanding wives. But a minority of hard-core traditionalists, perfectionists, and the insatiably curious make their own. The process: soak dried grains in lukewarm water, keep them damp, let them begin to sprout, then dry them, crush or grind them, and add the new malt to your mash. If you are using the malt immediately, there's no need to dry it.

That's a simplified explanation; for more thorough discussions of modern methods, refer to any good homebrewing book or website. In *Mountain Spirits* by Joe Dabney, the author tells of a traditional method as related by a retired Georgia moonshiner:

We put our shelled corn in a tow sack and poured hot water over it and put it in a sawdust pile. Just covered it up. In about three days, it'd have stringers about two, three inches long. All tangled up. You just spread it out and let it dry in the sun for two, three days. Carry it to the mill and have it ground.

Another way to sprout corn for malting was useful in the winter, but not necessarily for city folk. A burlap bag was filled to about two-thirds capacity with dried corn, sewn shut, soaked in water until the bag swelled—and then buried under horse or cow manure to assure enough heat to sprout the grains. One presumes the flavor didn't carry over.

malt after the flakes have had time to rehydrate, stirring occasionally, and allowing the mash to rest and cool before adding yeast (see The Process, page 75).

Whole grains, however, must first be crushed or milled into a coarse grind. Nearly any homebrew shop will do this for you with a specially designed grist or grain mill. You want each kernel free of its husk and broken into several pieces to expose its interior. Don't have it ground too small or you may end up with fine particulates you can't strain out that scorch the mash when you heat it.

Once it's crushed, you can add the grain—including malted grains—to heated water, stir, and let it rest (again, the recipe will indicate specific temperatures and time periods) to allow the starches to convert to sugars.

Traditional moonshiners at this point let the mash cool, add yeast, and allow the mixture to ferment "on the grain"—that is, with the grain still in the mash. The whiskey recipes in this book follow that same principle, particularly because flaked grains have already been processed for maximum starch conversion, and also settle neatly to the bottom of the container without leaving a lot of float-

Mash tun. This tricked-out cooler allows you to hold mash at a given temperature range and then draw off clear wash through a spigot. The bottom strainer (inset, upper left) separates mash solids from the liquid. You can make your own tun, or buy a commercial version such as this one at homebrew stores.

ing residue. However, some distillers—particularly those who come from a homebrew background, and perhaps especially those who use whole grains—prefer to ferment "off the grain" by first straining the liquid and then rinsing the grain and adding the rinse water.

To do this, after the grains have rested long enough to initiate starch-to-sugar conversion, strain the mash through a nylon brewer's bag into a fermentation vessel, keeping the grains in the bag. The strained, sweet liquid is now called *wort* (pronounced "wurt"). Next, *sparge*, or rinse, the grains to extract as much of the sugar as possible. In a separate pot, heat one gallon of the mash water to near boiling. Submerge the grain-filled brewer's bag in the hot water, agitate it gently, and remove it. Add this liquid back to the mash water, and repeat the sparging process once more. Discard the exhausted grains.

An alternative and more common technique relies on a tun, which is just a brewer's term for any large vessel that holds liquid. *Mash tuns* are specifically designed to hold, well, mash at a particular temperature. *Lauter tuns* allow liquids to drain from spent grains. Smaller operators often use the same vessel—a hybrid tun—for both purposes. The tun has a false bottom set just above the real bottom that allows the grains to settle and form a bed of husks and grain particles. Liquid wash flows through this bed into the space between the false bottom and the real one and is drawn off though a spigot. The grains are usually then sparged as described above.

You can buy a tun at homebrew shops or make your own; an insulated plastic picnic cooler tricked out with a false bottom and reinforced spigots is a common sight among distillers with beer-brewing backgrounds. If you want to take this more popular and practical route, you can find discussions of tuns and plans for building them in many homebrewing books and on the Internet. You will undoubtedly encounter other methods of separating fermented liquids from mash solids.

FRUIT

In the United States, spirits distilled from fruit are classified as brandy. By law, they cannot contain added sugar. But then, home distillers don't always cotton to legal distinctions, and often add white sugar to extend the mash. Peach brandy and applejack are two American classics, worth seeking out if anyone in your community is known for making them. The only thing better might be cherry bounce, a wallop-packing concoction of mixed sour and sweet cherries baptized in whiskey and honey, then left to mature for months on end (see page 146).

Grappa, eau de vie and some varieties of schnapps are all fruit distillates, though grappa refers strictly to spirits made of grape pomace (the skins, seeds, and other solids left after pressing grapes for juice or wine). Brandies often have specific names; kirsch is made from cherries, for example, and slivovitz is always made of plums. At one time or another, the spirits of pears, apricots, blackberries, tangerines, quince, strawberries, blueberries, huckleberries, jackfruit, cranberries, persimmons, raisins, prunes, limes, mangoes, gooseberries, raspberries, kiwis, cherries, currants, and rhubarb have wound their way through copper coils. What's good? Whatever tastes good—and whatever's fresh. Grow it, pick it, buy it wholesale, or cut a bartering deal with a local farmer, but always get your fruit in season for the best quality and best prices.

That advice, to obtain the "best quality" fruit, is a departure from some traditional approaches. Florida citrus farmer Benton McClintock once described for Eugene Walter, an irrepressible proponent of Southern foods, his recipe for wine using oranges that were "good and moldy." Mr. McClintock was in good company: Some of the most venerable recipes for fruit wines and home-style American brandies call for windfalls, or bruised and half-rotten fruits. In fact, bruised windfall peaches were once known and sold at market as less expensive "brandy peaches." Face it, stoning a peach is a lot easier when the thing's already mush. Besides, fruit mash is just rotten fruit anyway, right?

Well, not exactly. A pronounced trend among artisan distillers shows a different take on the rotten-fruit tradition. From Michigan to Austria,

Fruited Cock Water

◖◖◖○◖◖◖

Take a red Cock from ye Barn's door, pull it, take out ye Intrals & break all ye Bones, have in readiness of Rosemary, hops and Broad Time each 1 handful, red Pimpernel 2 handfuls, Raisins of ye Sun ston'd half a pound, Dates pick'd and ston'd a qtr of a pound, Currans wash'd and rubb'd dry a pound, Canary sack 2 qts; first lay most of ye herbs in ye bottom of ye still, then put in ye Cock, lay the fruit all about it, put ye rest of ye herbs over it, & pour ye sack in by ye sides, cover and past it close, begin the fire betimes & keep a constant heat under it. You may draw somewhat above 3 pints of very good [sic]; mix and sweeten it with Sugar-Candy to yr Liking.

Household manuscript
circa 1740
From the collection of
Chef Fritz Blank

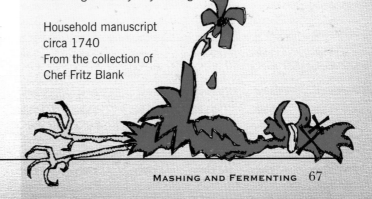

Whiskey Grades

Local whiskeys travel under different names depending on where and how good they are. The language of illicit distilling in America is far from universal, but I've never been misunderstood when using the following terms.

Courtin' whiskey: The finest grade of whiskey, suitable to assuage the misgivings of a beloved's father as one teeters on the cusp of asking for his daughter's hand.

Sippin' whiskey: Fine, handmade artisan whiskey, potent and sly. In small doses, a delightful conversational lubricant. Advisable to sip it neat or with a splash of water.

Sellin' whiskey: Low stuff indeed; when the distiller won't venture a drink because he knows it is shoddily made of inferior ingredients and possibly contaminated with adulterants. Usually shipped out of the maker's area, so he won't have to face his customers by the light of day.

Spittin' whiskey: Sellin' whiskey gone bad; for entertainment purposes only. Most common when infrequent imbibers buy gallon jugs of sugarhead whiskey and let it sit so long that the flavor of the plastic contaminates the drink. Wholly unfit for consumption, but kept on hand for spitting explosively into bonfires by skilled spitters (a trick that is emphatically NOT for amateurs).

Note that any of these whiskeys taken to excess degrades quickly into plain old **fightin' whiskey**.

Good versus ewwww. Although many old-time recipes called for rotten fruit, modern distillers strongly favor fruit that is in perfect condition and therefore less likely to harbor contaminating bacteria, yeasts, and other beasts.

people believe that only the very best fruits should be used when making brandies. Fruit for distilling, they proclaim, should be the very best, the ripest, the perfect fruits you might offer a guest in your home.

Although making fruit wines indeed involves a rotting process, these distillers prefer it to be a controlled one with known strains of yeast. Windfall fruit may be infected with wild yeasts and undesirable bacteria and may have begun spontaneous fermentation at high temperatures. The result? Some very funky tastes and smells. Banana, clove, plastic bandage, and dirty sock aromas are not unheard of. When a temperature difference of one degree can make dramatic changes in how a fermented beverage tastes, you want to have as much control over the process as possible. Using fresh, unblemished, wholesome, and sound fruit is a sure way to get better control over the type of yeast fermenting your mash and craft the right flavor profile. That's if you want to be safer. If you are afflicted with a pathological curiosity about these things, don't be afraid to try some rotten-fruit mashes, but do be aware that some of those brandies might not win medals.

Dried fruits such as prunes, raisins, apples, and peaches also may be pressed into service (see the sidebar, Fruited Cock Water, for one intriguing application). For most recipes, rehydrate or plump the dried fruit in lukewarm water, then use an immersion blender to reduce the entire mass to a dark slush and ferment as you would other fruit mashes. A few distillers advise adding acid blends (see page 73) to dried fruit mashes to make a more palatable product.

Preparing Fruit

To prepare fruits for fermenting, wash them gently. Remove stems, leaves, dirt, insects, and any other miscellaneous things that skeeve you. Don't worry about skins, pits, or seeds; you'll strain them out later. Crush the fruits. You may push them through a strainer or sieve, grind them in a meat grinder, crush them in a mill, even use a hydraulic cider or grape press if you have one (or use the shrimp boot method as described on page 57). The resulting slurry of fruit puree is called *pomace* or sometimes *pummie*.

Some recipes add hot or cold water and sugar. Others don't because the pomace is liquid enough or particular distillers don't like adding sugar. Either way, fruit mashes are almost never cooked.

Mash vs. Wash vs. Beer

There's no national moonshiner's union enforcing standard safety and conduct codes or glossaries. Consequently, the language they use to describe their tools and techniques varies from region to region and even among generations. A case in point concerns the words *mash*, *wash*, and *beer*. For some, they all refer to the fermented or fermenting mix of water and grains or fruit, whether the liquid has been racked or is still commingled with solids. Others insist that a mash is only called that when grains (not fruit) are steeping in hot water. A wash may refer to the liquid once the grains are removed before it's fermented, or the same after it has fermented and been transferred to a still. Others insist wash is appropriate only for sugar spirits such as rum or modern 'splo. Beer? It's the precursor to whiskey. But…also peach brandy…and sometimes applejack. I hope I don't get anyone's back up over it, but, as a lot of old timers do, I usually call them mash and hope that the context makes it clear what I'm talking about.

SUGAR

Sugar is a class of carbohydrates that includes dextrose, fructose, glucose, maltose, and others. Sugars fuel fermentation. Yeasts feeding in a mash convert sugars into ethanol and other products until the sugars are exhausted, the ethanol reaches a toxicity level that kills off the yeast, or the fermentation gets "stuck" some other way.

Table sugar—sucrose—is by far the most commonly used sugar among home distillers. It's cheap, it's widely available, and it's clean so it can be used right out of the package. When all you want to produce is a potent alcohol, table sugar is the way to go. A simple sugar wash using about 10 pounds of sugar per 5 gallons of water, fermented and distilled to 70 percent alcohol, will yield a ferocious distillate known as "sugar wash" or, more euphemistically, "sugar head" whiskey. Artisan distillers tend to hold it in low regard since it lacks subtlety, aroma, and taste. In the nomenclature of the South, where sippin' whiskey is particularly fine and fightin' whiskey is domestic disturbance in a jar, sugar head has been called sellin' whiskey because the primary virtue its makers recognize lies in the sheer volume of cash it can bring to their pockets. Since the days of American Prohibition, this is the moonshine most often found in urban markets.

Sugar wash whiskey (not really a whiskey at all since it is not grain-based) is still made in huge quantities in Virginia and North Carolina. Packed in one-gallon plastic milk jugs, it's shipped to eastern cities such as Washington D.C., Philadelphia, Miami, and New York. Once there, the 'splo (short for the explosion in one's head after drinking some) sells in shot houses by the glass at enormous profit. Its quality is suspect among artisan distillers, not because of any inherent fault of table sugar but because it is rarely of high quality, and because adulterants commonly contaminate batches destined for the poor clientele of inner cities.

Even among home distillers, whether and how much an individual uses table sugar is something of a litmus test. There are serious distillers who never use sugar, claiming it is a modern corruption of a respectable art, that spirits made wholly or in part with table sugar are thin and pallid reflections of those made from full fruit and grain mashes.

Then there are some whose entire aim is to produce neutral spirits as inexpensively as possible that they then spike with flavorings to emulate bourbon, tequila, Scotch, absinthe, triple sec, or whatever else they hanker. These distillers use reflux stills, which are designed to produce nearly pure (and largely tasteless) ethanol on a single

Alcohol fuel. Sugars power the process of fermentation. Grain and fruit yield their own sugars, but distillers also use other kinds of sugars such as (clockwise, from top left): malt extract, table sugar, brown sugar, molasses, honey, cane syrup, and maple syrup.

run, regardless of what's used as the sugar source: raspberries, apples, molasses, whatever. It all tastes about the same when distilled to 190 proof. The best product for a mash intended for running through a reflux still for maximum ethanol separation, then, is the cheapest you can lay your hands on. For those who sell their makings, that means plain old table sugar.

Other distillers use pot stills that produce a first run of about 40 percent alcohol that retains much of the tastes and aromas of the mash's individual sugars, whether those sugars are from grain or fruit or added in some form of sugar outright. I lean pretty heavily toward this side. But I've had some potent and decent sugar spirits, and some that used sugar adjuncts, so I don't get snarky about it. My advice? Use table sugar if you want to, but do also try using a pot still with grains and fruits and some of the more flavorful forms of sugar.

Rum, the American drink par excellence in colonial days, retains some of the character and body of molasses after fermentation. As a rule of thumb, some distillers use equal quantities of molasses and white sugar for rum; about 5 pounds of each per 5 gallons of water will yield a high-alcohol wash. Like all rules of thumb, it begs for tweaking and affixing with your own print. You could, for instance, go all old school and use nothing but molasses.

A distiller can also make good use of maple or cane syrup, brown sugar, demerara, sorghum, honey, or any of a number of other sugars. Some sugars ferment easily while others are notoriously difficult to ferment without added nutrients (see the next section on yeasts and yeast nutrients). Palm sugar, or jaggery, is common throughout India and Southeast Asia. Look for it packaged in small tawny pucks or paper-wrapped cones in Asian or specialty grocery stores. A supply is always good to have around the house for baking, but its ethereal butterscotch taste and floral nose carry through in the best *araks*, or distilled palm wine.

Malt extract, which is sold in homebrew shops in both powdered and syrup forms, and in dozens of varieties and brands of light, amber, and dark types, can also be treated for distillation purposes as a sugar. Get a light, unhopped variety and follow the package directions for fermenting. Once you've gained some experience, you may want to try experimenting with using hopped malt extract, or adding hops themselves during the fermentation. The hops' alpha acids, which provide bitterness in beer, don't distill out and can contibute smooth floral notes to spirits when used in moderation. Hops have long been used to curb unwanted microorganisms in mashes, so there is certainly a place for them in yours.

Homebrew stores also often sell granulated corn sugar, or dextrose, which many distillers use as a preferable substitute for table sugar. Despite common perception, ethanol also can easily be made from lactose, or milk sugar, but the fermentation requires *Kluyveromyces marxianus*, a species of yeast difficult to track down outside industrial settings.

YEASTS

Yeasts are not simply an ingredient—with the right temperature, acidity, nutrients, and fuels, these voracious little beasts devour sugars and energetically convert them to alcohol and carbon dioxide. In fact, fermentations can be so vigorous that they rip apart inadvertently sealed containers and blow air locks completely free of fermentation vessels. They shape the potential alcohol of your mash, the completeness of fermentation, and even the final flavors in your mash by acting on, and producing, a range of compounds.

Yeasts are unicellular microbes, fungi that can survive with oxygen or without it. In a normal *aerobic* fermentation cycle, they begin in an oxygen-rich mash and eventually consume all the free oxygen. The yeasts then turn to the sugars in the mash during this *anaerobic* ("without oxygen") stage to gobble up their oxygen. When they break apart glucose molecules to consume oxygen, the result is ethanol, carbon dioxide, and heat.

$$C_6H_{12}O_6 \rightarrow 2(C_2H_5OH) + 2(CO_2) + \text{heat}$$

Glucose   Ethanol   Carbon dioxide

Watch that heat. If you are running standard 5-gallon mashes, the heat generated will not be extreme, but in a sugar wash using turbo yeasts engineered to withstand high-alcohol mashes (see below), the mash temperature may rise enough to, 1) produce esters and higher alcohols whose off flavors can contaminate the final product or, 2) kill off the yeast before fermentation is complete. Use an instant-read thermometer or some other device to monitor and maintain a range of 60° to 75°F. This lower temperature helps assure a slower fermentation that reduces production of undesirable esters and higher alcohols. (See page 76 for ways to cool overly hot fermentations.)

What yeasts to use? Homebrew shops can outfit you with legions of species and varieties of yeasts that have been bred in laboratories to thrive in nutrient-rich solutions. Their sheer numbers can seem overwhelming, but as a novice, you will want to stick with just a few varieties until you get familiar with fermentation. Almost all the yeasts you'll

Not *That* Brewer's Yeast!

◗ ◗ ◗ ◯ ◯ ◗ ◗ ◗

If you frequent health food stores, you may be familiar with a dietary supplement called brewer's yeast that garnishes acclaim for its putative healing powers. It is not, not, not what you want to ferment your mashes and washes. Those yeast cells are dead and won't ferment anything. Instead, if you use brewer's yeast, you want to acquire it from reputable homebrew shops, beer and wine yeast labs, or a local brewpub that can assure live and active cultures.

be dealing with are in the *Saccharomyces* genus; *S. cerevisiae* are bottom-fermenting ale yeasts (that is, yeast that flocculates and settles near the bottom of the fermentation vessel toward the end of fermentation) while *S. carlsbergensis* are top-fermenting yeasts typically used in brewing lager beers.

The yeast you use will have a definite and predictable effect on the amount of ethanol you can produce and its aroma and flavor. The five most common kinds you are likely to encounter are:

Baker's yeast. Old-school moonshiners sometimes used ordinary grocery-store-variety baking yeasts, but with their low alcohol tolerance, better choices are out there for distilling.

Brewer's yeasts. These yeasts are ubiquitous among distillers because they're easiest to find; homebrew stores carry dozens of varieties. For distilling whiskeys, ask for dry ale yeasts. They're fine for most whiskeys and yield around five to eight percent alcohol. Many hobbyists prefer "whiskey" or "distiller's" yeasts (see below) when fermenting sugar because of their high alcohol yields. Brewer's yeast is not suitable for brandies. Note, too, that these are *not* the same products as the "brewer's yeast" sold in health food stores (see the sidebar).

Wine yeast. (including sherry, champagne, and mead yeasts). Mashes inoculated with wine yeasts typically ferment out at 12 to 16 percent alcohol, while champagne yeasts tolerate 16 to 20 percent alcohol at the extreme before dying off. Wine yeasts are what you want for most brandies.

Distiller's or "whiskey" yeast. These are actually brewer's yeasts, but strains with high alcohol tolerance and flavor profiles that are especially suited to making spirits from table sugar. Artisans and professionals frown on them, saying their only redeeming quality is yield.

Turbo yeast. An on-the-cheap distiller's dream. Turbo yeasts are designed specifically for fermenting sugar washes to yield 18 to 20 percent alcohol by volume—an unheard-of feat for Appalachian moonshiners. There's nothing inherently wrong with turbos, but you won't win many medals using

Ketchup on Yeast

Nothing is true, everything is permitted.

William S. Burroughs

Talk to enough distillers and your head may spin with contradictory advice: *Use rotten fruit; use only the best fruit. Ferment on the grain; ferment off the grain. Use baker's yeast; use turbo yeast.*

What goes in the pot, however, rarely surprises me: parsnips, pumpkins, medlars, wood, roots, animals (alive or dead), grains of paradise, juniper berries, lemongrass—nothing fazes me. That is, nothing fazed me until tomato paste smeared my notions of what makes a proper brew.

A North Carolina moonshiner, describing his mashing methods, dropped mention of something wholly new to me, when I interrupted and blurted out: "Do what now?"

"You mash in your tomato paste."

"Tomato paste?"

"Yep."

"The red stuff? Comes in little cans from the grocery store?"

"Yep. Best damn thing there is to feed your yeast. Makes the ferment good and strong, and your whiskey won't taste nothing like tomatoes."

So I looked into it. Turns out, he was on semisolid footing and certainly not alone in his praise of the canning industry's byproduct. About 6 ounces of the stuff per 5-gallon batch does in fact act as a primitive yeast nutrient and, in absence of nutrient mixes specially prepared for fermenting difficult mashes, can give yeasts enough of a boost to sustain a fermentation in an otherwise nutrient-poor mash. Australians have been using the yeast-spread product Vegemite for the same thing. Me? I can't help thinking that tomato ketchup-laced corn liquor is just plain wrong.

them. Some brandy recipes that are fortified with sugar call for them, but really their use should be confined to straight sugar spirits. Be sure to follow package directions exactly since turbos need different handling than do regular yeasts.

Another product you may need if you're making sugar-based spirits using anything other than turbo yeast is **yeast nutrient**. Sugar wash fermentations sometimes become stuck because brewing yeasts—adapted to thrive in nutrient-rich solutions—lack sufficient vitamins and nutrients to make complete fermentations. Adding yeast nutrients to the batch before *pitching* (adding) your yeast will help create a more hospitable environment and reduce the amount of undesirable byproducts of fermentation. Commercially available yeast nutrients often contain substances vital to healthy yeast growth; essential amino acids, vitamins, nitrogen, phosphorus (often in the form of the potent nutrient diammonium phosphate), zinc, free amino nitrogen compounds, magnesium sulfate and sometimes dead yeast particles (don't worry; they won't reactivate to interfere with your selected yeast strain). Turbo yeasts already include the nutrients necessary to sustain a robust fermentation, so there's no need to add further nutrients.

OTHER INGREDIENTS

A variety of other substances and products are at your disposal for nurturing a healthy, robust mash and coaxing an ever-more-vigorous ferment. Here are some you may want to consider adding to your palette.

Acids

Spirits made from insufficiently acid mashes sometimes taste bland or insipid. Acids also help to lower a mash's pH to an acceptable range that promotes enzyme activity and discourages bacteria growth. Most homebrew shops sell a premixed blend of citric, malic, and tartaric acids. While old-school moonshiners have historically made little use of such blends, some of the new breed of distillers dote on them. Plain lemon juice (which contains varying concentrations of citric acid) can be squeezed into a mash—anything from one to eight lemons per 5 gallons—to achieve a recipe's target pH. Regardless of whether you use lemons, acid blends, or whatever, remember to add only small amounts at a time, checking the pH after each addition, until you reach the right pH. If you just dump a big load of blends or juice into your fermenting vessel all at once, you risk creating an excessively acidic mash.

Sulfuric acid (H_2SO_4) is another option to lower mash water pH and is commonly available in 95 to 98 percent concentrations. It's a highly corrosive liquid, however, so if you decide to use it you must be extremely cautious not to get any on exposed skin or to inhale fumes. My advice for beginners? It's more of a tool for gearheads and lab rats. Skip it unless or until you're familiar with its use and laboratory safety in general.

Campden Tablets

Campden tablets are about 57 to 60 percent potassium or sodium metabisulfite and are sometimes used in brewing, winemaking, and distilling to kill off harmful microorganisms and wild yeasts in a mash before introducing cultivated yeast. Crush one tablet per gallon of mash, dissolve it in a little warm water, mix it into your mash, and let everything sit 24 hours before pitching yeast. Note that if you introduce your yeast too soon after adding campden tablets to your mash, those yeasts will also be killed off. For this reason, and because they feel the additives lend a bad taste to the final product, some home distillers refuse to use the tablets.

Gypsum or Hydrated Calcium Sulfate

Powdered gypsum ($CaSO_4$), also called hydrated calcium sulfate, is an essential part of yeast cell formation and helps to counter some substances that are toxic to yeasts. It can also lower a mash's pH. Some distillers put 1 teaspoon of gypsum in a five-gallon batch as a matter of course before fermentation.

Pectinase or Pectic Enzyme

Pectin in fruit, when combined with sugar, water, and acid under heat, can gel into marmalade, jellies, and jams. Many distillers add pectinase, an enzyme that specifically targets pectin, to fruit-based mashes for one reason: it breaks down the fruits' cell walls and increases the release of juices by as much as 17 percent. Pectinase is available in powdered or liquid form. In general, about ½ teaspoon per gallon of fruit mash is sufficient—be sure to check the package instructions, however, because strength varies according to the brand and form. Keep in mind, too, that adding pectinase also results in a greater production of methanol (toxic wood alcohol) and special care must be taken to purge it from your spirits (see page 120).

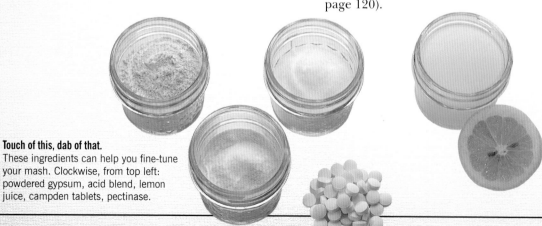

Touch of this, dab of that.
These ingredients can help you fine-tune your mash. Clockwise, from top left: powdered gypsum, acid blend, lemon juice, campden tablets, pectinase.

The Process

Once you've gathered together the equipment and ingredients you'll need, you'll be ready to have a go at mashing and fermenting. Individual recipes in this book may require their own particular procedures or variations, but these are the basic steps you'll need to follow.

1. Clean and sterilize all equipment that will come into contact with the mash using a weak chlorine bleach solution (¼ teaspoon per 2 gallons of cool water).

2. Make any necessary adjustments to the mash water with chemicals (if using) as described on page 60 before adding ingredients such as grains, fruit, or sugars.

3. Prepare the mash ingredients. Follow the directions given in specific recipes. Most of the recipes in this book follow these basic preparation procedures:

a. Fruit Mashes: Wash fruit gently in water. Cut, slice, smash, juice, or crush fruit to expose maximum surface area. Transfer to mash water as soon as possible to reduce oxidation.

b. Sugar Washes: Concentrated sugars such as molasses, sorghum, and cane or beet sugar must be completely dissolved. Heat the sugar in water to a low boil, stirring until all particles are completely dissolved.

c. Grain Mashes: All beginners' grain recipes in this book rely on flaked grains that are heated in mash water and held within a temperature range, allowing them to convert starches to sugars. Follow the recipes' instructions closely.

4. Combine the mash ingredients with the water in a fermentation vessel (if not heating) or in a stockpot (if the recipe calls for heating the mash). After the prescribed heating time, transfer any heated mash to a fermentation vessel or (if fermenting off the grain) to a tun.

5. Lower the temperature of the mash by topping it off with cool water to 60° to 75°F or using an immersion chiller (a specialized piece of equipment sold at some homebrew shops). The purpose is to reduce the mash's temperature to a range that promotes optimal yeast activity.

6. If a recipe calls for yeast nutrients, add them to the mash before pitching the yeast.

7. Pitch the yeast or yeast starter into the mash or wash (see page 130 for instructions on preparing a yeast starter). Before pitching the yeast, make certain that the mash in the fermentation vessel is between 60° and 75°F or the yeast will not survive. Many distillers simply allow the mash to come to room temperature; others chill the mash to between 60° and 75°F. Remember that, within this range, cooler temperatures lead to slower, more controlled fermentations with fewer opportunities for unwanted byproducts to form. Pour the yeast into the mash, and stir gently to distribute it evenly. (Some distillers first add their yeast slurry to an equal volume of mash, then stir in that mixture to the rest of the mash after a 20- to 30-minute rest to "atemperate" the slurry and minimize the risk of shocking and killing off some of the yeast.)

8. Cover the vessel with an airtight lid, and attach a water-filled airlock.

Air Lock

An air lock allows gases to bubble out of the fermenter while keeping potentially contaminating air from getting in. Fill the lock about half way with water, snap its cap back on, and insert the stem into the fermenter's lid.

> **If the weather becomes quite cold, the moonshiner reports each day and heats a bundle of iron objects (plow points, eye hoes, horseshoes, etc.) strung on a wire and 'souses' each barrel of beer to keep the temperature up.**
>
> Cratis Williams, "Moonshining in the Mountains,"
> *North Carolina Folklore Journal*, May 1967

Smoothing Temperature Spikes

If you're not using turbo yeasts or fermenting batches over 15 gallons, your mash probably will be just fine as long as it is off the stillhouse floor and away from heat and direct sunlight. Occasionally, however, a batch of fermenting mash or wash gets too hot too fast. If this happens, you can smooth the temperature spike a few different ways. One method is to immerse the entire fermenter in a sink of cool water. Another is to keep sterile, closed containers of ice on hand to place in the mash if needed as a quick and dirty emergency measure. To make these, sterilize one-liter plastic soda or seltzer bottles in a weak bleach solution, then fill them about three-fourths of the way with water, recap them, and put them in your freezer stored in plastic zip-closure bags. Slip one or more of the frozen capped bottles into overly warm mash to lower the temperature.

A trick from the homebrewing crowd involves putting the entire fermentation vessel in a shallow pan of water, covering it with a cotton t-shirt that droops into the water, and pointing an electric fan at it. As the shirt wicks up water, the moving air causes it to evaporate, effectively cooling the mash.

9. Check to make sure the yeast is doing its job. You should start to see evidence of fermentation within one to twelve hours of pitching the yeast: a *raft* consisting of murky foam and mash solids should begin to form on the surface of the liquid. Air bubbles (carbon dioxide) will begin to gurgle through the airlock and eventually a sound not unlike sizzling bacon may emanate from the container. Occasionally stirring your mash during fermentation with a sanitized spoon will help achieve a more complete fermentation and flavor extraction.

10. At its peak, the raft is a thick, bubbly puck of fruit or grain solids mixed with yeast residue that floats on top of an increasingly liquid and effervescent mash. If you're fermenting a fruit-based mash, **you may want to fold the raft back into the mash** from time to time. Opinion is divided: some distillers fold fruit rafts back into the mash because they believe the raft, if left floating on top, may harbor unwanted microorganisms. But others following older traditions don't bother, feeling that this "cap" protects the fermenting mash. In all likelihood, an undisturbed cap promotes the formation of acetobacters, which can turn your mash into vinegar.

11. Watch for signs that the process of fermentation is complete. After a matter of days, depending on the amount of sugars, the yeast type and population, the ambient and internal mash temperatures, and available nutrients, fermentation activity

About Specific Gravity

Professional distillers and amateurs with brewing backgrounds do one thing regularly that traditional folk distillers almost never do: they measure the *specific gravity* of their mash. Did I say one thing? Excuse me. They also measure its *degrees Plato*, *Balling*, or *Brix*; its *original gravity*; its *Belgian degrees*; or possibly its brewer's pounds—depending on where they learned their trade and their recipes' provenance. These are intimidating-sounding systems for the beginner, maybe, but not when you keep in mind that they all do that one thing: each measures the density of a liquid compared to that of pure water.

Pure water has a specific gravity of 1.000. Knowing the mash's variation from that number allows distillers to track the course of fermentation; to gauge, for instance, how much sugar is present and whether those sugars are completely converted to alcohol. Measure specific gravity by floating a weighted but buoyant hydrometer in a strained liquid. The liquid's density will dictate the degree to which it sinks. When the hydrometer comes to rest, compare the liquid's level against the internal scale for a specific-gravity reading.

There are (of course) some kinks. The first is that hydrometers are typically calibrated at 60°F. Measurements at other temperatures yield skewed, but predictable, results, and must be compared against hydrometer correction charts—which you'll find in reliable homebrew books and on websites.

The second kink is that most small-scale liquor recipes—unlike many beer recipes—do not specify the initial and final "target" specific gravities for the fermentation stage. While small-batch distillers who regularly measure density do ply their trade, moonshiners and old-school artisans disregard specific gravity almost entirely and rely instead on their powers of observation to tell them when a mash has fermented satisfactorily. Consequently, none of the recipes in this book calls for measuring specific gravity during fermentation. The people who shared them with me simply don't follow the practice.

will slow and eventually cease altogether. Bubbling sounds will stop and CO_2 will no longer glug through the airlock. In cool weather, a fermentation may take a week or more to complete; in warmer weather or with a "hotter" yeast or mash, the fermentation may wind down within just two or three days. Note that fermentations are not always 100% efficient and some stop before all the available sugars convert to alcohol. For a more accurate assessment of the completeness of the fermentation, you may measure initial and final specific gravities (see the sidebar, About Specific Gravity).

12. Strain the mash to prepare it for distillation. Uncover the mash and gently lift away any raft using a mesh strainer. From this point, you can take either of two routes:

The first method is an all-purpose procedure suitable for whole- or flaked-grain mashes, fruit mashes, and sugar washes. Insert a racking cane into the mash, and siphon or rack the clearer liquid off the muck of sediment (spent yeast, grain pulp, fruit pits, etc.) on the bottom of the vessel and into another sterilized container such as a glass carboy or second fermentation vessel.

The second method calls for transferring grain or fruit mashes to a tun. The solids are left behind as the liquid drains through a false bottom and out a spigot into a second sterilized container. Fruit pomace and flaked grains may clog tuns or drain only slowly, so watch them closely and stir gently to assure a continual flow if you decide on this method.

13. Let the strained mash rest for one more day, to allow suspended particles to settle. Then rack the liquid into the still's boiler. Important note: never distill an unracked mash, especially not in smaller stills, because the mash solids are likely to burn and scorch the alcohol. More importantly, they may clog the tubing, creating a dangerously explosive steam-driven bomb.

CHAPTER 5

STILLS
and
How to Build One

You can build or buy a still from hundreds of available styles and designs. Some are more effective than others, but each rig does the same thing: it separates liquids of varying boiling temperatures to achieve more concentrated—sometimes even pure—distillations of those liquids. Essential oils, perfumes, medicines, and alcohol all can be made in a still. For a simplified explanation of how a basic still works, see page 13.

In this chapter, we'll first take a look at basic still types and materials, and discuss their pros and cons. Then we'll get some experience both building and using a very simple conical still made from little more than a stockpot and a wok. This still has its limitations, but it really can produce some respectable fruit-based beverages such as grappa, and serves nicely as a simple but elegant introduction to the fundamentals of distilling.

Finally, we'll go step-by-step, in detail, through the process of constructing a traditional Appalachian-style pot still. Some would say the design is archaic, but they'd be right only in the sense that the design is venerable; it is also quite capable. Using this humble pot still, you can make superb whiskeys and brandies. If you understand the basics of working with metal and brazing, you can use the instructions to build a still yourself; if you don't have those skills, you may be able to find a metalworker who'd be willing to do it for you.

Still Designs

Stills of one design or another have been around since the early seventh century. The first European distillers weren't after moonshine, nor contemplating wily midnight liquor runs. Before alcohol distillation grew into a business in the mid-seventeenth century, alchemists—the fore-runners of today's chemists—analyzed and tested the world around them. When an understanding of Arab distilling arts began to circulate in Europe, alchemists were at the fore of research and development using small distillation devices made of glass and ceramics. Because they were working in a time when magic was still thought to affect everyday life, their experiments in understanding the natural world were tinged with spirituality and pre-Christian mysticism.

For them, high-proof alcohol was not just an extract; it was the purified essence of mellifluous wine. This essence was deemed so powerful that it was called *spiritus*, a fleeting ethereal quiddity ascribed with miraculous powers and capable of unmooring a man's mind that he might nearer approach divinity.

Recipes from alchemical manuscripts and, later, household account books indicate that alcohol was almost never used as a recreational beverage,

Timeless design. The basic components of a pot still haven't changed much over the centuries. This variation of a pot still was submitted to the U.S. Patent Office in 1808.

I've been a moonshiner for seventeen long year

I've spent all my money on whiskey and beer

In some lonesome hollow I'll build me my still

And I'll make you a gallon for a two dollar bill

"Kentucky Moonshiner," Traditional

but as a solvent and base for barks, roots, flowers, seeds, salts, metals, and animals (whole or parts, live or dead). The resulting concoctions, decoctions, infusions, and tonics were medicines meant to cure everything from bad luck to leprosy. Housewives from the seventeenth century on made these home remedies in small conical and coffin stills (see page 84).

In the search for ever-purer spirits, alchemists tweaked still designs and sometimes radically re-invented them. The most basic stills of the time—alembics—were little more than long-necked flasks heated over open flames. More complex models involved double boilers and water baths. Though simple, the designs were so effective for distilling small batches that they are still used in laboratories around the world.

POT STILLS

As herb-infused medicinal spirits and "strong waters" such as genever became popular beverages in the mid-1600s, canny distillers tapped the profit by fashioning bigger-bellied stills from metal, since large glass and ceramic stills would have been too heavy or too fragile (or both). These were the first pot stills, and the design hasn't changed all that much since.

Colonial American towns exhibited a marked tendency for large pot stills because towns could support relatively large commercial distilling operations. As settlers moved into the American interior, the stills they brought were not the 800- to 3,000-gallon commercial behemoths of Philadelphia, Baltimore, and Manhattan, but smaller household models and side yard pot stills that were easily packed on horseback and in wagons.

The American copper pot still was the runaway favorite still of pioneer families throughout the Appalachian mountains from the eighteenth to early twentieth centuries. Popular and romantic history holds that the small farmers and householders who operated them generally put out high-quality whiskeys and brandies in small batches. Because they allowed substantial amounts of congeners to pass into the distillate, the old homestead pot stills were ideal for producing full-flavored whiskeys.

Endless variations. All pot stills work on the same fundamental principles, but over the years distillers have devised countless design variations. Known for the distinctive shape of its cap and boiler, this 150-gallon "submarine" still could produce 10 gallons of whiskey a night. Notice the small middle container between the boiler and flake stand, a device known as a "thump keg," (in this case, a metal barrel). The thump keg probably contains a "charge" of beer or feints to boost the vapor's alcohol content as it travels to the flake stand (see page 106). One hopes that most home distillers will strive for higher standards in still quality and cleanliness than are reflected in the commercial operation shown here.

In Praise of Copper

Stills can be made with iron, glass, aluminum, clay, brass, copper, galvanized or stainless steel, even-food grade plastic. Just because something can be done, though, doesn't mean it should. Galvanized steel's potential to leach toxic salts into the vapor, for instance, makes it imperative to avoid. Plastic in general isn't safe in contact with high-proof alcohol, though food-grade plastic is fine for a fermenter. Brass? Difficult to work with. Aluminum? Same. Glass? Very pretty. Allows you to see what's going on in the still. It's not for you, though. Glass still components are extremely fragile and, unless you are a skilled glassblower or work in a chemistry lab, prohibitively expensive. Save it for a vanity project after you've become a seasoned distiller.

Most stills these days are made of either stainless steel or copper. Both are excellent conductors of heat, something you need to consider when bringing your beer to distilling temperatures. Although stainless steel rigs are difficult to create without advanced welding experience, ready-made models are available for purchase. They're relatively lightweight, strong, and easy to clean. Furthermore, most of the designs for stainless steel stills lend themselves to attaching a reflux column for ultrapure spirits.

Copper is so common that any well-equipped hardware store or contractors' supply house can outfit you with what you need to make a beginner's still or to have one made for you. Like stainless, it's relatively easy to clean. Unlike stainless, it's easy to work with. Copper is malleable and forgiving. And there's no difficult welding involved since all the connections can be sealed with soft lead-free material.

But the biggest advantage of copper is its chemical properties. It has been the choice of distillers for centuries because stills without copper at least somewhere in their construction—the condenser, the arm, the boiler, etc.—are thought to put out an unpalatable whiskey. Some call the resulting spirit flabby, some say it smells of rotten eggs or skunks, but whatever you call the result, those who taste the difference don't come back for more.

Chris Morris, Master Distiller at Woodford Reserve, explains the mysteries of copper in making bourbon. "Our copper stills continually sacrifice themselves on a molecular level. The primary reason for copper is that it reacts with sulfur. Sulfur compounds smell bad. Nobody adds sulfur to the mash; it's there as a natural part of the grains, and it's released as yeasts go to work. Copper binds with hydrogen sulfide and isobutyl mercaptans and forms copper sulfate. The copper sulfate tends to bond with fatty acids and oils to eliminate skunky and rotten-egg smells from the spirit."

new designs that could handle hundreds and even thousands of gallons of mash were thrown up in secluded locations, from the deep woods to urban basements. Traditional, less capacious pot stills, and the small-batch distillers who used them, retreated to near-obscurity.

When Prohibition was repealed in 1933, advanced, higher-capacity stills fueled by cheap sugar dominated illicit alcohol production. Pot stills had become less common, but they didn't fade away entirely. Traditional artisan distillers continued to craft small batches of grain- and fruit-based spirits in home-size designs, and legal distilleries have always used massive copper pot stills for whiskeys.

Few home distillers actually go through the bother of making a fully copper pot still today, though. Instead, many "repurpose" other containers such as stockpots, pressure cookers, industrial coffee urns, beer kegs, and even point-of-use water heaters for their boilers because the boiler in particular can seem expensive to produce. In the opinions of many, however, including myself, a copper pot still is unsurpassed for producing whiskeys and brandies (see the sidebar, In Praise of Copper, previous page).

High output. This column still, discovered in 1940 in an abandoned brewery off Fifth Avenue in New York City, turned out 1,500 gallons a day.

When national Prohibition was ratified in 1919 and ever-thirsty Americans developed an unslakable mania for alcohol in any form, all of that went out the window. Distillers who could produce booze in quantity came to dominate the moonshine market. Sugar came on the scene as the preferred base for moonshine because it was cheap, plentiful, and had a higher ethanol yield than corn or other traditional grains. Stills became larger;

REFLUX STILLS

Each time a liquid with a relatively low alcohol volume is sent through a pot still in a process called a run, its water concentration drops and its ethanol concentration rises until the distiller intentionally stops the process or the distillate reaches its maximum practical concentration. On the first run, the resulting *low wines* or *singlings* contain around 40 percent ethanol and pack a potent kick, but still also contain a generous dose of impurities. Old-school moonshiners collect low wines from several runs and distill them together, or distill them a second and sometimes third time (thus the terms double-distilled and triple-distilled).

Modern distillers sometimes take this route with small pot stills, but often employ a device known as a "thumper," "thump keg," or "doubler" (see the sidebar on page 106) that essentially distills ethanol vapor a second time to produce straight moonshine on a single run.

Reflux stills operate on a similar principle and are even more efficient at yielding pure, high-proof alcohol. Reflux stills are capable of cleanly drawing off specific compounds at exact temperatures through a top-mounted column. All stills reflux—that is, allow ethanol-rich vapors to condense inside and flow downwards and revaporize—but a reflux still's column is designed to maximize that action. In place of a head as you'd find in a pot still, a reflux still incorporates a vertically mounted hollow copper column on its boiler. On home-sized rigs, such columns are generally around 2 inches wide and from 42 to 62 inches long to assure efficient operation. Vapor rises and collects inside this column, swirling over and around packing material such as copper scrubbers or ceramic rings. The huge surface area of its packing allows rising vapor and condensing liquid to commingle, stripping them of unwanted volatile substances, and creating very pure liquids in a single continuous run.

Truly excellent spirits are possible with a columnar reflux still. If you're curious about them, check out any of the books and websites that provide more details on them (see Resources starting on page 156).

My beef with reflux stills has nothing to do with their capabilities; they are marvels of ingenuity. What disappoints me is how they get used. Way too many distillers make the highest proof liquor they can without regard to the subtleties of crafting small-batch spirits. The reigning ideal of a fan-tastically high-proof sugar spirit that is supposedly tasteless, odorless, and colorless yields examples that, once cut with water, are mixed with ersatz flavorings to emulate bourbon, Canadian whiskey, cognac, peach brandy, peppermint schnapps, and, tragically, pound cake and key lime pie.

MY PREFERENCE

A reflux still in the right hands can crank out masterpieces, no doubt, especially when the distillate is aged in wood. A pot still, though, captures the essence, "the true and uncontaminated fruitage," as Irvin Cobb put it, of the fruits and grains that go into the pot. By using a pot still and distilling carefully nurtured mash to a lower final proof—say, 100 to 140—much of the individual sugars' tastes and aromas carry through to the distillate. Why salvage artless sugarhead whiskey with compounds meant to evoke rye, rum, or peach when you can actually handcraft the real deal from genuine ingredients?

Don't let gearheads tell you otherwise: a pot still is not a perplexing cornpone vestige of backwoods inefficiency. It is a tool for extracting and preserving everything we love about apples, peaches, cherries, and the amber waves for which America is justly famous. It lets the taste of molasses and sorghum shine and it is the only fitting vessel for cooking a corn mash.

As homage to centuries of proven excellence, we'll spend most of the remainder of this chapter exploring the construction of a small Appalachian-style pot still, a tool that deserves a place of honor among the gear of serious artisan distillers.

But first, let's take a look at what has to be the simplest still of all.

Making and Using a Conical (Wok) Still

A conical still gives you a great introduction to making spirits and is particularly popular for making German and Austrian home-style schnapps. It's also one of the simplest contraptions you may ever build; putting one together is much easier than assembling a child's bicycle, making a birdhouse, or building bookcases. Its main advantage is that it can be assembled in short order from everyday kitchen items and requires no soldering, brazing, welding, or metal cutting. For the utter novice, there really is no more satisfying foray into making alcohol than learning distillation principles firsthand with one of these simple alky cookers.

A simple conical (or wok) distillation rig is made of three stainless steel components that can be assembled in under one minute: a mixing bowl in a stockpot covered with a wok. At its most basic, the apparatus works like so: as mash simmers gently in the stockpot, ethanol and other alcohols escape and rise as vapor, condense on the underside of the wok, and drip down into the bowl floating on the surface of the simmering mash. There's your alcohol.

Despite its simplicity, some folks can't leave well enough alone and try to improve on the design by adding internal braces and stands, drilling holes for circulating water, and inserting thermometers in places they don't belong. Forget all that. The idea of the conical still is that it is simple. Period. Can it be improved upon? Of course! Use one, and immediately you will begin to realize ways it could be made more efficient. That's expected; an insatiable curiosity is one of the hallmarks of a good distiller. That curiosity drives many distillers to constantly tinker with still designs to increase efficiency or improve flavor. If you're among them, feel free. Be aware, however, that very nice spirits can be routinely made with nothing more complex than a pot, a Chinese wok, and a floating metal bowl. Here's how.

YOU WILL NEED

Large (about 7 gallons) stainless steel stockpot (see Note)

Medium stainless steel mixing bowl (see Note)

Stainless steel wok with round bottom (see Note)

Chlorine bleach

Water

Fermented mash (see recipes starting on page 128)

Electric hot plate with temperature control

Ice cubes (about 20 pounds)

Bowl gripper (optional)

Funnel

Glass jars or bottles

THE COMPONENTS

Note: Best known for its use in Chinese cooking, a wok is a thin metal skillet shaped like a broad bowl with one or more handles. Those made of dark, high-carbon steel (the kind that rusts if left wet) are wholly unsuited for your still. They impart a nasty, metallic tang that absolutely ruins your spirits. Instead, hunt down a bright, shiny stainless steel wok with a rounded—not flat—bottom. It should be big enough to cover the mouth of the stockpot, but small enough that its bottom extends into the pot itself (see the illustration, next page). The stockpot should be large enough to hold the entire volume of a 6-gallon fermentation, minus the mash solids (grains, peach bunkers, tangerine rinds, plum pits, yeast byproducts and assorted sludge) that you've strained out. The bowl should be about two-thirds as wide as the stockpot, so it'll fit inside without touching the pot's sides. Also, the bowl should be light enough to float in water or, in this case, a mash.

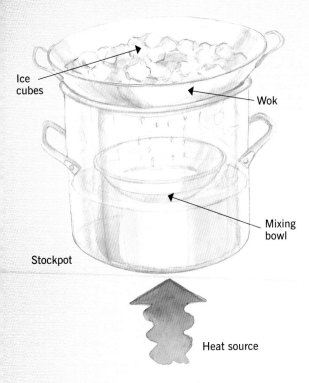

Ice cubes

Wok

Mixing bowl

Stockpot

Heat source

Assembling the Still

1. Test the components for fit. Place the stainless steel bowl in the stockpot. The bowl should be large enough that a portion of it is always under the center of the wok, so that condensation dripping from the bottom of the wok doesn't allow ethanol to drip back into the mash.

2. Now place the wok over the mouth of the stockpot and again check for fit. The wok's edge should fit seamlessly within the stockpot's opening. Later, you'll fill the wok with ice, the weight of which will distend the wok's moderately flexible rim a bit, providing a snug fit. Consequently, ethanol vapor that might have escaped into the room will condense into spirit. *Important:* Do *not* succumb to the temptation to seal the connection between the wok and the pot with masking tape, flour paste, glue, or any other substance: You're making a still, not a bomb.

Operating the Still

3. Make a solution of two tablespoons of household chlorine bleach in five gallons of water. Let it stand for 10 minutes, then soak all of your equipment in the solution for half an hour. Remove everything from the solution and let it drip dry completely.

4. Gently pour your strained and cleared mash into the stockpot and place it on the heating element. Do *not* use an open flame source, and keep the room well-ventilated.

5. Turn the heat to high and float the stainless bowl on the surface of the mash. Cover the opening of the pot with the wok, bottom side down.

6. When the mash begins to boil, turn the heat down to a bare simmer and fill the wok with ice. Monitor progress by lifting the wok now and then and examining the bowl's contents.

7. Discard the first 4 fluid ounces (½ cup) of distillate that falls into the bowl; it may contain methanol and other potentially dangerous (or at least headache-causing) compounds.

8. Collect the remaining distillate in the bowl, pouring and funneling it off occasionally into a glass bottle or jar (keep the container covered otherwise, to minimize the dissipation of ethanol fumes) until what collects in the bowl no longer smells or tastes strongly of alcohol. Some schnapps-makers test the rough alcohol content of the distillate in the bowl by dipping the handle of a wooden spoon into the clear liquid and setting it aflame. As long as it burns, they continue to collect. With experience, your nose and eyesight will tell you when to stop collecting.

Congratulations; you've just made your first batch of homemade hooch. Pour your spirits into glass bottles through a funnel and age them no less than four weeks (see page 125).

Building a Pot Still

Though eminently simple and easy to use for producing spirits, a conical wok still is clearly a rudimentary device. Ethanol vapor inevitably escapes from the gap between the wok and pot into the surrounding space; it affords only crude separation of fusel alcohols and congeners; and you have to keep opening it to check the status of the floating bowl's contents, thereby losing even more ethanol vapor. Purists will also contend that the absence of copper in the design means that more unpleasant-tasting congeners remain in the distillate. One could sidestep this argument by substituting a copper egg-white mixing bowl for the wok, but that stretches the boundaries of what constitutes a cheap and affordable still.

Pot stills resolve most of the inherent inefficiencies of conical stills. They're necessarily more complex, but not as difficult or expensive to construct as you might think.

THE COMPONENTS

First, let's look at the components of our pot still, which has a boiler capacity of 6¾ gallons, just the right size for distilling 5 to 6 gallons of wash, the quantity that most of the recipes in this book yield. Keep in mind that this is only one design. Hundreds of variations and thousands of tweaks exist, so you may well encounter other pot stills that look nothing like this, yet produce fine, nuanced whiskeys and brandies.

The first and bulkiest component is the *boiler* that is heated externally from below and holds fermented mash.

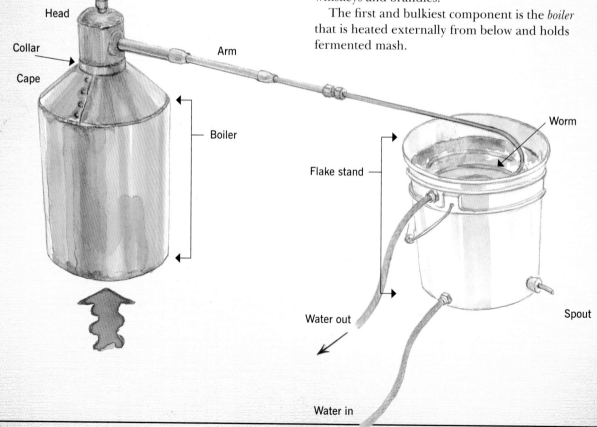

A sloping ring called the *cape* (or *shoulder*) forms the top of the boiler and leads to a *collar* encircling an opening for rising ethanol vapors.

Above the collar, vapors collect in the *head* of the still and pass through a connecting *arm* to a cooled condenser where hot ethanol-rich vapors revert to liquid. Although a variety of condensers is used by distillers, the simplest to construct is made of copper tubing coiled into a tight spiral called a *worm* submerged in a container of flowing cool water called a *flake stand*.

The three main procedures for constructing the main body and arm of the still are: 1) cutting the individual pieces from a sheet of copper, 2) forming the various components by bending, crimping, and riveting the pieces, and 3) brazing the components. (*Brazing* is essentially the same process as soldering, but involves using material—in our case, a silver-based alloy—that melts at a higher temperature, and provides a more durable joint and seal, than ordinary solder.)

After that, you need only to put together a simple worm and flake stand (see pages 103 and 104 for those instructions), and attach it to the still. Let's get started by building the boiler/head/arm assembly.

YOU WILL NEED

MATERIALS

20-ounce (22-gauge, 0.027 inch thick) copper sheet, 3 x 3 feet

Round-head copper rivets, ¼ inch long, ⅛-inch-diameter stems

Brazing alloy (see page 97)

¾-inch-to-½-inch copper pipe reducing coupler

1-inch-to-½-inch internal diameter (ID) copper pipe reducing coupler

10-inch length of copper pipe, 1 inch diameter

10-inch length of copper pipe, ½ inch diameter

½-inch-to-⅜-inch internal diameter (ID) copper pipe reducing coupler

6-inch length of ⅜-inch outer diameter (OD) copper tubing

Flake stand materials listed on page 103

TOOLS

Straightedge

Measuring tape

Pencil, nail, or ultrafine permanent marker

Tin snips

Drawing compass

Makeshift compass (optional; see step 6)

C-clamps

Small pieces of felt or fabric, for padding

Scrap piece of 2x4, approx. 18 inches long

Electric drill with bits

Machine-head screws, ⅛-inch diameter, with matching hex nuts

Metal bar, 2 inches square, about 2 feet long

Ball peen hammer

Adjustable (slip joint) pliers

Towel

Brazing equipment and supplies (see page 97)

Step drill bit, with steps for drilling ⅝- and 1-inch holes

Flake stand tools listed on page 103

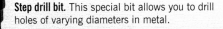

Step drill bit. This special bit allows you to drill holes of varying diameters in metal.

CUTTING THE COMPONENTS

You'll start by cutting the 3-foot-square copper sheeting into the still body's various components, following the instructions and the diagram (figure 1) shown here. Remember: Measure twice, cut once.

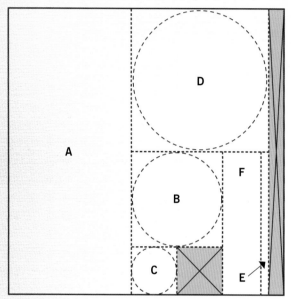

Figure 1

Description	Initial Cutting Dimensions	Final Cut Dimensions
A Boiler Wall	16" x 36"	Same
B Boiler Bottom	12" x 12"	11¾" diameter
C Head Cap	6" x 6"	6" diameter
D Cape	18" x 18"	17½" diameter
E Collar	1" x 18"	Same
F Head Wall	5" x 18"	Same

Cutting the Boiler Wall and Basic Template Pieces

1. Lay the copper sheet flat on the floor or other work surface and, using the straightedge and measuring tape, measure 16 inches in from one end, along one of the long sides. Mark the spot with a pencil or ultrafine permanent marker, or lightly scratch it with a nail. Repeat on the opposite side. Connect the two marks with the straightedge and lightly scribe a line connecting the two marks. Use the tin snips to cut along the line carefully so that the cut is as smooth and straight as possible. This is piece A; make sure it measures 16 by 36 inches. Later, when the two short ends are joined to form a cylinder, it will serve as your still's boiler walls. Set it aside for now—but just before you do, use the straightedge to mark a line that extends fully across one long edge, ⅛ inch in from the edge itself. You'll use this mark as a guide in step 14.

2. Next, measure 2 inches in from the other (uncut) end of the copper sheet on both long sides, mark a line between those two points, and cut the 2-inch strip away from the copper sheet. For your immediate purposes, this is waste; you can recycle it or save it for some other project.

3. Now, while following the template and the "initial cutting dimensions" on the chart, measure, mark, and cut out the basic squares and rectangles for pieces B through F from the copper sheet. When you're finished, the collar (piece E) and the head wall (piece F) will require no further cutting; set them aside for now.

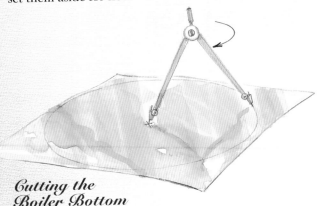

Cutting the Boiler Bottom

4. Place piece B, the 12-inch square, flat on the floor or work surface. Position the straightedge diagonally across the piece, connecting one corner's outermost point to the opposite corner's, and mark a line about 2 inches long in the approximate middle of the square. Make a matching mark with the straightedge positioned diagonally between the other two corners, so that the two lines intersect, forming a small "X" that marks the dead center of what will be a circle. Using a center punch or small nail, lightly mark (don't puncture!) the center point. Set your compass to a radius of 5⅞ inches, place its point on the center mark, and inscribe a circle with a diameter of 11¾ inches. (See the cutting diagram.) Then set your compass to a radius of 5⅝ inches, and again using the center point, mark a slightly smaller inner circle—you'll use this mark as a guide later, in step 15. Cut along the inscribed outer circle and discard or recycle the trimmings. Set the disc aside.

Cutting the Head Cap

5. Referring to the diagram and using the same technique described in step 4, find dead center of piece C, the 6-inch square. Mark it, and use the compass to inscribe a 6-inch-diameter circle. With the tin snips, cut out the circle and discard or recycle the trimmings.

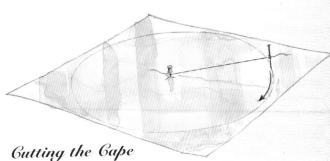

Cutting the Cape

6. The process of cutting the cape (piece D) from the 18-inch square is trickier than the previous steps—but not all that tricky. If you're unsure of your cutting skills, you may want to draw and cut a mock-up cape to scale on paper or card stock first, and test-fit it to the top of the boiler wall (piece A) before cutting the real thing.

In any case, using the same technique described in step 4, mark an "X" in the center of the 18-inch square and use a center punch or nail to lightly mark their intersection. Next, you'll need to mark a 17-½-inch diameter circle on the square. If your compass isn't big enough to do this, you can create a large makeshift compass using a piece of string at least 20 inches long, a nail, and a thumbtack. Tie one end of the string to the nail; then, from the nail, measure out along the string 8¾ inches, and stick a thumbtack through the string at that point. Put the thumbtack at the marked "X" center point and, with the string extended and taut, gently scribe the 17-½-inch circle with the nail. Check with the tape measure to make sure the circle is indeed 17½ inches; then cut out the circle using tin snips. Discard the trimmings.

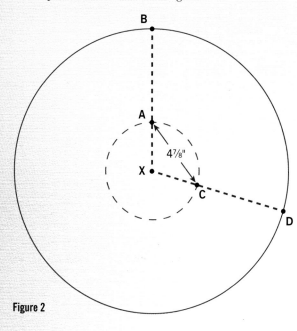

Figure 2

7. Set the disc on a flat surface and, again using the circle's center mark (point X) and a compass, scribe a 6-inch inner circle. Then, using a straight-edge, mark a line extending straight from the center point and across the inner circle (point A) all the way to the disc's outside edge (point B).

8. Now, from point A, using a straightedge or a compass set to the proper distance, mark another point (C) on the inner circle exactly 4⅞ inches from the first point (A). Next, draw a line straight from the center point and across point C to the outer edge of the disc (point D)—see figure 2. Cut along lines X-A-B and X-C-D and discard the wedge-shaped piece that comes off. Then carefully cut around the remainder of the inner circle. Now the piece looks like a big letter C. Set it aside.

FORMING THE COMPONENTS

With all the components cut, it's time to shape the pieces you've made to create your pot still's various components (figure 3).

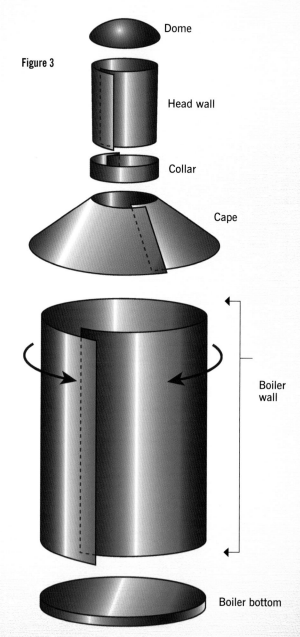

Figure 3

Dome

Head wall

Collar

Cape

Boiler wall

Boiler bottom

Forming the Boiler Wall

9. Begin a slight bend at one short end of the boiler wall and gently roll the copper into a cylinder. Allow a ½-inch overlap and secure each end with C-clamps. (Put a small piece of felt or fabric between the clamps and the copper to avoid scratching the metal.)

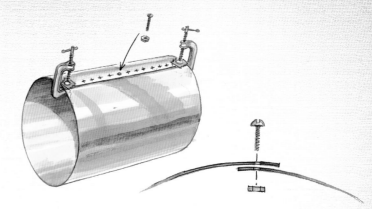

11. Insert a machine-head screw—head side out—through the hole and twist on a hex nut from the other side until it's finger tight. Next, drill another hole at one of the adjacent 1-inch marks, and tighten down a screw and nut through it. Repeat this process on the other side of the center hole, and then along the entire seam until all the holes have been drilled and fastened together. This will keep the overlapping ends together and properly aligned while you fasten them with rivets. Remove the C-clamps.

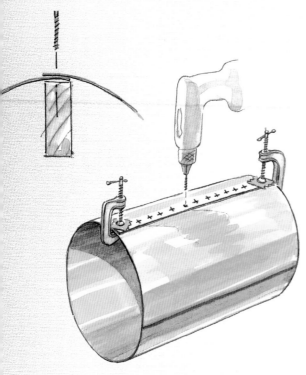

10. On the outside of the boiler wall, mark 1 inch in from the top and bottom of the overlap area. From those points, mark 1-inch intervals along the overlap for your rivets. Brace the wooden 2x4 under the seam, and drill a hole at the center mark through both layers of copper.

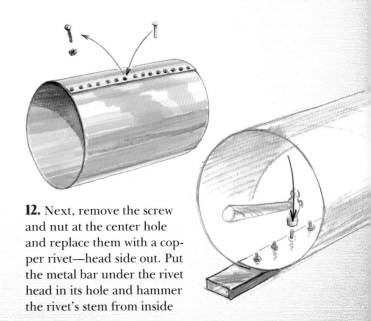

12. Next, remove the screw and nut at the center hole and replace them with a copper rivet—head side out. Put the metal bar under the rivet head in its hole and hammer the rivet's stem from inside the cylinder so that it flattens and secures the overlapping ends. Be sure the overlapping copper is pressed firmly together before hammering.

13. Repeat the process along the remainder of the seam on each side of the center rivet, removing the screws and nuts one at a time and replacing them with rivets.

14. Using the slip joint pliers and following the line you marked on the copper sheet as a guide in step 1, crimp a ⅛-inch inward-bending lip all the way around the top of the boiler wall at a 45° angle.

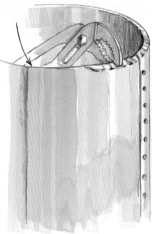

line you marked in step 4, carefully and gradually bend a ¼-inch lip to about a 45° angle all the way around the disc. Yes, the process is tedious—but not hard. Now go around with the pliers two or three times more, bending the same lip again to form a 90° angle. (Don't try to form the 90° lip in less than three or four passes; bending copper needs to be done in stages. If you try to bend the lip to 90° all at once, you risk snapping or breaking the metal or bending it out of shape.) When you're finished, the disc should be an 11¼-inch platter with a ¼-inch rim.

Forming the Boiler Bottom

15. The 11¾-inch disc you cut for the boiler bottom (piece B) needs to be reshaped just a little to ensure a snug fit with the boiler wall. Using adjustable pliers and following the inner-circle guide

16. Insert the bottom into the uncrimped end of the cylinder (piece A) with the lip's edge facing out, so that the lip aligns with the bottom edge of the boiler wall. Stand the boiler upright. Tap the bottom into place with the hammer handle. Turn the boiler upside down and eyeball the fit. Make any necessary minor adjustments to assure a snug fit by clamping or crimping the copper where the ¼-inch lip and boiler wall come together with the pliers, going around the entire perimeter. You should end up with what looks like a flimsy stockpot with walls that extend ¼ inch below the bottom. This space provides a convenient lip to grab when dumping spent mash after using the still.

Forming the Cape

17. Bring the open ends of piece D (the cape piece) together, aligning the curves along the top and bottom edges, to create a broad cone with a 1-inch overlap (the overlap at the bottom may need to be greater to align the sides and create a circular cone). Clamp the cone's ends into place. See the round aperture at the narrow end? That's what you want. Ethanol-rich vapor will rise and exit the boiler from that opening.

19. Remove the cone from the boiler cylinder. Beginning 1 inch from the small aperture's edge, mark rivet holes at 1-inch intervals along the overlap area. Drill and rivet the hole nearest the cone's bottom, then work your way upward and remove the C-clamp. Use the snips to trim uneven edges.

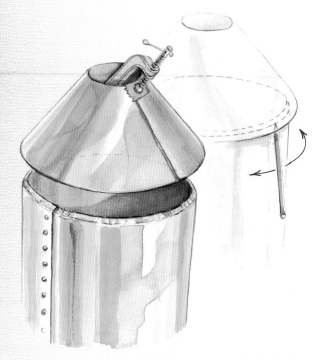

18. Place the wide end of the cone onto the boiler's open top. It should extend slightly over the edge of the boiler wall. Mark the overhang by scribing a circle around the cone's underside where it meets the boiler wall.

20. Using adjustable pliers, bend the inner edge of the cape's smaller top opening slightly downward about ⅛ inch, to a 20° to 30° angle. Use a metal file to clean off any burrs or sharp edges from snipping; you'll need to reach your arm through this hole when cleaning the fully operational still, and unsliced arms are always better than sliced ones. Later, the collar and head will rest on this lip.

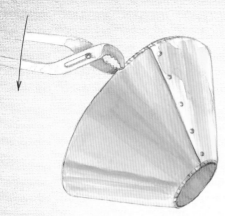

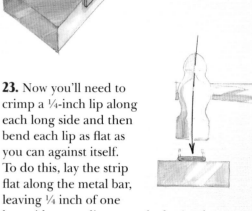

21. Bend the bottom rim inward ⅛ inch to a 45° angle. When assembling your still, this bottom rim will be brazed to the top of the boiler wall, and their two 45° angles should meet to form a flat joint.

23. Now you'll need to crimp a ¼-inch lip along each long side and then bend each lip as flat as you can against itself. To do this, lay the strip flat along the metal bar, leaving ¼ inch of one long side extending over the bar's edge. Tap the overhanging copper lip down 90°, then hammer it flat. Repeat the process on the other long side. Finally, pound the entire strip flat with a hammer so that you are left with a reinforced ½-inch-wide length of copper.

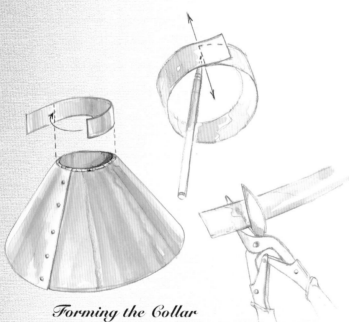

24. Bend the strip back into a circle (use the mark you made before to get your ¾-inch over-lap). Drill a hole at the overlap and place a single rivet there. Be sure to hammer the rivet as flat as possible on the inside of the collar so that it won't in-terfere when you try to slip the head in place.

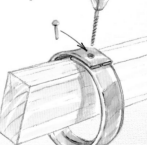

Forming the Collar

22. Using the cape's top aperture as a guide, bend the copper strip (piece E) into a circle that is about ⅛ inch larger than the hole. Mark it so that the ends form a ¾-inch overlap. Cut off the excess and flatten the strip back out.

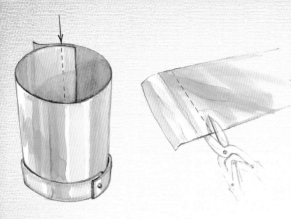

Forming the Head Wall and Dome

25. To make the head wall, roll piece F into a 5-inch-tall cylinder and insert it into the collar. Give it some slack to expand as far as the collar will allow. With the cylinder still in the collar, measure 1 inch in from the end of one long edge of the inside layer and mark that point on the outer layer. Do the same on the opposite long edge. Remove the loose cylinder from the collar and lay it flat. Scribe a straight line between the two marks and use the snips to cut away the excess. The remaining piece will be large enough to fit inside the collar, with a 1-inch overlap.

26. Roll the cylinder (which will be approximately 13 inches long) inside the collar again, overlapping the ends by about 1 inch. Using a straightedge or measuring tape, mark holes for rivets at the 1-, 2-, 3-, and 4-inch points, centered along the overlap area.

27. Remove the cylinder from the collar and clamp both ends; then drill and rivet the two center holes. Remove the clamps. Drill and rivet the end holes. Set the head wall cylinder aside.

28. Now it's time to form the dome of the head, using a technique I borrowed from stillmaker Thee King's narrative in *More Mountain Spirits* (see Resources, page 156). Place piece C flat against bare dirt ground (in a garden or flower bed, for instance) outdoors. Using the rounded end of the ball peen hammer and starting in the center, begin pounding the disc into a shallow cup.

29. Continue shaping the dome, hammering outward. The idea is to stretch the metal, so don't hit repeatedly in the same spot. Move in a spiral from the center to the outer rim, then begin again and repeat until you've created the cup. (You may have to move the disc a few times so you don't pound a hole in your lawn or garden.) The dome doesn't need to slope steeply; instead, create a gentle curve so that, when your still is operating, vapors that have risen and condensed on the head cap will flow to and down the sides of the head before being redistilled.

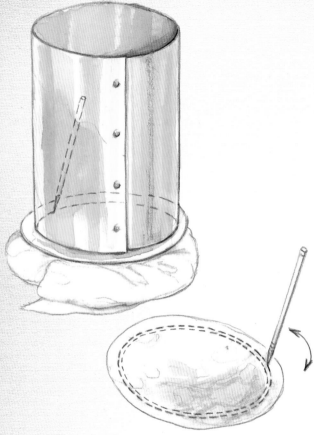

BRAZING THE COMPONENTS

Now it's time to seal all seams and connect the components using silver-based brazing alloy (also sometimes called "silver solder"). Remember, if you don't already have basic brazing skills you might be able to find a metalsmith to do this part of the process for you.

YOU WILL NEED

Leather welding gloves

Welding safety goggles

Acetylene or oxyacetylene brazing torch set with gas tank and regulator (see Note)

Silver/phosphorous/copper brazing alloy containing 6% silver

Igniter

Locking pliers (two pairs)

Scouring pads

Note: An oxyacetylene torch produces a hotter and smaller, more precise flame, but an atmospheric-air acetylene torch will also work acceptably.

30. Wash the dirt off the dome and dry it. Then coil a soft towel into a circle on a flat surface. Put the dome on the towel concave side up to hold it in place. Center the riveted head wall on the circle. Reach into the cylinder and scribe a circle on the dome where it meets the inner surface of the cylinder wall. Remove the cylinder. Carefully scribe another circle ⅛ inch outside and around the first circle. Using the tin snips, trim the dome to the outer circle's circumference.

31. Using the inner mark as a guide and working gradually in several passes, bend a 90° ⅛-inch lip around the edge of the dome. Fit it against the cylinder to assure a snug fit. Make any necessary adjustments with the pliers.

Welding goggles such as these help protect against burns. Check with your brazing supplier for a suitable model.

Brazing: Play It Safe

A good brazing job seals the joints in the still, eliminating dangerous ethanol leaks, and also makes those joints very strong. It needs to be done with care and skill, or it might as well not be done at all. Sturdy, leak-free joints are essential. If you don't already have the basic skills and know-how for brazing copper, take the time to learn first on a simpler project before attempting this one. Or, as I've suggested, enlist the help of someone who already has the necessary skills and equipment.

Do not attempt to braze the still using lesser equipment or materials than those specified here. Silver/phosphorous/copper brazing alloy can be expensive, but it is used on the still for two important reasons: 1) its high melting point means that it creates an especially durable seal, and 2) more importantly, it is lead-free. Acetylene gas burns at 4618°F; oxyacetylene at about 6000°F. At such temperatures, copper glows a fierce cherry red and the brazing alloy flows like water. A propane gas torch will not heat your copper sufficiently to work with brazing alloy, nor will the dinky little heaters that come with hobbyist soldering kits.

Keep in mind, too, that no matter how experienced you are, it is imperative always to wear both appropriate safety goggles and leather welders' gloves when using acetylene or oxyacetylene. Make sure your work area is well-ventilated, and keep it uncluttered and organized so that you can work efficiently—and therefore safely. Open the tube of alloy so that the individual rods are within easy reach. As you melt one rod to the point where the heat is too great to comfortably handle it, discard it in a safe, out-of-the-way place and reach for another so that the copper remains glowing red as you continue to play the flame on the spot you are brazing.

Brazing equipment. Clockwise from top: Oxyacetylene tanks with regulators and hoses, igniter, torch, brazing alloy rods, leather gloves.

Brazing the Boiler Walls and Bottom

32. The first seam to braze is the overlapping joint of the boiler walls. On a heavy steel or earthen surface that can withstand intense heat, turn the cylinder (with the bottom snugly fitted in place) on its side so the seam faces upward. Make certain the piece will not roll or move of its own accord. Working from the bottom to the top on the outside, heat a small patch of the seam—an inch and a half or so—until it takes on a light of its own, like a muted ember whose heat you can feel just looking at it. Touch the end of a brazing rod to that area. If the joint is hot enough, the silver alloy will, after a beat, melt and be drawn into the joint like water up a straw. Move toward the open end, heating, melting, and sealing as you go, always playing the flame just ahead of the rod.

33. After the piece cools, turn the cylinder upside down and braze the boiler (piece A) to the bottom (piece B) from the outside. Allow the pieces to cool.

34. Next, braze both seams on the inside to assure a complete seal and to fill in any little crevices in which organic matter could stick and scorch a simmering mash. This inside work is a considerably hotter task; you'll probably want to hold the brazing rod with locking pliers to keep your hands farther from the heat (or you can melt two rods together to create a longer one). Pause as necessary to ensure your safety and comfort while working with this superhot material.

If the heat warps the boiler wall out of a true circle, simply bend it by hand to the correct shape after it cools. Fill the boiler with water to test for leaks. Fix any you find by rebrazing that section of seam. Using scouring pads, gently but thoroughly clean the carbon off the boiler's inside surface (regardless of how hard you scrub, you can expect some permanent discoloration of the copper as a result of the heat). Rinse away every last bit of ash and cleaner before you even think about putting your precious mash in the boiler.

Say No to Sizzle!

◗ ● ◗ ○ ◖ ● ◖

At some point you may need to turn the pieces you're brazing. Turn off the gas and use two pairs of locking pliers, one pair in each gloved hand, to reposition the pieces carefully. The metal will be extremely hot and will sear disfiguring burns if it even lightly grazes unprotected flesh. Ssssszzzzz is never a good sound to hear when working with hot copper.

Brazing the Head, Cape, and Collar

35. Next, braze the side seams of the head (piece F) and set it aside.

36. While the head is cooling, braze the riveted overlapping edge of the cape (piece D) and set it aside.

37. While the cape is cooling, braze the riveted seams of the collar and set it aside.

38. Go back to the head and insert the dome into place on the top of piece F. Depending on your measurements, it may fit better with the overlap either inside or outside the head walls. A good seal makes either a decent choice. Braze it and set aside to cool. Fill the head with water to test the seals, and rebraze as necessary.

39. Place the cape wide end down. Test fit the collar by placing it onto the cape's smaller, top aperture. The collar should rest just outside the cape's top opening, leaving a thin ⅛-inch rim of cape protruding inside the collar. This rim will support the still's head once it's inserted. Look for spots where the rim of the aperture does not actually meet the collar, and if necessary use pliers to bend the rim downward, creating a small lip, to ensure a closer fit.

40. Lock the collar into place using two pairs of adjustable clamping pliers, one at 3 o'clock and one at 9 o'clock. Spot braze the outside juncture of the cape and collar at 12, 3, 6, and 9 o'clock to secure the collar in place. Then remove the pliers and braze the seam all around both the outside and the inside.

Brazing the Cape/Collar to the Boiler

41. Fit the brazed collar/cape piece down into the boiler and pull it gently upwards, so that the cape's bent rim fits snugly inside and flush against the bent rim of the boiler. Tap the rims gently with a hammer to close any gaps between them. (If necessary, brace the inside of the seam by holding a small block of wood against the spot you hammer.) From the outside spot braze around the seam every 4 inches or so to prevent the cape from popping out of place when it heats. Then braze the entire seam from the outside.

42. As you're brazing, the juncture of the boiler wall seam and the cape may form a particularly large gap because of heat distortion. If so, cut a small piece of copper to fit, and braze that in place. You can also try spot brazing in several places, hammering the cape and side walls closer together as you work, to reduce the gap. In any case, do not try to fill a large gap with brazing material.

43. With the boiler upright, fill it to near capacity to check for water leaks. Rebraze as necessary.

Figure 4
Thermometer Coupling

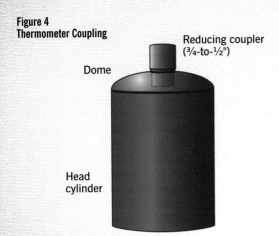

Dome

Reducing coupler
(¾-to-½")

Head
cylinder

Figure 5
Arm Assembly

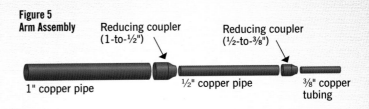

Reducing coupler
(1-to-½")

Reducing coupler
(½-to-⅜")

1" copper pipe

½" copper pipe

⅜" copper
tubing

Brazing the Optional Thermometer Coupling

Note: You may prefer to omit this element. Although it is not traditional in an Appalachian-style pot still, a built-in thermometer coupling—really just an opening into which you can insert a thermometer to gauge the still head's interior temperature—will be of great help to the novice distiller. If you want to run batches without it, plugging it is a simple matter of snugly inserting a silicone plug (heat resistant to 500°F).

44. Mark the center of the still head's dome and, using the step bit, carefully drill a ⅝-inch hole. File any burrs from the edges and insert the ½-inch end of the ¾-to-½-inch copper tube reducing coupler (that is, a single piece that is ½-inch diameter on one end and ¾-inch diameter on the other, used to join pipes of different diameters). Braze it in place. When cool, seal the opening with a ¾-inch silicone plug. Test the assembly for water leaks.

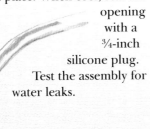

Brazing the Arm

The arm is composed of three lengths of copper pipe of decreasing diameter (see figure 5). The arm carries vapors from the head to the worm, and its angle can affect the flavor of the distillate; an upward angle causes more vapor to reflux (see pages 82 and 83); a downward angle has the opposite effect, thus allowing more congeners to pass into the worm. An arm that extends straight out from the head at a 90° angle is common among small modern home stills, but if you choose you can alter the design so that the arm tilts up 10° to 20° for a product with a more subtle flavor profile, or turn the arm down slightly for a full, robust liquor. Don't let rampant testosterone get the better of you, though: "full and robust" can entail wicked hangovers and a design that encourages mash to puke, or bubble up and spew into the distillate.

45. Braze the 1-inch end of the 1-inch-to-½-inch copper pipe reducing coupler to one end of the 1-inch copper pipe. When cool, braze one end of the ½-inch copper pipe into the free (½-inch) end of the brazed coupling. Let the assembly cool. Then braze the ½-inch end of the ½-inch-to-⅜-inch copper pipe reducing coupler to the remaining free end of the ½-inch pipe. Finally, braze a straight 6-inch length of ⅜-inch copper tubing (the same you'll use for the worm) in the free end of the ½-to-⅜-inch coupler. *Note:* Keep in mind that the coupler measurements are internal diameter, while the pipe measurements are outer diameter (OD). A ⅜-inch pipe, therefore, will fit snugly into a ⅜-inch coupler.

46. Turn the brazed head on its side, seam down, and, again using the step bit, drill a 1-inch hole through the side, centered 3½ inches up from the bottom edge. You may have to drill or file the hole out just a little larger to accommodate the 1-inch copper pipe.

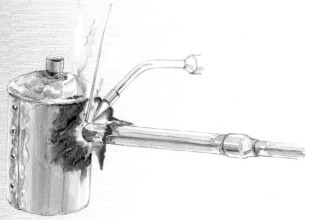

47. When the assembly is cool, insert about ½ inch of the large 1-inch pipe into the hole you drilled in the side of the head. Brace it in place and braze the connection on both the outside and inside. The arm is complete.

MAKING THE WORM AND FLAKE STAND

Figure 6
Flake Stand

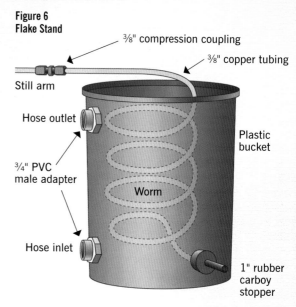

A still's worm and flake stand are where the transformational "magic" of distilling takes place. Inside, mere wisps of alcohol vapor are converted into droplets of liquid ambrosia—or eye-popping firewater, depending on the distiller's skill.

The coiled copper-tubing worm is, of course, the still's condenser. In the cat-and-mouse days of mountain moonshining raids, diligent revenuers destroyed pot still worms that fell into their hands. Distillers fleeing raids did their best to spirit away that valuable copper to use another day.

Valuable though a worm is, it is worthless without its flake stand—essentially a container (ours is a bucket) that holds the copper coil in a jacket of cold running water. As ethanol vapor spirals down the chilled coil and cools, it reverts to liquid. The water absorbs the heat of the vapor and is replaced continually with new chilled water that flows in from the bottom of the stand.

Flake stands come bigger than the model described here, and some designs are much more compactly engineered, but this easy version is fine for small batches on a pot still.

YOU WILL NEED

MATERIALS

32 feet of ⅜-inch copper tubing

Sturdy, clean 5-gallon plastic bucket (such as an olive or pickle bucket)

2 8-foot lengths of ⅝-inch (inner diameter) garden hose

⅝-inch female hose coupling with matching hose clamp

¹⁵⁄₁₆-inch male thread faucet adapter (optional)

2 PVC male adapters, ¾-inch

Clear silicone sealant

1-inch rubber carboy stopper with airlock hole

⅜-inch brass compression coupling

TOOLS

1-gallon glass jug

Copper tubing cutter (or substitute a hacksaw, and use a round file to smooth cut edges)

Electric drill

Hole saw drill attachment, 1-inch diameter (or use step bit)

Flathead screwdriver

Adjustable or open-end wrenches

Making the Worm

48. The copper tubing comes already coiled, but you'll need to coil it more tightly. To do so, place the jug or other round container (about 6½ inches in diameter) in the middle of the loosely coiled copper tubing. Beginning with the inside end of the tubing, wrap the copper by hand tightly around the jug, moving previous coils upward on the jug as you go.

49. Keep wrapping until you have a nice, tight coil of about 15 loops. Leave approximately 3 feet of unwrapped copper at the end before cutting the tubing from the main coil with the tubing cutter or hacksaw. This will be the top of the worm, which will attach to the still arm. Straighten a 6-inch length of tubing at the bottom of the coil to project through the flake stand's base.

Making the Flake Stand

50. First, you'll need to cut three holes in the plastic bucket. The first two are for the water output and input hoses respectively. The third will accommodate the rubber plug through which the end of the copper worm passes from the inside of the bucket to the outside.

Set the bucket upright. Mark a spot on the outer surface 2 to 3 inches from the top rim. Center the hole saw or step bit on that mark and drill a 1-inch hole. Discard the cutout plug.

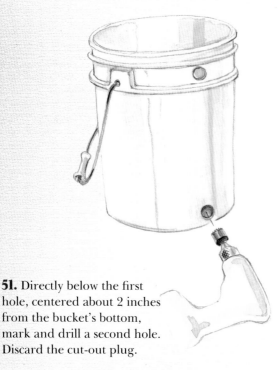

53. Next, you'll prepare the flake stand's input hose; the other hose needs no alterations. Slip the female hose coupling's clamp onto one end of one 8-foot hose length. Then push the coupling into the same end until the threaded ring sits flush against the hose ending. Slip the clamp back up the hose and tighten it down on the coupling with the flathead screwdriver. Attach the hose to a faucet (if necessary, attach the male faucet adapter to your faucet first). Put the open end in a sink or over a drain. Turn on the water, letting it run through the hose, and check for leaks. Tighten the clamp as necessary. Drain the hose.

51. Directly below the first hole, centered about 2 inches from the bucket's bottom, mark and drill a second hole. Discard the cut-out plug.

52. Turn the bucket 90° to the left to drill the third hole, which should be at the same level as the second, about 2 inches from the bucket's bottom. Discard the cut-out plug and brush out any plastic filings. Set the drilled bucket aside.

54. Now you're ready to assemble the flake stand's components. Make certain the bucket is clean and completely dry. Twist the threaded end of one ¾-inch PVC male adapter into each of the two hose holes, so that the larger unthreaded end is on the outside of the bucket. The adapters should fit snugly.

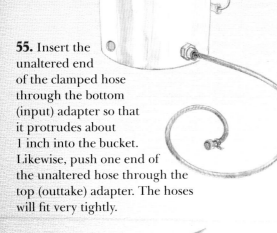

55. Insert the unaltered end of the clamped hose through the bottom (input) adapter so that it protrudes about 1 inch into the bucket. Likewise, push one end of the unaltered hose through the top (outtake) adapter. The hoses will fit very tightly.

56. Working from the bucket's interior, squeeze a bead of clear silicone sealant between the top (outtake) hose and the adapter. The juncture around the adapter where it meets the bucket wall shouldn't need a seal, but if it's not perfect, squeeze a bead along that joint as well.

57. Repeat step 56 on the bottom (intake) hose and adapter.

58. Insert the coiled worm into the bucket and position the spout end of the coil so that it protrudes about 2 inches through the remaining hole to the outside.

59. Press the end of the spout through the hole in the rubber stopper, and then work the stopper over the tube until it fits snugly in the hole. There's no need for sealant here because the rubber forms its own watertight seal.

60. As a final step, after the silicone dries, run water into and through the flake stand, checking for leaks. If you find any, empty the stand, dry it and seal as necessary with silicone sealant.

CONNECTING THE STILL'S MAIN BODY AND FLAKE STAND

61. Using the pliers, attach one of the brass compression coupling's two nuts to the ⅜-inch tubing on the still arm, and screw in the coupling's threaded middle connector.

62. Attach the compression coupling's other nut to the straight upper end of the worm's ⅜-inch tubing. Position the still and flake stand so that they're aligned, and screw the worm-end nut onto the coupling's middle connector. Tighten both nuts with pliers.

Congratulations; your still is complete.

Home distillers who use pot stills frequently install an additional component variously called a thumper, thump keg, or doubler to eliminate the need for second runs.

The thumper is an ingenious device that sits between a pot still's arm and worm. Before a run, it's charged about half full with unheated mash (whether beer or wine) or the low-alcohol feints (liquid remaining in a boiler after a run that may have residual ethanol). The lid is then affixed to trap steam inside. Hot vapor from the arm of the heating still enters through a pipe that passes through the lid and extends into the liquid, almost to the bottom of the charged container. Another pipe, shorter and positioned above the liquid's surface, also passes though the lid, but leads out of

the thumper and to the worm. High-ethanol steam entering the thumper through the first pipe reverts to liquid when it hits the beer, thus driving up the beer's proof. Building steam heats this higher-proof liquid enough to drive off an even higher-ethanol vapor. As the steam heats the keg's contents, the bubbling liquid produces a low thump thu-thump that gives its name to the device. This new vapor escapes through the second, shorter, pipe and into the worm where it condenses as usual, but at such a high proof that it eliminates the need for a second distillation.

Sheer genius.

Not everyone uses them. The distillers re-creating traditional spirits tend not to, for instance, even though such contraptions have been around since the last

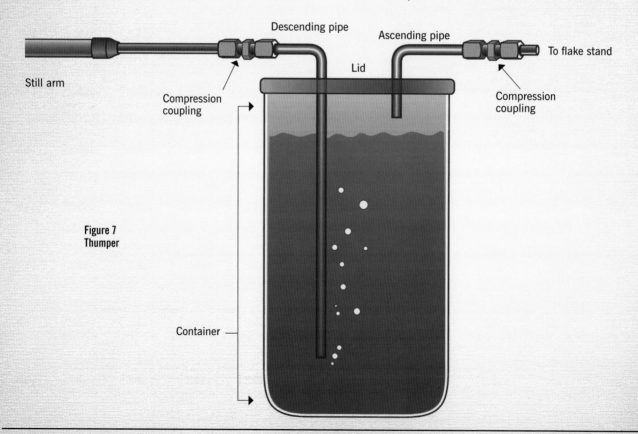

Descending pipe

Ascending pipe

To flake stand

Lid

Still arm

Compression coupling

Compression coupling

Figure 7
Thumper

Container

century. Fantastic spirits are possible without resorting to using a thump keg, but if less work captures your fancy, here are some general notes for adding one to a pot still such as the one we've shown you how to build.

First, you'll need a container suitable to serve as the keg. This can be any food-grade container as long as it's capable of withstanding temperatures up to 200°F and has a removable airtight lid that can be drilled. Most thump kegs are smaller than the stills they're attached to. A still that can hold a five-gallon charge, for instance, doesn't need anything larger than a two-gallon thumper, though some setups involve boilers and thumpers of equal volumes. Among home distillers, I have seen modified soda syrup canisters, three-liter bottles, gallon pickle jugs, paint cans (not recommended), plastic buckets, silicone-stoppered glass flasks, metal beer kegs, and stockpots with C-clamped lids. A copper version could be fashioned following the general principles laid out in this book for building a pot still's boiler.

Once you have the container, you can install the simple plumbing, as shown in figure 7. First, cut two lengths of copper tubing the same diameter as the worm (in the case of our still, 3/8 inch). Make the first pipe long enough to reach from the still arm's coupling joint (where it would normally attach to the worm) over about 12 inches, then bend south 90° and continue down to within 2 inches of the thumper's bottom. To create the 90° turn, bend the tube gently around a beer or soda bottle to prevent accidentally flattening the tubing. Attach half a compression coupling to the tube's other end, and connect it to the half on the still arm.

The second pipe should penetrate the lid and reach into the container only about 1½ inches, while its other end extends up and over to reach the worm's coupling joint. Attach half a compression coupling to that pipe too.

Drill two holes in the lid 1/16 inch larger than the pipes themselves (7/16 inch for our still). Insert the pipes (it's okay to bend them slightly to position them properly), and seal the holes with silicone sealant. Let the silicone cure for 24 hours.

To use your thump keg, make sure it's clean and resting on a heat-resistant surface. Charge it to about half capacity with beer, wine, or feints. Make sure the tubing is properly aligned, and affix the lid. Secure and tighten the couplings to the still arm and the worm. Assure yourself that all joints are airtight. Fire the still. Collect the distillate emerging from the worm as usual (discarding the poisonous foreshots, separating the heads and tails, and focusing on the middle run). There's no need to redistill the resulting high-proof spirit, but cut and age it as normal.

CHAPTER 6

DISTILLING

This chapter covers the basics of operating a small pot still. Keep in mind that the procedures for operating other kinds of stills, such as column stills more commonly used to produce vodka or gin, differ radically.

Even among pot stills, because of materials and structural variances, each behaves a little differently. Those differences can affect such things as flow rate (the quantity of distillate coming out of a condenser over a certain time), the time it takes a still to come to temperature, its tendency to scorch mash, and more.

Some might say that each still has its own personality. Get to know your still by following the directions here and taking meticulous notes on flow rate, temperature, taste, smell, and the amount of spirit produced. With experience, you'll come to understand how your particular still behaves and how you can adjust your recipes and procedures to fit your circumstances and tastes. By all means, research and experiment.

Fundamentals of Distilling

The scientific principles behind distillation remain the same from still to still. The primary alcohol that distillers tease from grains, fruits, and sugars is ethyl alcohol or ethanol (C_2H_5OH). Ethanol is the base of all alcoholic beverages you encounter: wines, beers, brandies, whiskeys, sangria, sidecars, and vodka martinis. Even the suspect artistry of a pousse-café owes its kick to it.

Stills separate ethanol from the water in a mash or wash because each liquid boils at a separate and predictable temperature. Ethanol vaporizes at 172°F; water, at 212°F. If a wash were made only of water and ethanol, distillation would be simplicity itself; you'd just heat your still's contents to 172°F and keep the simmering mixture between that temperature and 211°F. Pure ethanol vapors would rise, waft to the condenser, revert to a liquid, and exit into your eagerly awaiting containers.

However, when you set a mash to fermenting, it produces—in addition to ethanol—a range of byproducts known as *congeners* that includes amyl, butyl, methyl, and propyl alcohols as well as esters and aldehydes. Congener means, literally, "born with." These byproducts are created at the same time as ethanol, except that they are often a result of unintended fermentation processes, and also may be present in a wash.

Daddy made whiskey

and he made it well,

Cost two dollars

and it burned like hell.

"Brown Eyed Woman,"
Robert Hunter

These substances, too, have their own particular boiling points, most of them between 174° and 212°F. So as a wash is heated inside a still, these substances also are released in turn, according to their boiling points. At any given time during a run, depending on the temperature of the still's contents, the vapor entering the condenser, and the liquid exiting, is a mixture of substances. Some (such as ethanol) are good, some not so much. One—methanol—is famously poisonous.

SEPARATING THE GOOD FROM THE BAD

If ethanol is a rambunctious lapdog that occasionally acts up, causing household mischief, methanol or methyl alcohol (CH_3OH) is pure Cujo. Methanol is a frequent, though not inevitable, product of fermentation. Also known as wood alcohol, it is a powerful poison that can utterly and irreversibly destroy optic nerves. When you hear of people going blind from drinking bad moonshine, bet on methanol as the culprit.

Although the small amount of methanol that appears naturally in foods such as apple or grape juice (and unnaturally in diet soda) is easily metabolized by humans and poses no threat, it is essential to purge the substance from distilled beverages. Methanol is in fact such a potent toxin that during Prohibition the American government issued explicit formulae to render industrially produced ethanol poisonous by adding about 10 percent methanol. Scurrilous bootleggers who got hold of such denatured alcohol sold it to unsuspecting drinkers, who then suffered blindness, nausea, nerve damage, and even death.

Methanol is not the only potentially unruly sibling to ethanol produced by fermentation. While some of the other congeners in the final distillate give whiskeys their sublime nose and taste, most are regarded as undesirable because they can lend a hot, solventlike flavor to your finished beverage. One kind held in particularly low esteem is *fusel alcohols*, known among old-timers as fusel oil (from the German *fusel* for "rotgut"), grain oil, or bardy grease. Fusels are the main components of alcohol that cause misery and vows of abstinence from intemperate drinkers left sweating and heaving in the aftermath of excess.

The good news for distillers is that levels of methanol and other congeners can be kept to an acceptable minimum. The first line of defense is to begin fermentation with a yeast strain cultured by a well-regarded, professional lab.

Professionally cultured yeasts tend to produce ethanol cleanly without creating high levels of undesirable congeners.

The second line of defense—and this is vital—is controlling the temperature of your mash during fermentation (see page 75). Higher temperatures cause molecules within a liquid to move faster and collide with greater force. If they collide with enough force to bond with the "wrong" molecule, the result might not be ethanol, but some funky-tasting miscreation. If you take care to keep your fermenting mash nearer the lower end of a 60° to 75°F temperature range, you'll get a slower, cleaner, and more controlled product to distill.

The third defense is distillation itself. As vapor rises from the surface of the mash inside a still's boiler, some of it falls back—or refluxes—into the mash again, slightly purified from unwanted congeners through molecular interaction with the copper. This is why, in the age of stainless steel appliances, copper rigs remain the undisputed monarchs of the stillhouse.

What's more, because vapor coming into the condenser is almost always a mixture of substances with known boiling points, home distillers can discern the approximate makeup of the distillate—that is, the percentage of ethanol and the likely presence of particular congeners—by noting

Still Head Temperatures

	Begin cut	End cut	Percent of Ethanol
Foreshots	<174°F (<79°C)	175°F (79°C)	Poisonous methanol; discard
Heads	176°F (80°C)	195°F (90°C)	>80%
Middle run	196° to 198°F (91° to 92°C)	201° to 203°F (94° to 95°C)	80 to 65%
Tails	201° to 203°F (94° to 95°C	208.4°F (98°C)	Residual alcohol

the temperature within the still at any given time during a run. By collecting the distillate separately in stages, each determined by monitoring the temperature within a still or the percentage of alcohol exiting it (or, with experience, by noting changes in the liquid's appearance, smell, and feel) you can separate the bad, the not-so-bad, and the good. These stages are known among distillers as: foreshots, heads, the middle run (or heart of the run), and tails. The chart on the previous page shows the approximate temperatures and alcohol percentages at which you begin and end each "cut," or stage.

By collecting the distillate in stages, each in its own glass jug or jar, you can use taste, smell, and feel—or, if you want to be scientific, the liquid's proof (see the next section)—to gauge the strength of the alcohol before transferring it to a main container. Anything that smells or tastes off should be set aside, except the foreshots, which contain

methanol and should be discarded entirely.

Finally, you can redistill the spirits from all or some of the stages (except the foreshots) to produce spirits with a higher percentage of the good (ethanol) and a lower concentration of the bad and/or ugly (congeners). Each distillation removes more congeners from the spirit. This is why highly distilled beverages such as vodka, gin, and grain alcohol (what old timers called Cologne, velvet, or silent spirits, regardless of its base) simply have fewer congeners. At the same time, redistilling increases the alcohol content.

When fermenting a grain- or fruit-based mash for distilling, you generally can expect no more than 20 percent alcohol by volume before running it through a still—and that's by using the most alcohol-tolerant yeast strains on the market today under optimal conditions. The first run of spirits through a still results in what traditionalists call low wines or singlings; higher ethanol content than beer or wine, but still containing lots of impurities and flavor. Modern distillers often use a thump keg or doubler (see page 106) to create strong spirits in one run in a pot still, but traditionalists rely on two distillations to yield a clean, if initially harsh, spirit of around 70 percent ethanol. Some prefer a triple distillation for particularly smooth whiskeys. Anything more than that begins to strip the taste of your spirit. In any case, the practical maximum ethanol concentration you can expect regardless of the number of runs is around 96 percent, or 192 proof.

MEASURING PROOF

What, exactly, is proof? For distillers, it's an important concept, a measurement predating modern scientific tools that gauges a spirit's alcoholic content. The term originally comes from Great Britain, where one early measurement involved "proving" a spirit by mixing it with gunpowder and attempting to ignite it. Too much water in the mix meant that the gunpowder would not burn, and the spirit was said to be under proof. If, on the other hand, the gunpowder lit readily and burned evenly, it was regarded as "proof" of the spirit's potency.

Today, proof is measured in the United States by determining the parts of alcohol per 200 total parts in a beverage at 60°F. The resulting "proof" of an American beverage is exactly twice its alcohol content. A 100-proof beverage is thus 50 percent alcohol by volume, while a 60-percent alcohol drink is 120-proof. Commercial spirits often rank around a respectable 80 proof. American moonshine typically thunders in at 100 proof or higher.

Although the proof of finished spirits is significant information, modern home distillers also apply proof as a measure of the progress of a distillation in its various stages, using the readings to tell them when to begin and end cuts. While monitoring the temperatures inside a still during a run is useful for the same purpose, still temperatures can vary and fluctuate. Modern small-batch distillers measure proof by regularly sampling distillate emerging from the condenser with a temperature-sensitive instrument called a *proof hydrometer*.

Figure 1

Proof Hydrometer. Read a proof hydrometer at eye level, noting where the hydrometer emerges at the flat (center) portion of the liquid's surface. This hydrometer reads 120 proof; the "percent alcohol" scale on the opposite side reads 60.

Using a Proof Hydrometer

A proof hydrometer measures a spirit's alcohol content by volume, expressed as *abv*. It looks a lot like the floating hydrometers commonly used in homebrew operations for gauging beers and wine, and it works similarly by measuring the specific gravity (SG) of the spirit; more alcohol means a lower SG and a lower-floating hydrometer. Please note, however, that a hydrometer designed for beer and wine will not measure spirits. Instead, distillers use a proof hydrometer that is marked in both "proof" and "percent alcohol" sides.

Here's what you do: Place the hydrometer in a narrow glass cylinder filled with the distillate in question, and spin it gently with your thumb and forefinger to release any adhering air bubbles. Read the level of liquid at eye level (not where the spirit climbs the cylinder wall); then check the reading on the hydrometer's scale to determine the corresponding proof. Then, since the "proof" readings may be in one of several scales depending on where the instrument was made, double-check the reading against the side labeled "percent alcohol."

Because American alcohol content is measured at 60°F, a matter of a few degrees can derail the accuracy of hydrometers calibrated to that temperature. Immediately after withdrawing the hydrometer, measure the temperature of your distillate, note the difference from 60°F, and make any necessary corrections from the conversion chart that comes with your hydrometer. If you don't have a conversion chart, refer to the graph on page 154 to get an accurate final reading.

A note on the cylinder: Since you will be dealing with small amounts of spirit, look for a narrow glass cylinder that allows the hydrometer to float freely but uses a minimal amount of precious spirits. Any source selling new hydrometers should also supply the appropriate cylinder.

Measuring Proof: Old School

◗ ◖ ◗ ◯ ◯ ◗ ◗ ◖

How did the old timers know when to make cuts for good whiskey? Through experience and practice, many acquired a set of skills that let them know what was happening within the still at any given moment.

The smell of a distillate, for instance, was a constant indicator of quality; the nose-wrinkling, solvent-like stink of the foreshots would be a warning to anyone but the most desperate alcoholic not to drink. When the run began smelling and tasting sour, when it had taken on an oily feel, and when it no longer burned when put to a flame, it was time to stop collecting that spirit with the middle run and start collecting it to add to the next batch. Later in the run, smelling and tasting the distillate—or even rubbing a small portion into the back of the hand—could let a moonshiner know whether the "strength had gone" out of his mash and it was time to shut down the run.

Most commonly, though, whiskey makers (and drinkers in the know) still shake a jar or small vial of the spirit under consideration from side to side. As the agitated beverage settles, bubbles congregate near the surface where the liquid meets the glass wall. The size and duration of this "bead" tells savvy folk the general proof. One-hundred proof alcohol bears a larger, lasting bead that sits half-in and half-out of the whiskey. Lower proof alcohol bearing smaller, shorter-lasting beads are often passed over as suspect or impure.

Figure 2

Reading a Bead. To use the traditional method for judging a spirit's alcohol content, give a jar of spirits a side-to-side shake and watch the bubbles form where the surface meets the glass. This sample's large, long-lasting, half-in-and-half-out bubbles promise potency.

Operating a Pot Still

Have a seat and take some time to carefully review and understand these next steps before you try your hand at distilling. Your first forays into distilling ethanol can be divided into half a dozen primary stages: 1) cleaning the still; 2) preparing the fermented mash; 3) heating the still; 4) monitoring alcohol content and drawing off the distillate, or low wines; 5) emptying and cleaning the still; and 6) "smoothing" the product by making additional runs and filtering or aging the product.

Of course, before you do anything, you'll need to make sure you have all the proper equipment.

EQUIPMENT AND MATERIALS

Naturally, you'll need a still to distill. But you'll also need to take a few moments to make certain that you have all the other equipment you'll need on hand.

Fire extinguisher. Once again I've placed this first on the list. If you don't understand why, go back and read about the need for a fire extinguisher on page 55. You shouldn't have to, though: common sense tells you that when you're making a highly flammable and potentially explosive product, you should have a fire extinguisher on hand. Remember to get one rated for class B fires.

Heat source. A flameless source such as an electric stove or a 1,000-watt hotplate is best. Although it's true that since its inception, distillation has been carried out over open fires, and also true that many of today's home whiskey makers use propane-fired rigs, wood-fired furnaces, and gas stoves to create first-rate spirits safely and affordably, I recommend playing it safe. There is no getting around the fact that an open flame increases the risk of fire.

Racking cane and hose. For transferring liquid from the fermenter to your still's boiler (see page 59).

Cool running water. You'll need to be able to run a continuous stream of cool water through the still's condenser. Unlike mash water, the quality of this water is of minimal import because it never contacts the mash or distillate, though it should be at least drinkable.

Wheat flour. Remember way back in elementary school, when you made paste from flour and water? Well, you're about to do it again. Distillers use wheat paste to seal the joints on their pot stills, an ancient practice called *luting* (see page 119).

Thermometer. A standard glass lab thermometer that measures up to 110°C and about 220°F will suit you here. It should fit snugly in the drilled silicone stopper that plugs the optional thermometer housing in the still head and be long enough to project about 1 inch into the head.

Proof hydrometer. See the section on measuring proof, on page 112.

Timer or stopwatch. You want to note how long the various stages of distillation take and incorporate those into your procedures as you develop your own recipes.

Funnel. So that you won't lose a single precious drop of that hard-earned elixir you distill when transferring it between vessels.

Receiving and storage vessels. Glass canning jars are, of course, standard issue for moonshine containers. You'll need at least four glass pints to use as receiving vessels for the distilling process itself, plus as many storage vessels—glass jars, jugs, bottles, or whatever—as you need to keep up with your production. Label the glass pints "foreshots," "heads," "middle run," and "tails."

Orderin' the Quart

An old joke still current in distilling circles maintains that confirmed corn drinkers are easy to pick out of a crowd: just look for the crease on the bridge of their noses, right where a fruit jar rim bumps during deep quaffs.

Time was, locally made liquor was stored in wooden barrels and was served by the drink from the tap. For a portable container, a stout pottery jug became a favorite and is still featured as part of the stereotypical moonshiner's standard-issue paraphernalia, complete with a triple X on the side.

But in the twentieth century, the classic moonshine container became a glass jar or jug. Why glass? Because of production innovations, glass containers could be made cheaply and in uniform shapes for packing in cases. Glass is also lighter than pottery, contributes no off flavors, and carries an unspoken implication of purity. Glass still reigns as the preferred material among artisans and home distillers.

The old moonshiners' favorite containers were canning jars, especially the pint and big half-gallon sizes. Though originally intended to preserve summer's bounty as jams, jellies, and chowchows, small-time distillers found the containers perfect for marketing their wares. Those who sold in their own communities sometimes even referred to their sideline as the *fruit jar trade*. The fruit jar is so closely associated with local whiskey that one Kentucky distillery widely markets its commercial corn whiskey in fruit jars with screw-on lids.

Canning jars remain in favor among modern home distillers, though repurposed liquor bottles are just as likely to show up. Unfortunately, much moonshine today—at least, the skeevy stuff made cheap to sell fast—is packed in thick-gauge plastic gallon jugs. Many plastics are soluble in high-proof ethanol, so aging in such containers makes the product—usually already inferior—go south quickly as the moonshine takes on the special tang of petrochemicals and joins the ranks, so to speak, of genuine *spittin' whiskey* (see page 68).

> My ancestors never saw a mint julep, but they sipped five-day-old likker out of ceramic jugs and Bell jars until they could not remember their Christian names.

Rick Bragg, *All Over But The Shoutin'*

Clear evidence. There can be no denying the long-standing status of the canning jar as the moonshiner's container of choice, as evidenced in this well-attended post-bust photo-op taken in the 1940s.

GETTING READY

Like almost any do-it-yourself job, distilling requires a certain degree of prep work before you can get to the good part, in this case the actual distilling. These initial steps are important, though—don't hurry through them.

1. Clean the Still

Clean your room; clean your plate: odious chores and sometimes undesirable undertakings. Cleaning your still, though? Why, that's simply a matter of pride and good housekeeping.

When copper reacts with airborne or liquid contaminants, it forms substances such as copper sulfate, copper chloride, or cupric oxide that can turn a still green or even a blackish color. You can't cook with that nasty stuff. Regardless of whether your rig is brand new and shiny, or is so tacky with oily deposits from previous distillations that it could stand in for flypaper, it's a good idea to give it a once-over before firing it up to ensure that no off-tastes from the still will affect your distillate.

Though my mother didn't know a still from a water heater when I was young, she did raise me in a house with a lot of copper and showed me how to clean the pots and pans. The technique applies nicely to our purposes, too. She would slice a lemon or lime in half, sprinkle the cut surface generously with table salt, and use the fruit as a scrubber on her copper. The acid, the salt, and the scrubbing work like a charm to clean the metal. Another, and perhaps more common, method employs vinegar (four to seven percent acetic acid) and table salt: spray the vinegar on a soft cloth, sprinkle salt on the moistened cloth, reach your arm through the still's opening, and scrub the interior surfaces lightly. With either method, as a final step, rinse the scrubbed still thoroughly with clean water, and you'll be good to go.

2. Prepare the Mash

You'll find thorough instructions for mashing and fermenting in chapter 4. Before you put that carefully nursed mash in your still, though, you need to make dead certain that it embodies one particular quality. Distillers may be divided on the best ways to prepare mashes for distilling, but the good ones agree: a crystal-clear wash is imperative. Because an unstrained mash contains solids such as spent grains and fruit residue, it can scorch easily and could clog a still. So the first order of business is clearing the mash of particulates. When you're making beverage alcohol, *never fire the still with solids in the boiler* unless a recipe specifically calls for it. For those who prefer to ferment a clear wash off the grain, this means clearing before even adding yeast.

If floating material such as fruit pulp or spent grains has formed a raft on top of the liquid portion of your mash, carefully lift it out of the vessel using a mesh skimmer or large slotted spoon. Some squeeze the raft through a muslin brewing bag back into the fermenter before racking, to extract every last bit of alcoholic liquid. Others don't because it reintroduces fine particulates. Your call.

Next, use a hose and racking cane to siphon the mostly clear liquid off any sediment accumulated at the bottom of the vat into another, lower, container such as a carboy. Although the mash is ready to be transferred to the still and heated now, you may want to let it rest, covered, one more day to let any residual suspended particulate settle out before racking directly into the boiler.

In especially big moonshining rigs—the illicit commercial kind—the boiler sometimes pulls double duty as a fermenter. Once the mash has completed fermentation, it—including spent grains, dead yeast, fruit skins, pits, and all—is merely boiled in the same container. Don't ever do that; it's a malevolent shortcut borne of ignorance and greed that yields some true rotgut. Besides, if all that gunk plugs your still, you'll likely be scrubbing scum off your ceiling until the wee hours—if, that is, you were lucky enough to have avoided a trip to the nearest emergency room.

An excess of solids in your boiler also can lead to pits, skins, foam, and other material getting into the still's pipes and condenser if the mixture boils over, a situation delicately referred to as *slobbering* or *puking*. If your mash pukes, turn down the heat, toss whatever contaminated distillate you already collected back into the still's boiler, and redistill. If it comes out cloudy or with solid bits, turn off the still, clean out the tubes with a mild vinegar solution, and start over. A few distillers use mineral, canola, or almond oil—about 1 tablespoon per 5 gallons—to keep foaming down within a heated still. Paying close attention and maintaining a low heat eliminates most of the rationale for antifoaming oils, but grain-based mashes seem more prone to foam if the temperature gets too high.

3. Transfer the Mash to the Still

When your mash is completely fermented, draw the liquids off the solids using either a racking cane or by draining them through a tun (see page 66). Particularly thick mashes drain more easily from a tun. If you use a racking cane and hose, make sure you place a receiving vessel (such as a carboy) that will hold at least 6 gallons below your fermentation vessel. Remember, too, that although you can transfer the liquid directly into the boiler and begin distilling, putting it in another container for a day lets particulates settle out for a clearer wash.

To use a racking cane, put the rigid end of the cane assembly into the mash, all the way to the bottom of the fermentation vessel. Holes an inch or so up the cane's side prevent it from sucking in an excess of solids settled on the bottom. Next, hold the hose end up to your mouth and suck on it to draw liquid into the hose. Now cover the end of the hose with your thumb, and quickly insert

Don't Let Your Still Slobber

Babies may slobber, drunks may puke, but your still has no business doing either. Stills *puke*, or *slobber*, when solids are somehow forced into the condenser. It really mucks things up, and there are three main causes.

The first is solids in the mash. If you've left in grains, fruit skins, or other excessive particulates, you increase the chance that some are going to clog the pipes. Not only will this ruin the spirit, but it presents a very real danger of creating a steam bomb, since vapor pressure in the still will continue to build until something blows.

Second is overfilling the boiler. A boiler filled beyond three-fourths capacity runs a much greater chance of puking. Keep your boiler charged appropriately—in other words, less than three-fourths full—and you'll end up with a cleaner run.

Third is allowing the wash to boil. I can't say this emphatically enough: *do not boil the wash*. Boiling encourages foam, which sometimes can clog your pipes—but even if it doesn't, the foam will run out into your distillate, and you'll have to dump the spirits back in the boiler and start over.

Some distillers guard against puking by attaching a device called a *slobberbox* between the boiler and condenser. A slobberbox is a container that traps solids emerging from the still arm and allows

them to settle out as the vapor passes into the worm. Some have a plug like a trumpet's spit valve that drains accumulated gunk. The plug may or may not lead back into the boiler so the gunk can be redistilled. Regardless, vapor goes into the worm clean. Nimble-minded distillers will realize that a thump keg (see page 106) performs much the same function, while also helping to produce a higher-proof distillate.

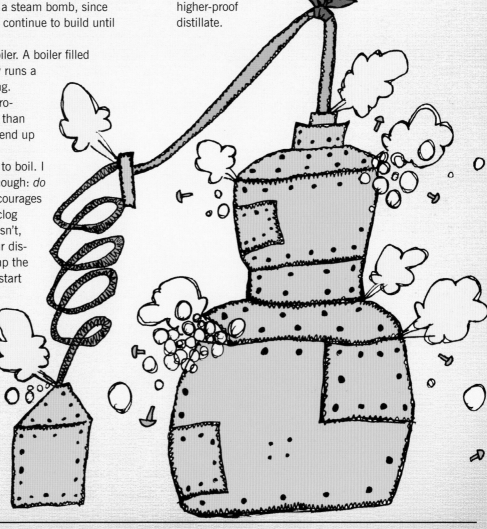

it into the lower container while removing your thumb. If you did it right, you created a siphon, and the liquid will gush forth from the primary container into the lower container.

To transfer wash from a secondary container after allowing it to settle, either siphon it with the racking cane or pour it directly into the boiler, being careful of course not to pour in any sediment remaining on the bottom.

4. Assemble the Still

Everything from this point on assumes that you've already water-tested your still for leaks when you finished making it or otherwise obtained it.

First, connect the flake stand's input water hose to a faucet, and make sure the output hose is positioned to drain into a sink drain, garden, or wherever you don't mind clean waste water. Now turn on the water and run cool water into the flake stand, submerging the worm. You're checking for leaks, but also preparing the worm for when you need it. You'll turn the water on to a slow trickle once the still begins heating.

Next, affix the head and the cap and arm to the still, making sure all the fittings are snug. Likewise, connect the arm to the worm. Of course, if your still also includes a thumper or slobberbox, you'll want to include those components in the setup, too. You're not filling the boiler or sealing anything yet, just making sure you have the entire rig set up properly. Make sure the boiler is firmly seated on the heat source and that the entire setup, from boiler to flake stand, is stable—and I mean rock steady. You don't want anything spilling or leaking from this point on.

Once you're satisfied that everything fits together and isn't going to blow steam or gush hot liquids, you are ready to transfer the cleared mash to the boiler. Remove the head (it should remain attached to the condenser pipe, though) and set it aside. Center the boiler on the heating element (you don't want to move it once it's charged) and,

using a racking cane or simply by pouring, gently transfer the cleared mash from whatever container it's in to the boiler. Try to avoid splashing.

DISTILLING A RUN

OK; settle back and get ready to do some serious studying here. You'll want to read through this part a few times because now, finally, you're ready to transform your mash into the potent liquid you've been pursuing ever since you first picked up this book. Yes, that's right: it's time to make some moonshine.

5. Heat the Still

Once you've transferred the cleared mash to the still, the rig is ready to be heated. It takes a while to get a still and its contents up to temperature, so give yourself plenty of time. Ready? Okay, turn on…wait. Forgive me for repeating myself, but here I go anyway. Before you fire up your still, keep this thought foremost: ethanol is flammable, and high concentrations of its fumes are outright explosive. Also, look around. Is your still site clean, free of clutter, and well-ventilated to minimize the possibility of accidents? Do you have a fire extinguisher at the ready? Don't even think about starting unless you've checked all these things.

Alright. Now turn the heat on to full power (it takes a lot of energy to heat this much liquid) and bring the mash almost to a boil. This could take anywhere from 90 to 120 minutes depending on the volume of liquid in your still and the heating source. Then reduce the heat so that no large bubbles rise, and the mash just barely simmers. A low, steady simmer produces a cleaner distillate, and this is what you want for a long, controlled run. In this state, the surface heaves, swirls, and quivers—some say it "smiles"—but never actually breaks into large bubbles. This is the ideal state for running off first-rate liquors.

6. Slap That Cap and Lute Them Joints

So, the still is heating, the liquid inside is beginning to swirl and churn, wisps of vapor are rising off the surface, and the still's giving off odd pings and occasional thumping sounds as it warms. Now you're ready to seal it so you can trap all that alcohol goodness. Allowing ethanol vapor to escape from the joint between the still cap and shoulder will mean two things: 1) of negligible import, you'll have less whiskey or brandy when all is said and done because the vapor isn't condensing in your worm; 2) of much greater concern, you'll be creating the potential for an explosion of ethanol vapors. All the whiskey in the world can't drown the sorrow of a lost house or limb, so you need to seal those joints and seal them tight.

Insert the head—with the condenser arm tightly attached to it—back into the collar aperture and push it snugly into place. Don't worry if it's not an airtight seal—you're going to make it one soon.

It's time now to lute, or seal, the joints with flour paste. The procedure is undeniably sloppy and low-tech, but appropriately so given the traditional pot still you're using. Besides—and more significantly—the method works. The earliest stills were sealed, or essentially caulked, with lute or luting, a general name for clay, ashes, or fine flour mixed with water. This thick paste is smeared heavily onto joints on the still—anywhere the metal parts are put together, but not soldered. As the still heats, the paste bakes and hardens in place, making an effective seal. When you complete a run, you simply break away the heavy crust and clean it from both parts of the joint.

The amount of water called for depends on the type of flour, its grind, and the ambient humidity. Luting is one of those things you learn by doing. For a thick paste, combine about one cup of white, all-purpose flour with ½ cup of water in a bowl, and mix thoroughly. Add more water or flour as necessary for a good, sticky consistency.

Using your fingers, thickly apply luting at the joint between the collar and head to assure a snug seal with no gaps. Try not to slop it about on the sides of the boiler or your work surface. Don't be startled if you smell something like fresh bread; it's just the paste cooking. Look for any places that need some extra sealing, too. For instance, if your compression coupling between the still arm and condenser (and optional thump keg or slobberbox) is not airtight, try tightening the seal with pliers, but as added insurance you may also choose to coat it in paste. The extra paste makes cleaning the still at the end of the day a little more difficult, but only a little.

The last assembly routine? If you've built a still with an optional thermometer housing and are using a thermometer, gently

---

MADE PLAIN AND EASY. 377

How to use this Ordinary Still.

You muſt lay the plate, then wood aſhes thick at the bottom, then the iron pan, which you are to fill with your walnuts and liquor; then put on the head of the ſtill; make a pretty briſk fire till the ſtill begins to drop, then ſlacken it ſo as juſt to have enough to keep the ſtill at work. Mind to keep a wet cloth all over the head of the ſtill all the time it is at work, and always obſerve not to let the ſtill work longer than the liquor is good, and take great care you do not burn the ſtill; and thus you may diſtil what you pleaſe. If you draw the ſtill too far it will burn, and give your liquor a bad taſte.

To make Treacle Water.

Take the juice of green walnuts, four pounds of rue, carduus, marigold, and baum, of each three pounds, roots of butter-bur half a pound, roots of burdock one pound, angelica and maſter wort, of each half a pound, leaves of ſcordium ſix handfuls, Venice treacle and mithridate, of each half a pound, old Canary wine two pounds, white wine vinegar ſix pounds, juice of lemon ſix pounds; and diſtil this in an alembic.

Keeping the flame. When you fire up a still, you're carrying on a tradition that stretches back for centuries. Like the book you're holding now, this page from an eighteenth-century cookbook was intended to advise newcomers to the craft.

insert it into the drilled silicone plug (see page 101) and firmly push the two into the housing on top of the head so that the weighted end protrudes about an inch into the head and the plug seals the aperture. If you've made your still with a thermometer housing but have decided not to use a thermometer this time, place an undrilled silicone plug firmly into the opening to seal it; luting shouldn't be necessary. Obviously, if you opted out of making a thermometer housing for your still, there's nothing there to plug, so don't worry about it.

Turn the water through the flake stand to a slow trickle. Right underneath the part of the worm protruding from the bottom of the stand, place your first receiving vessel (labeled "foreshots") to catch exiting liquids, making certain that the end of the tube will not be submerged once the spirit flows.

Now it begins.

7. Draw Off the Foreshots

MAKING THE CUT: FORESHOTS

**Approx. Still Head Temperature
Begin Cut:** <174°F (<79°C)
End Cut: 174°F (79°C)

Percent alcohol: Doesn't matter; discard first 3 to 5 ounces exiting still.

Physical Properties: Smells awful. Sharp, hot, fuel-like odor.

The first distillate to come out of the worm is known as foreshots. In a pot still, these low-boiling-point compounds are tricky to separate cleanly from the heads that follow, but you're going to do it because they are composed of volatiles such as acetone, methanol, and a range of undesirable esters and aldehydes. *Foreshots are poisonous. You must not drink them. Throw them out.* Under no circumstances should you let them pass your lips.

A Word on Boiling

Talk to enough distillers and you will surely hear talk of "boiling" mash. I like to think that these are cases of careless language rather than actual big, rolling boiling going on. Let's be clear: the mash should never boil. Oh, the *ethanol* comes to a boiling temperature before the water when the mixture is heated—that's why distillation works, after all—but whether you call it beer, mash, or wash, the liquid in the boiler should not come to the same kind of boil that you'd expect in a pot of water for pasta or in a tea kettle.

Instead, monitor the optional thermometer to gauge the internal temperature and compare that with the chart on page 110, or bring the wash just to the point of boiling, but turn down and level off the temperature so that the boil never breaks forth, but slowly churns and rolls with wisps of vapor beginning to rise. This is the state the more poetically inclined describe as smiling.

Never leave your still untended. You'll need to watch the temperature (if you are using a thermometer) and occasionally adjust the heat to make sure it doesn't get too hot. Thermometer or not, you'll also need to listen to the sounds the still makes; if you hear bubbling and boiling, you need to turn down the heat. Hissing? A bad sign. Very bad. Turn off the heat immediately, find the leak, and fix it.

Their harsh, solvent-like smell should be enough to warn you off drinking them.

As the first beads of clear liquid begin to drip from the end of the worm, let them fall into the glass pint jar or measuring cup marked "foreshots." They will come drip by drip, not in a gush. Once you've collected an inch or so in the container, take a whiff (do not inhale deeply). Remember that smell. File it in your active memory. If you *ever* come across moonshine that has that smell, politely decline even the smallest sip.

Once you've collected 3 to 5 ounces (here's where the measuring cup is handy) or the temperature rises to 176°F (80°C), remove the container, set it aside, and replace it with another glass container marked "heads."

Now you're ready for the next step.

8. Collect the Heads

Drips of clear distillate will be coming from the end of the worm faster now, but still not gushing—maybe one drop per second. Smell. Notice that the liquid is decidedly less skanky; it's still strong-smelling, but without that nose-crinkling paint thinner bouquet.

This stage is called the heads. Heads are high in ethanol as well as the congeners that lend some desirable flavor and aroma to spirits. Whether to draw off the heads in a container separate from the next stage—the middle run—is a matter of personal taste. Some distillers make no distinction between the heads and the purer middle run and just run them together. For now, you're going to separate them and make up your own mind later after you've done this a few times. You may decide to add small portions of the reserved heads to the finished spirit for a final flavor boost before diluting to drinking strength. Or, you could pour the heads in with the tails—the last of the usable alcohol coming from the still—and redistill the combined liquid as feints after collecting them from several runs.

Those are decisions for later. For now, collect the drips of distillate in a glass pint jar labeled "heads" until the temperature climbs slowly up to about 196°F (91°C); the alcohol percentage should read above 80. If you find the temperature is not rising (it should), increase the heat a very small amount. Watch carefully how your still responds, and take notes. You'll rely on them when you make subsequent batches to know how to set your heating element and whether to adjust it, how much volume to expect from each stage and what smells to expect.

Once the temperature hits 196°F (91°C) or the alcohol percentage drops to 80 or below, take away the "heads" container and switch to one marked "middle run" under the worm.

9. Collect the Middle Run: Best of the Batch

The main volume of alcohol coming from a mash distillation is known as the middle run. When the middle run first emerges, it's around 80 percent ethanol and contains fewer congeners than the heads do. As the run progresses, the ethanol content of the emerging distillate gradually drops until, after about 65 percent or so, the spirit no longer tastes so strongly of its ingredients. Peach brandies lose their peachiness, corn liquor is not so corny, and applejack's nose fades away.

By now, the distillate emerging from the still will have increased volume. Instead of the drip-per-second you watched earlier, don't be alarmed to see a thin, steady stream of distillate. Let me repeat: You never want a gusher, just a gentle flow. You may feel like lowering the heat to slow the flow back to a drip-drip pace if you're more comfortable with that. The lower flow rate will produce a cleaner spirit. On the other hand, this is your maiden run and you can be excused a certain degree of eagerness; a slightly higher flow rate will produce a perfectly passable spirit, too. It's your decision. Just be sure to take notes, so that if you want you can make changes based on them on the next go-around.

Collect the distillate in the "middle run" container. It's especially important to smell and taste at this stage. Oh, yes—you should taste it now. Remember, this is pure white liquor, and it's strong. If you're expecting subtlety, look elsewhere. It's harsh and raw. But notice that it also carries some sweet notes. Keep smelling, keep tasting—a dab off your finger, not a shot glass full. Collect an inch or so in your container, and when you are satisfied that it's good quality, transfer that smaller amount to a larger container such as a half-gallon glass jug. Use a funnel so you don't slosh.

This is also an especially good time to use that spirit hydrometer you bought. Test small samples of the middle-run distillate to gauge their proof. It's alright if they vary; you're interested in the final proof of several samples combined in that big jug.

Do that repeatedly until you begin noticing changes. You will notice after a while that the smell becomes less intense, less interesting. The strength is beginning to go from your spirit as the ethanol content drops. If you're watching your thermometer, it should register around 201°F (94°C). The proof should be around 130 (65 percent ethanol). Stop collecting the middle run. You've gotten most of what you need from this mash—but you're not finished wringing the last of its usable alcohol. You're going to bring this thing to a close by collecting the tails.

10. Collect the Tails

MAKING THE CUT: TAILS

Approx. Still Head Temperature
Begin Cut: 201° to 203°F (94° to 95°C)
End Cut: 208°F (98°C)

Percent alcohol: Residual

Physical Properties: Runs more thinly from still; lacks sweetness, tastes like an abandoned cocktail filled with melted ice. Towards the end of the run, can feel oily. Rank odor, sometimes cloudy.

At this point, the tails—characterized by lower ethanol and higher congener concentrations—have begun emerging. Use the pint container marked "tails" to collect the distillate from the worm. Regular measuring of the emerging liquid with a proof hydrometer will tell you when the bulk of ethanol has been extracted from the mash as the internal temperature hits 208°F (98°C). But honestly, after the first few times you won't need tools to know when the mash is spent. Smell for it: there's little nose and what's there is slightly foul-smelling, like a sick mop. The distillate has gone all watery. Watch for it. The emerging trickle changes consistency, becoming less sinewy and serpentine, and sometimes a bit cloudy, as it twists out the spout. Keep tails separate from the middle run and, for now, from the heads. Maybe later you'll redistill them, but for now you're done collecting alcohol.

Turn off the heat. Set all the sealed jars and containers aside in a safe, out-of-the-way place. Turn off the flow of water to the flake stand. It's time to clean up.

11. Empty and Clean the Still

When the run is over and before the still cools, break off any cooked-on luting from the joints and uncap the still to allow it to breathe as the liquid inside cools. This step is vital in a reflux still, but it's just a good idea for a pot still. If ambient air cannot get into a cooling still quickly enough, a powerful vacuum forms that can crush stout stills as easily as an adult crushes aluminum beer cans.

Either siphon away or pour off the spent liquid remaining in the still—the slops are not fit for any practical use except that livestock may enjoy it. In fact, in the folklore of revenuers, stumbling cows and sideways-staggering pigs have led to many a still seizure.

Rinse the still with warm water and a soft scrubber. You may notice a greasy residue on the inside upper surfaces. This "bardy grease" is normal and a byproduct of the fusel alcohols that were extracted from the mash. If it's present on the boiler's inner surface, it's a sure bet to be in the tubes as well. Not a problem. Clean out the head/arm assembly and worm by running through a mild vinegar solution (about ½ cup per gallon of water). Subsequent distillations of the singlings should come out considerably less oily.

You may choose to make a second run of those low wines right now (see the sidebar, upper right). If so, just clean the inside of the still and any pipes as necessary, and don't worry about cleaning the outer surface just yet. If you are finished for now, clean the entire still's exterior with salt and lemon or vinegar, rinse it, dry it, and then store it wherever it lives when it is resting.

A Second Run Now, or Later?

After you've successfully made your first batch of low wines, you want to distill the product a second time to produce a cleaner-tasting, higher-proof spirit. Don't worry; the procedure's the same except that you charge your boiler with low wines instead of cleared mash. (If you've attached a thump keg to your still, your spirit is already double-distilled and there's no pressing need to take it further.) Your options are to redistill now, while all your gear is out, or to wait and redistill a day, a week, a month later.

The advantage of waiting is that you can collect the heads, tails, and middle runs from several batches and redistill each kind all at once. This is, in fact, a smart way of using this style of pot still. If you combine the middle run of, say, four or five low-wine runs, you save energy and time. Plus, you get a substantial amount of high-proof liquor that's already been stripped of many impurities.

Combining the heads and tails from several runs is definitely worthwhile. This way, you wrest the last bits of usable alcohol from several combined batches. If you don't want to wait until you have four or so gallons of feints, just add the heads and tails to the next batch of mash you distill.

Another Option: Beer Stripping

Some distillers essentially *predistill* their mash—a technique called *beer stripping*. The idea is to reduce a large volume of low-alcohol beer quickly to more manageable, higher proof, low wines by roughly wresting the bulk of alcohol from beer without much regard for separating good parts from the bad. Here's what you do: Follow the instructions for heating a still and distilling as outlined, *except ignore all the parts about drawing off stages*. That's right; just heat the still, and collect every bit of distillate that comes out in one large container. Once the alcohol is expended (determine either by sense, hydrometer or when the still head temperature hits about 208°F, or 98°C), turn off the heat, and put aside the low wines until you are ready to distill them into proper liquor. When you've collected four to five runs, combine them and follow the instructions below for drawing off heads, tails, and whatnot.

12. Blend and Cut the Final Product

Though they're all more likely to cause hangovers, not all congeners are bad. Some, in fact, are essential for lending particular whiskeys their characteristic flavors. For a flavor boost, you may add a small portion of the heads (this is why you saved them in a separate container) back to the middle run. How much to add is a matter of personal taste, but start with a small portion and add more if you think your spirit will bear it. Combine any heads you don't use for blending with the tails in a tightly sealed glass container, and add them to the next batch of fermented mash you distill. Or, you can add some heads back to the next mash you make, before fermenting; as the mixture ferments, yeasts metabolize the aldehyde congeners in the heads.

The last step is cutting—or diluting—your final high-proof, double-distilled spirit with pure water. Fifty percent alcohol (100 proof) is the usual dilution, although some distillers leave their spirits uncut. Use the spirit hydrometer to measure the proof properly. Not only are cut spirits less flammable (in the case of an accident) when they are diluted to 80 or 100 proof, but volatile aromatics are more easily released, increasing the perception of aroma and taste. In short, if the 'shine is good, it tastes better when it has been cut.

Unless you're blessed with outstanding tap water, avoid it for cutting. Instead, use distilled water or spring water, even if you used tap water for your mash. Because half of your product is going to be this water, you want to make sure it's a taste you enjoy.

Finishing Touches: Filtering and Aging

Moonshine's reputation as skull-splitting firewater often stems from the failure of profit-seeking distillers, in their rush to get products to market, to take the time to "smooth" their products. Fortunately, polishing 'shine is not difficult. If you can calm babies and put them to sleep, you'll be a master at taming rough spirits and laying them up.

FILTERING

Distillers routinely filter their spirits, sometimes through activated carbon, to improve the taste and smoothness. The carbon cleans or "polishes" liquor by removing excess congeners. This adsorption (not absorption) relies mostly on electrostatic attraction to trap contaminant molecules within its millions of tiny holes and crevices as unfiltered liquor passes through. Household water filters operate on the same principle.

A lot of beginners could stand to filter their makings.

Filtering becomes less called for as distillers gain experience and develop surer hands operating their stills. Ultimately, it's a personal choice. I'm less inclined to enjoy filtered brandies, but that's just my personal taste. Even with the more full-flavored whiskey recipes in this book, you won't want to run the spirits through too much filtering, or you just end up with bland hooch bereft of the special tastes of grains and fruits you were after in the first place. By all means, experiment to find the degree of filtering that suits you.

If you decide to take the filtering route, check online or in the books listed in the Resources section for information on activated carbon, including suggestions for cleaning and reusing it, and ways to create homemade filters. Most homebrew shops also can show you how to set up a filtering system. At least one commercial pour-through device for filtering liquor is available, too. In any event, if you're purchasing activated carbon be sure you get only the *granulated* form. The stuff sold for aquarium filters is no good for what you want; pellets are too big and powders pack too tightly.

AGING

It's easy to understand why commercial moonshiners would rush their wares to market as fast as possible: to beat revenue agents intent on seizing and destroying shipments. Even among old-time artisans, the demands of making respectable whiskeys were balanced with the need to avoid detection. The more expediently one fermented, distilled, and sold one's alcohol, the less risk one ran of explaining the family business before a magistrate.

Unfortunately, those spirits invariably deliver a less-than-desirable one-two punch: harsh, fuel-like taste, and a lick-of-fire lung explosion that can leave a drinker gasping for breath. Aged whiskeys and brandies, by contrast, can become mellow, smooth elixirs with clear notes of fruit or grain dominating. At the same time, their fire cools from an ear-nose-and-throat cauterization to a gentle, warming blossom that unfolds in one's chest.

There's simply no reason not to age your product—unless, of course, you prefer young whiskeys. Some folks do. But it doesn't take a snooty, sophisticated, or refined palate to appreciate the differ-

> **I'd buy old felt hats, tear the lining out of 'em and what not, and I had a rack I'd put that on. It was strained through an old felt hat. That's all that was run through, before it went into the keg...It went through that very slow, and into the kegs. And there'd be absolutely nothing, it came out a there as clear as water. But to make sure there was nothing, we strained it through the hat...preferably they were white.**
>
> Pennsylvania moonshiner
> "Memories of a Moonshiner," *Pennsylvania Folklife*, Fall 1976

ence. You owe it to yourself to at least try aging your moonshine. After all, it's either legal where you live or you've secured the proper authorization, so there's no need to rush the process for fear of getting caught.

Fortunately, aging your moonshine is not complicated; it just tests your patience. Just remind yourself that the wait is worth it. Spirits become more mellow and flavorful as time goes by because many of the long-chain alcohols present as congeners evolve into fruity esters and a host of other pleasant-tasting compounds. In the case of bourbon, Scotch, and other whiskeys, such maturation lasts years.

The simplest way to age moonshine is just to pour it into glass jars or bottles (*never plastic*) and tuck them away into a cool, dark place. Maturation as short as a single month can alter rocket fuel to the pride of your pantry.

Some spirits require aging in wood. Bourbon, for instance, is generally aged for at least four years (though in practice most distillers age it longer) in new, charred, white oak barrels. As the barrels sit over years in warehouses, the colorless spirit slowly moves into and out of the wood with the change of seasons and becomes the famous red likker of Kentucky, all the while picking up tastes from the wood, altering its chemistry, and becoming a more distinguished and palatable drink.

Wooden barrels are available in smaller sizes for small batches, but because they can lie outside the budget of many home distillers, many prefer wood chips or ½-inch cubes as an affordable alternative to help age, color, and flavor their product. American white oak (*Quercus alba*) chips—both new and toasted or charred—are by far the most

commonly available in homebrew shops. Since the desired degree of wood and char in a whiskey or brandy is a matter of personal taste, it behooves you as a novice distiller to experiment and develop proportions that fit the profile of what you like in a drink. About two ounces of oak chips per quart is a decent place to begin your research.

Additional woods to consider include beech, French oak, red oak, pecan, sugar maple, cherry, and other fruit woods. Not all woods are suitable, however, so please check with local horticultural societies, university botanists, or field guides to determine whether the woods you consider are safe or tasty. Pine, cedar, juniper, spruce, and birch, for instance, are not universally beloved tastes. To toast your own woods, cut them into ½-inch cubes, wrap them in heavy aluminum foil, and pop them in the oven on a sheet pan at 280° to 400°F until it reaches the degree of char you like (anywhere from heavily tanned to black). See "Baby Step Bourbon" on page 131 for one recipe that calls for wood chips.

Keep in mind that the character of the wood becomes more pronounced over time and that it's always possible to add more chips to a batch. If you find that your whiskey becomes too bosky, the most practical way to correct the taste is blending it with less strongly "oaked" whiskey. Of course, the best way to guard against extra woodiness is to sample your spirit occasionally; when it comes to a taste you enjoy, filter and rebottle it. Use muslin to filter it; activated carbon would strip it of all the taste you just put in.

Graceful aging. Small wooden casks are available for aging your makin's, or you can use oak chips to imbue woody flavors, bouquet, and color.

The Angels' Share

◖●◖◖○◖●◖

Whoever coined the phrase "smells like a distillery" for a wretchedly hung over, stinking drunk apparently never spent time in distilleries before maligning them so unjustly. One of the most magical things you're likely to encounter traveling through Kentucky is, in fact, the smell of a bourbon distillery. From malty, yeasty fermentation vats full of bubbling mash to the heady aromas of the bottling line, these places are wonderlands of intoxicating aromas. None, however, compares to that of an outdoor bourbon warehouse with its racks upon racks of wooden barrels stretching into the dark recesses of its ceilings.

Because wood is a semi-porous material, spirits aging in the barrels slowly seep back and forth into the charred wood with seasonal temperature variations. Warm weather causes barrels to open and breathe, allowing them to take on whiskey a little like a sponge. With the coming of winter, the barrels constrict and force the whiskey back into the center. A small percentage of the spirits actually escape the barrels entirely, evaporating to fill the atmosphere of loosely closed warehouses. This lost whiskey distillers call "the angels' share." Close your eyes in a dark warehouse, inhale its sweet, clear, grainy bourbon essence, and you will understand the heavenly metaphor instantly. And, please, out of respect for generations of Kentucky distillers, let's find something else to say about those drunks.

CHAPTER 7

Recipes

Now that you know how to mash, ferment, and distill, you can turn your attention to deciding just *what*, precisely, you'd like to mash, ferment, and distill. Distilling recipes are unlike traditional cookbook recipes, for they are never truly meant to be duplicated—no two batches, whether produced by the same or different distillers, are likely to be exactly the same. Any given distillation yields a product that is unique to the sum of its ever-variable parts: the ingredients, of course, but also the specific nature, quality, and source of those ingredients; the distiller's skills; the still's intrinsic idiosyncrasies; and more.

Because of this, the ingredients listed here and the instructions given should be regarded more as guidelines than as specifics to follow precisely each and every time you make a certain recipe. Instead, view each recipe as an evolving work in progress, to be tweaked and adjusted according to your particular situation and observations. Make mental or, better yet, written notes as you go: what kind of yeast did you use and how did it react? Precisely how long did the mash take to ferment completely? At exactly what temperatures did the foreshots begin and end? Would a little more or this or a little less of that improve the flavor? Every observation, every experience, contributes to the ongoing process of creating an ever-better end product. After all, it's not just the recipes that will evolve and improve over time, but your skills as a distiller, too.

Whiskeys: Grain-Based Recipes

In the parlance of American distillers, grains such as wheat, barley, corn, rye, oats, rice, and millet yield *beer* when fermented with yeast and water. Once distilled, those beers become whiskeys. The traditional whiskey recipes in this chapter have been drawn from interviews, personal observations, and historical research, but some are modified for the novice distiller by using mostly precooked flaked grains.

Unlike grains for regular mashes, flaked grains do not need to be crushed. They also yield more ethanol in a single fermentation than crushed uncooked grains do. In all instances, your initial mash pH for whiskeys should be between 5.2 and 5.5. As you become a more proficient distiller, you may wish to experiment with cooked whole-grain recipes, try your hand at Appalachian-style corn whiskeys, or reuse grains in a no-cook, slop-back sour mash recipe. See the resources section (page 156) for taking those next steps.

> **Kentucky, oh, Kentucky,**
> **How I love your classic shades,**
> **Where flit the fairy figures**
> **Of the star-eyed Southern maids;**
> **Where the butterflies are joying**
> **'Mid the blossoms newly born;**
> **Where the corn is full of kernels,**
> **And the Colonels full of corn!**
>
> William James Lampton

BEGINNER'S CORN WHISKEY

Every moonshiner has particular recipes tweaked over time to suit individual tastes and local circumstances. This take on *corn likker*, the primal American whiskey, is ideally suited to novice distillers because it relies on flaked maize, a processed grain that eliminates more complex techniques called for in other recipes. The path to making good whiskey is sometimes a lifelong trek. Getting the hang of this recipe will equip you well for that journey of developing your own, more advanced recipes.

Ingredients
    8 pounds of flaked maize
    20 ounces of two-row barley malt, ground
    1 teaspoon of gypsum
    1 teaspoon of acid blend
    5 gallons of water
    Yeast starter using ale or distillers' yeast

In a large (7- to 10-gallon) stockpot, mix the water, gypsum, and acid blend. Measure the pH to ensure that it's within range; if the pH is too high, add as much as a teaspoon of gypsum. Cover the pot and heat the mixture to 165°F. Turn off the heat and add the flaked maize. Stir about five minutes to ensure even distribution (it will turn thick and slushy). Stir occasionally until the mass cools to 152°F, then stir in the malt. Allow the mixture to cool to 149°F, cover the pot, and let everything rest for 90 minutes, stirring occasionally. Cool the mash to under 76°F and add the yeast starter (see next page), stirring gently. Allow the mash to ferment. When fermentation is complete, rack off the liquid and distill.

Don't Forget the Yeast!

If you've ever baked bread by reactivating dry yeast in a liquid, you already know what's coming. Most of these recipes call for a yeast starter—in other words, a slurry made of dry yeast rehydrated in warm water. Starters allow a distiller to introduce a big, robust yeast population into a nutritious mash to begin a proper fermentation before any harmful microbes get a foothold.

Follow this easy-to-remember rule of thumb for making a starter: For every 1 gallon of mash, rehydrate 2 grams of dry yeast in ½ cup of blood-warm (100° to 105°F) water.

For a 5-gallon batch, that means adding two standard 5-gram packages of dried yeast (available in homebrew stores) to a sterilized container with 2½ cups of water.

Stir the mixture gently, and let it rest about 10 to 15 minutes. By then, the starter should be foamy on top and have turned a cloudy, tannish gray. If your starter does not appear to be activated after a half hour or so, your yeast may be old or dead. Get new, fresh yeast pronto because dead yeast will do you no good.

Once the starter is activated, add, or "pitch", it to the cooled (under 76°F) mash, and stir the entire mass gently to distribute it throughout.

Many, if not most, small-batch distillers rely on this method or some close variation. Some distillers, eager to get fermentation underway, buy dry yeast in bulk and use as much as 2 ounces for a 5- to 10-gallon batch. This is cautious overkill, but certainly won't harm their fermentations.

Still others use liquid or turbo yeasts, which are designed for particular applications (turbos are used primarily for sugar washes, for instance) and come with instructions that are specific to their brand and yeast type. Follow the instructions carefully, and you should get good results.

Take the blood out of an alligator. Take the left eye of a fish.

Take the skin off of a frog and mix it up in a dish.

Add a cup of grease swamp water. And then countin' one to nine,

Spit over your left shoulder. And you got alligator wine.

"Alligator Wine," Screamin' Jay Hawkins

THIN MASH (50/50) WHISKEY

Some liquor revisionists say that old-timers would never add sugar to their mash—it just wouldn't be the real McCoy. The truth is, cheap refined sugar has been around so long that generations of moonshiners have embraced it as necessary and desirable. Some gullible drinkers swear they can taste maize in whiskey that is corn in name only. Can you taste the difference?

Note: Because this recipe produces twice the amount of mash created in the other recipes in this chapter, you'll need two fermenters or enough freezer space to freeze about 3 gallons of unfermented mash to ferment and distill later. Or, see the recipe for Split Brandy (page 132) for another way to use half of the corn whiskey.

Ingredients

Ingredients for Beginner's Corn Whiskey
  (see page 129)
20 pounds of corn sugar (dextrose)
  or 16 pounds of table sugar
Enough cool water to make 10 gallons
  total volume
Yeast starter

Begin by making a full batch of Beginner's Corn Whiskey (page 129) but stop just after you've let the mash rest for 90 minutes, before you've cooled the mash and pitched the yeast. Instead, split the mash evenly between two fermentation vessels and add half the sugar to each. Stir to dissolve the sugar; then top off the vessels with enough cool water to create a total volume of 5 gallons in each. Chances are the mash will have cooled to under 76°F by then; if it has, pitch the yeast and ferment to completion. When fermentation has ceased, rack off the liquid, allow it to settle, and distill.

BABY STEP BOURBON

If bourbon is an old man's drink, then I am nearly ready for the grave. I dote on the Kentucky spirit and always keep a clutch of various bottles on hand to break out, depending on who's visiting. This recipe employs a scaled-down home version of traditional no-cook mashing. By definition, bourbon must be at least 51 percent corn. Though grain bills typically call for two to three parts of corn to one of rye, one popular premium brand substitutes wheat for rye with excellent results. Here we sidestep *de jure* aging in charred oak barrels with more accessible oak chips.

Ingredients

7 pounds of flaked maize
¾ pounds of flaked rye
1 pound of flaked wheat
2 pounds of malted barley, ground
1 teaspoon of gypsum
1 teaspoon of acid blend
5 gallons of water
Yeast starter
Charred white oak chips

In a large (7- to 10-gallon) stockpot, mix the water, gypsum, and acid blend. Measure the pH to ensure that it's within range; if it's too high, add as much as a teaspoon of gypsum. Cover the pot and heat the mixture to 165°F. Turn off the heat and add the flaked maize, rye, and wheat. Stir about five minutes to ensure even distribution (it will turn thick and slushy). Continue stirring occasionally until the mash cools to 152°F, then mix in the malted barley. Let the mash cool to 149°F, cover the pot, and allow the mixture to rest 90 minutes, stirring occasionally. Cool the mash to under 76°F and add the yeast starter (see page 75, step 7); then allow to ferment. When fermentation is complete, rack off the liquid and distill.

If you have new charred oak barrels, then by all means use them to age your white liquor. Otherwise, once distilled, age the white spirit in glass containers with 2 to 3 tablespoons of charred American white oak chips per quart to approximate bourbon's characteristic amber hue and complex flavors. After a few weeks, taste the bourbon from time to time, and when the flavor suits you, remove the oak chips. (You can either let the chips free-float and then remove them with a strainer, or put them in a small, undyed muslin bag before adding them to the distilled spirit. Small straining bags are available at homebrew shops, or you can substitute reusable cloth tea bags sold at health food stores.)

SPLIT BRANDY

Split brandies—so-called because they're part fruit- and part grain-based—are a popular way to reuse partially spent grains from a traditional no-cook mash of whole grains. This version is especially easy for the novice distiller.

Ingredients

> Same ingredients for Beginner's Corn
> Whiskey (page 129) *except*:
> 6 pounds (not 8 pounds) of flaked maize *plus*
> 10 pounds of dead-ripe peaches, washed
> and crushed

Follow the instructions for making Beginner's Corn Whiskey. Just before cooling the mash to fermentation temperature, add the peaches to the mash, stirring them in completely. Then continue following the instructions.

GEORGE WASHINGTON'S RYE WHISKEY

Scotsman James Anderson made whiskey at George Washington's Mount Vernon estate in a distillery that operated in a brief but fantastically profitable run from 1797 to Washington's death in 1799. By 1809, there were no records of sales. With help from the Distilled Spirits Council of the United States, that distillery is being reconstructed and employs a replica of an eighteenth-century still captured in 1940 in Fairfax County, Virginia.

Washington's grain bill was 60 percent rye, 35 percent maize, and 5 percent barley malt. To make an approximation of his whiskey, use these ingredients:

Ingredients

> 6 pounds of flaked rye
> 3½ pounds of flaked maize
> ½ pound of malted barley, ground
> 1 teaspoon of gypsum
> 1 teaspoon of acid blend
> 5 gallons of water
> Yeast starter
> White oak chips (or wood strips from a used
> port-wine barrel)

Follow the procedure for making Baby Step Bourbon, but use only the grains listed here. After distilling, age the spirit with uncharred white oak chips or wood from a used port-wine barrel to suit your taste, then remove the wood.

MALT EXTRACT WHISKEY

When you just can't be bothered to make a batch of all-grain whiskey, do what legions of sneaky homebrewers do when they're in a hurry for a barley fix: use dried malt extract. This sweet, powdery shortcut to a fermentable wort is quick and easy, and the key ingredient is available at any homebrew shop. If you decide to use malt syrup instead of dried malt extract, make certain it's un-hopped, and multiply the dry-malt weight by 1.25.

Ingredients
    8 pounds of light dried malt extract (or 10 pounds
    of light unhopped malt syrup)
    5 gallons of water
    Yeast starter

In a large stockpot, heat 3 gallons of water to boiling. Put the remaining 2 gallons of cool water in your fermentation vessel. Add the malt extract to the boiling water, and stir until thoroughly dissolved. Turn off the heat and transfer the hot malt/water mixture to the cool water in the fermenter. Cool the mash to under 76°F and add the yeast starter; then cover and allow to ferment. When fermentation is complete, rack off the liquid and distill.

What Is Koji?

Koji is the Japanese name for rice inoculated with the spores of *Aspergillus oryzae*, a mold that breaks down rice starches into glucose for more efficient fermentation. It's also used to make *miso* and Japanese pickles. In western-style fermentations, malt enzymes are usually used to convert grain starches in one container before the wort is fermented in another. A koji-based fermentation combines the steps in a single container, because enzymes are produced as the mold spreads, and yeasts pitched in the container consume the resulting sugars. Koji is available refrigerated at some homebrew shops and in many Asian and health food groceries.

RICE WHISKEY

In Korea, Japan, and other Asian countries, rice is as well-known to distillers as corn, barley, and rye are to their American counterparts. In the north of Thailand, where locals believe that sticky white rice is central to their mellow outlook, *lao khao* (literally "rice whiskey") is a pillar of the rural economy. Ask for sticky rice in bulk at your nearest Asian grocery. This version of rice whiskey relies on both yeast and *koji*, a specialty ingredient that converts rice starches to sugar (see the sidebar at bottom left).

Ingredients
    15 pounds of uncooked sticky rice *(khao neuw)*,
    crushed (see Note)
    1 pound of koji
    1 teaspoon of gypsum
    1 teaspoon of acid blend
    Enough water to make 5 gallons total volume
    Yeast starter using champagne or sake yeast

Dissolve the gypsum and acid blend in the water; then cover the rice with the water in a fermenter and let it rest overnight. Making sure the rice mixture's temperature is between 68° and 76°F, add the koji and pitch the yeast at the same time. Stir until the whole mass resembles a watery porridge. Ferment for five to seven days or until the rice sinks to the bottom and fermentation seems to cease. Rack the liquid into a carboy or other clean container and strain the remaining bottom sludge through a mesh brewer's bag, squeezing as much liquid as possible into the container. Let the liquid settle and, once it's clear, rack it into the still boiler. Distill twice in a pot still, or once if your still is equipped with a thumper (see page 106).

Note: Homebrew stores sell grain mills and sometimes even grind grains for customers on-site. For this recipe, you want each rice grain crushed or cracked into three to five pieces, not pulverized into powder.

Rums and Washes: Sugar-Based Recipes

Rum in the morning, rum in the evening, rum at suppertime; America was once fueled on rum. Though the molasses-based spirit is nowhere near as popular as it once was, it remains a staple at all liquor stores. Recently, small distilleries have begun turning out batches of North American artisan rums. Home distillers and former homebrewers are following step by experimenting with yeast strains, flavorings, and types of sugars, pulling the craft back ever so slightly from its "sugarhead 'splo" reputation.

In cane-growing regions such as Louisiana, the Caribbean, and well into South America, sugar spirits are central to any distiller's toolkit. Molasses-, sorghum-, sugar-, and honey-based washes (rather than grain or fruit mashes) produce lovely, well-rounded, complex spirits. Sugar, however, is sometimes tricky to ferment because, though rich in oxygen for growing yeast populations, it is notoriously deficient in other nutrients. Without additional help, sugar-wash fermentations can get stuck before fermenting completely, leaving sugar unconverted to ethanol.

Yeast nutrients (see page 73) are one way around obstinate fermentations. Other methods, such as adding massive amounts of yeast to the wash in stages, are useful, but adding nutrients is easier and more efficient for the beginner. Nutrients are available in most homebrew shops. Some may also carry turbo yeasts, which are designed specifically for sugar washes. If you use turbo yeasts, be especially sure to follow the package directions carefully.

HOME BATCH MONKEY RUM

Monkey rum is rarely a term of endearment, as it's used here. More often, it's given to hair-raising hooch made by desperate distillers using blackstrap molasses, a viscous goo left over from sugar refining. Blackstrap molasses is just too strong to my taste for distilling, though some swear by it.

Instead, this more palatable version of monkey rum calls for amber molasses, which should have a sugar content of 60 to 69 percent and is available from health food stores and food distributors. Better yet, don't take my word for it. Try this recipe using different varieties of sweeteners—amber, blackstrap, cane syrup, corn syrup, agave nectar, or others—to see what you like. Take notes and make the recipe your own. Temperate additions of brown, palm, piloncillo, or muscovado sugars can also lend their own distinctive characters to rums.

Ingredients
  1½ gallons (about 19 pounds) of unsulfured amber molasses
  4½ gallons of hot water
  Yeast nutrients
  Yeast starter

Mix together the molasses and hot water until the molasses is thoroughly dissolved. If you're also adding small amounts of sugars, make certain

Spirit of Honey

Put one part of Honey to 5 parts of water: when the water boyleth, dissolve your Honey therein, skimme it, and having sodden an hour or two, put it into a wooden vessel, and when it is but bloudwarme, set it on worke with yeast after the usuall manner of Beere and Ale: runne it, and when it hath lyen some time, it will yield his Spirit by distillation, as Wine, Beere and Ale will doe.

Sir Hugh Plat, *Delightes for Ladies* (1627)

AGUARDIENTE
(AKA CACHAÇA, FLOR DE CAÑA, ETC.)

Lighter than rum, *aguardiente* is slightly more complicated to make than the nearly idiot-proof home rum recipe on the preceding page. Since this aguardiente is made from cane juice rich in sugars, it needs no malt to begin fermentation. It does, however, benefit from an initial boiling to drive off excess water and increase the concentration of fermentable sugars in the wash.

The disadvantage of cane juice, of course, is that it's generally available only in those regions—the Deep South and points southward—where sugar cane is pressed. If you don't live in such an area, search out fresh-squeezed cane juice in Cuban fruit stands and some Latin markets, where it's known as *guarapo*.

Ingredients
8 gallons of freshly pressed cane juice
Yeast nutrients
Yeast starter

In a 10-gallon stockpot, boil the cane juice down to 5 to 6 gallons. Cool the reduced, sweeter juice to under 76°F, and add the yeast nutrients and yeast starter; then allow the mixture to ferment. When fermentation is complete, rack off the liquid and distill.

they're completely dissolved before proceeding. Cool the mash to under 76°F and add the yeast nutrients and yeast starter; then allow the mixture to ferment. When fermentation is complete, rack off the liquid and distill.

Try Caipirinha
◗ ● ◗ ○ ○ ◗ ◗

For a refreshing summer drink from Brazil, one that's kin to mojitos and daiquiris, and traditionally based on the Brazilian cane spirit *cachaça* (ca-SHA-sha, a version of aguardiente), try this: cut a green lime (or two creole/key limes) into a dozen pieces and distribute them among two tumblers. Sprinkle heavily with table sugar, and muddle them together to form a pulpy green conglomeration. Drop in several ice cubes, fill two-thirds full with *aguardiente* or 21st Century Moonshine (see page 136) and top with a splash of soda water.

SKIMMIN'S

In the fall throughout the American South, fresh sorghum is crushed and its sap boiled down to make a sweetener for biscuits, candies, and breakfast foods. As the liquid boils in large, flat pans, the foam and scum that rise to the top are skimmed off to leave a dark, molasses-like syrup. Plenty of fermentable sugars remain in the skimmings, though. If you know folks who boil their own sorghum, plead your case to get some of the skimmings before they're tossed out. Given a choice between throwing them away, feeding them to the hogs, or running them though a still, which way would you jump?

Ingredients

    5 gallons of sorghum skimmings
    1 gallon of water
    Yeast starter

Add the skimmings to a fermentation vessel. Heat the water to boiling in a pot. Carefully add the hot water to the vessel and stir to distribute it evenly. When the temperature drops to under 76°F, pitch the yeast, cover, and ferment to completion. Rack and distill.

> ## You don't buy
> ## 300, 400, 500 pounds of sugar
> ## just to can huckleberries.
>
> Vernon Still,
> Sheriff of Barry County, Missouri

SUGAR SPIRITS: 21ST CENTURY MOONSHINE

I have to be honest: I'm ambivalent about using table sugar to make spirits. There's nothing wrong with well-made sugar spirits, but because so much of the truly bad and flat-out dangerous moonshine on the market relies on granulated sugar to provide its kick, I've become leery of them all. Sugar, though, is the darling workhorse of modern moonshiners and home distillers alike. It has been part of the moonshiner's toolbox so long that many consider it essential to traditional distilling.

There's no reason that double- or triple-distilled sugar-based ethanol can't be part of your larder. Sugar spirits are usually distilled to such a high proof that, once cut with water to a drinkable state, they really don't have much inherent taste. Home distillers regard this as an advantage, however, because this same blandness allows them to flavor their "whiskey" with commercial essences that emulate Irish whiskey, Scotch, bourbon, applejack, Armagnac, wintergreen schnapps, cinnamon shots, root beer, or even candy apples. I'd rather have the real thing when it comes to bourbon and Irish, but for a collegiate indulgence in funky flavors or if you want to just get high as a kite, why not?

Go on and make some for preserving fruits, making cordials, and turning into vanilla extract. But for your sippin' whiskey, you'll be happier developing your own real fruit- and grain-based recipes, which have more enduring and endearing character.

Ingredients

    10 pounds of white granulated table sugar
    5 gallons of water
    Yeast nutrients (see Note)
    Yeast starter using distiller's yeast (or turbo yeast;
      see Note)

Put 2½ gallons of cool water in a fermentation vessel. Heat the remaining water to boiling. Add the sugar to the hot water and stir to dissolve;

then, while continuing to stir, add the hot sweetened water to the cool water. When the temperature drops below 76°F, add the yeast nutrients and yeast starter. When fermentation is complete, rack off the liquid and distill.

Note: This recipe calls for distiller's yeast, which has an expected 14 percent alcohol yield and relies on added yeast nutrients to sustain the yeast population. If you use turbo yeasts (as most hobby distillers do when fermenting sugar), refer to the package instructions; you will omit the nutrients and use more sugar because turbos contain their own nutrients and tolerate higher alcohol content.

You take a little trash and you mix it up with ash,

And you throw in the sole of a shoe,

Then you stir it awhile with an old rusty file,

And they call it that good old mountain dew.

"Mountain Dew," lyrics and music by Bascom Lamar Lunsford/Lulu Belle and Scott Wiseman, 1973

Brandies, Schnapps, and Grappa: Fruit-Based Recipes

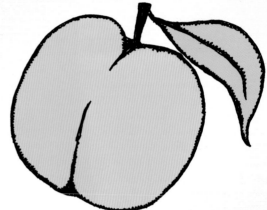

The United States federal government maintains strict definitions of beverages and prohibits any distilled spirit made of anything except fruit wines from being called a brandy. Apples and peaches are the runaway favorites of distillers, but cherries, pears, plums, raspberries, blackberries, quince, bananas, mangos, huckleberries, figs, grapes (particularly those large-bore American muscadines and foxy Concords), tangerines, and persimmons have all breathed their last through a copper worm. Grappa and fruit-based schnapps are brandies, too. Grappa is made specifically from the skins of grapes. Although some kinds of schnapps are made from grain, many boast the same fruity heritage that other brandies claim. There's a good reason why brandies are expensive: 20, 40, even 50 pounds of fruit to produce each bottle of brandy is not unheard of among commercial distillers.

New School thinking holds that only the most perfect fruit at its peak of freshness should be fermented for brandy. Old Schoolers sometimes use fruits that would never make it past a health inspector. Which is right? A strong advantage of the fresh-fruit method (used in the first two recipes here) lies in the ability to replicate closely a brandy every time you make it. Half-rotten fruit (called for in the third recipe) may produce sublime brandies, but be aware that, because of the unpredictable wild yeasts and bacteria present, each making is a unique adventure. There's always a chance that you'll produce a beverage best consumed only mentally, as a learning experience.

Also, because home distillers have not always been fond of the federal government telling them what can and cannot go into their products, ingredients other than fruit—sugar in particular—have found their way into some so-called brandies. Whether you include sugar in your recipes is a matter of personal choice. Bear in mind, however, that traditionalists frown on the practice. When these recipes call for sugar, that is because that is how they were shared with me; I have tried to preserve the recipes as close to their original rendering as possible. In general, though, sugar-fortified brandies (and whiskey) make sense only for two groups: 1) those selling their spirits illegally who use it to increase ethanol output cheaply and thus make even bigger margins, and 2) beginners who haven't yet graduated to hand-crafted, artisan products. Of course, spirits always have a place as a base for cordials and bitters, for preserving fruits, or for other kitchen uses. Following the guidelines for Peach Brandy II (facing page) would put you solidly in the most venerable American distilling traditions.

Brandies are, of course, colorless when they escape the still. Many moonshiners, though, insert fruit in the jar with the brandy; jars with skinned peaches, stemmed cherries, pierced Damson plums, or whole Seckel pears are traditional gifts around Christmas and the winter holidays, when exchanges of the summer and autumn runs are common among some families. Particularly wily children learn to snatch a boozy cherry or two when no one is looking.

PEACH BRANDY I

Ingredients

    25 pounds of ripe peaches
    13 pounds of sugar
    1 tablespoon of pectinase
    Enough water to make 6 gallons
        total volume
    Acid blend (if needed)
    Turbo yeast

Wash the peaches and thoroughly crush them in a fermentation vessel. Let the pits stay in the mash (you'll strain it later). Add 5 quarts of boiling water and 6½ pounds of sugar, stirring to dissolve it completely. Allow the mixture to cool to 122°F; then add the pectinase and let your mash sit loosely covered for one hour. Add enough cool water to bring the total liquid to 5 gallons. When the temperature drops below 76°F, check the mash's pH; it should be between 4.0 and 5.0. If it is not, add acid blend to adjust it. Then pitch the turbo yeast according to the manufacturer's instructions. Replace the lid.

Ferment the mixture for two to three days until the bubbling subsides, then strain out the floating solids by pouring the wine through a muslin or nylon bag into a separate, clean container. Be certain to squeeze the solids hard to remove as much liquid as possible. Discard the pulp and return the liquid to the fermentation vessel.

In a small stockpot, dissolve another 6½ pounds of sugar in 1 gallon of water over high heat. Stir until all of the sugar is dissolved. When the sugar solution cools to 76°F, add it to the wine in the fermenter. Using cool water, top off the liquid to 6 gallons and cover the fermenter loosely with a lid. After seven to ten days, rack off the liquid and distill.

PEACH BRANDY II

Ingredients

    1 bushel (about 35 pounds) of ripe peaches
    Up to 1 gallon of water (optional)
    Yeast nutrients
    Yeast starter

Wash the peaches and thoroughly crush them in a fermentation vessel. Let the pits stay in the mash (you'll strain it later). If the peaches are completely ripe, they'll provide enough juice to make a slushy, chunky liquid. If not, add up to 1 gallon of boiling water to create that consistency.

Check to be sure the peach mash temperature is below 76°F; then pitch the starter, and stir briefly and gently.

After fermentation begins, the fruit pulp will rise to the surface of the liquid as a raft. Allow the mixture to ferment for five to seven days, but gently fold the effervescent raft in on itself once a day using a sterile, long-handled spoon—be sure the spoon is sterile, because the liquid is a particularly rich environment for unwanted bacteria to form. When fermentation has ceased, rack off the liquid and distill.

PEACH BRANDY III

Ingredients

    21 to 25 pounds of partially rotted, windfall,
        or "brandy" peaches
    3 pounds of sugar
    3 gallons of water
    ⅓ cup of distiller's yeast

The peaches may be soft, bruised, or even moldy; do not wash them; simply crush them directly into the fermentation vessel. Let the pits stay in the mash (you'll strain it later). In a stockpot over high heat, dissolve the sugar in the water; then pour the liquid over the mashed peaches. When the temperature falls below 76°F, pitch the dry yeast directly into the mash and stir gently to distribute it thoroughly. Loosely cover the vessel and allow the liquid to ferment to completion, about three to six days. Gently lift away the raft, then strain the liquid and distill.

NEW ORLEANS PLUM BRANDY

Though plums have never enjoyed as much popularity among small distillers in the United States as peaches or apples, canny European distillers have long used them to make truly outstanding brandies. This version, from an anonymous New Orleans distiller, uses sugar to bump up the final alcohol volume. Traditionalists who disavow added sugar as an abomination should simply omit it and expect a lower alcohol yield.

Ingredients

> 25 pounds of very ripe plums
> 5 pounds of sugar
> 5 gallons of water
> Yeast starter

Wash the plums, then crush them and place the fruit pulp, juice, skins, and pits into a fermentation vessel. Boil 3 gallons of the water and add the sugar. Turn off the heat and stir until all the sugar particles are dissolved. Add the boiled sugar solution to the fermentation vessel, and top it off with the remaining 2 gallons of (room temperature) water. When the mash cools to under 76°F, pitch the yeast starter, cover the vessel, and allow the liquid to ferment to completion. Strain the mash by pouring it through a muslin or nylon brewer's bag, squeezing the pulp thoroughly to extract all the liquid. Rack off the liquid and distill.

APPALACHIAN STYLE APPLEJACK

It wasn't just pies that Johnny Appleseed had in mind. Applejacks—spirits made of fermented and distilled apples—were once ubiquitous throughout New England, the Mid-Atlantic states, and the mountain South. Now you have to hunt for good examples.

This is the style of applejack that converted me to brandy drinking. The man who gave it to me was surely an underhanded Appalachian missionary, spreading the Gospel of camaraderie and good spirits. In sparse northeastern Missouri where we celebrated Derby Day, Mother's Day, Tuesday, the anniversary of the end of Prohibition, and any other day that needed commemorating with a raised wrist, he was a welcome addition. This is a brandy to be shared.

Grinding and pressing apples—the usual procedure—can be a daunting task for the novice distiller who may not have a full complement of necessary equipment, including an apple grinder. This recipe uses already-pressed, unpasteurized apple cider. Ask the owners at your local orchard what varieties are best for making hard cider. They'll know.

Ingredients

> 6 gallons of fresh, unpasteurized sweet apple cider
> 5 pounds of sugar
> Yeast starter

Pour 1 gallon of cider and all of the sugar into a stockpot. Heat and stir the solution to dissolve the sugar completely. Pour the remaining 5 gallons of cider into a fermentation vessel; then stir in the sugar/cider solution. Check to be sure the mixture's temperature is below 76°F; then pitch the starter, and stir briefly and gently. Cover the vessel and allow the mash to ferment to completion; then rack off the liquid (you should have a little more than 5 gallons) and distill.

Note: If not using sugar, simply ferment, rack, and distill.

NEW ENGLAND STYLE APPLEJACK

Two methods for making applejack are traditional to North America's frigid North and Northeast. The first is essentially the same as—and predates—the distilled Appalachian variety. The second is a decidedly low-tech invention with a distinctly high-tech name: fractional crystallization (also known as freeze distillation). A tub of fermented (or "hard") apple cider is placed outside and allowed to freeze partially during sustained subzero temperatures. Water freezes at 32°F; the ethanol doesn't freeze until minus 178.6°F. Ice crystals that form are skimmed from the container, and the process is repeated until the alcohol content rises so much that the beverage simply stops freezing.

In other words, ethanol is not extracted from a solution; instead, the water is removed from the ethanol in the form of ice. A fiery and flavorful spirit is left in the tub, but be warned: it contains not only ethanol, but all the methanol, esters, aldehydes, fusel alcohols, and hard-cider particulates. Drink too much of this applejack, and a mere hangover would seem a blessing compared to the Armageddon in your head. It sometimes requires years of storage in oak barrels or with oak chips to tame this fiery Yankee antifreeze.

Here's the recipe:

Ingredients

Approximately 5 gallons of fermented ("hard") cider

When winter weather allows for sustained freezing temperatures, place the hard cider outside (or in the freezer if you have access to a walk-in model) in a plastic bucket large enough to allow for some expansion. Cover the bucket and leave the cider alone until large ice crystals form along the sides and top. Using a mesh strainer, skim out the slurry of ice. Put the cover back on the container.

Repeat this process until ice no longer forms and the quantity of cider (now applejack) is much reduced. Strain the liquid through a muslin or nylon brewer's bag, and age.

Alternatively, you can simply freeze a 1-gallon jug of hard cider in a freezer or outside in cold weather (leave about 2 inches of headspace for the cider to expand without breaking the jug). Once the cider has frozen, uncap the jug and turn it upside down over a container such as a glass jar. Because of ethanol's lower freezing point, the water will stay largely frozen while the spirit drips out bit by bit into the jar. Strain it, age it, and break it out next winter.

MUSCADINE MOONSHINE

Throughout the American South, summer is the season for putting up preserves and pickles. Making wines from local grapes, berries, and other fruits is an old tradition, even in areas that are "dry" (at least, on the books). Muscadines—large, wide-ranging grapes with almost leatherlike skin—are often eaten out of hand, but remain a favorite ingredient for jams, jellies, wines … and moonshine.

Ingredients
> 25 pounds of muscadine grapes
> Yeast starter

Crush the grapes using the Shrimp Boot Method (see page 57) or some acceptable substitute (using a potato masher and a large stainless steel bowl will work, but requires crushing multiple batches). Pour all of the juice, skins, and seeds into a fermentation vessel. Pitch the yeast starter; then cover and allow the mixture to ferment to completion. Strain the wine, rack off the liquid into your boiler, and distill.

Note: You can add 2 pounds of sugar dissolved in 2 gallons of warm water to the mash before pitching the yeast if you like. Just be certain that the mash temperature is below 76°F before adding the starter. Also, after straining the mash, don't throw out those skins and seeds. See the recipe for Dumpster Grappa on page 144.

TANGERINE SCHNAPPS

Oranges work fine for making wine, but if you have access to a load of tangerines, forget the oranges and run off a batch of tangerine schnapps.

Most cooking recipes and some winemaking directions call for separating the pith, that fibrous white membrane between the pulp and the outer skin of citrus fruits, from the juice or zest because it can impart a bitter note to pastries and delicate sauces. I say just leave it in: the bitterness is there, but it's not an unpleasant background note.

Ingredients
> 18 pounds of tangerines, washed and cut
>   into quarters
> 8 pounds of sugar
> 4 gallons of hot (107°F) water
> 130 grams (about half a package)
>   of turbo yeast

In a 7- to 10-gallon stockpot, heat the water to 107°F. While the water is heating, use a meat grinder or food processor to grind the tangerines and pour everything—juice, seeds, pith, rind, and all—into your fermentation vessel. Cover the vessel. Stir the sugar into the hot water until it's completely dissolved. The solution should be sweet, but not syrupy, and free of any sugar granules. Carefully pour the hot sugar water over the ground tangerines, and stir briefly to distribute the fruit.

When the temperature lowers to under 76°F, pitch the dry turbo yeast directly into the mash, cover the vessel loosely, and allow the liquid to ferment. Each day, gently fold the fruit raft that rises to the top back into itself. When fermentation has ceased, strain the solids from the mash, rack the liquid, and distill.

Note: Tangerines spurt, and grinding them is messy work. Be sure to wear a long-sleeved shirt and long pants; sugar-rich tangerine juice drying on your bare skin redefines the word "itchy."

DR. STULGIES'S WEINTRAUBE

An informal Bourbon Trail linking whiskey distilleries meanders through Kentucky's bluegrass country. After a recent trip on the Trail, chemist Baldur Stulgies was inspired to distill his own spirits. Dr. Stulgies's grandfather made his own wines from raspberries, cherries, and apples in Germany, but occasionally, those wines were mere steppingstones on a path to stouter beverages.

This recipe highlights a history parallel to folk distilling, but it is one of professional chemists and pharmacists creating their own spirits, rather than one of cherished family traditions passing through generations. Based on wine, it eliminates one of the beginning distiller's more time-consuming tasks: fermentation.

Dr. Stulgies bypasses the entire fermentation stage by buying cheap red wine in boxes and distilling it, one liter at a time, in a laboratory-style glass flask while inviting friends over to sample the results. Since there is no fermentation in this recipe, the only ingredient is the wine itself. I've increased the quantity to take advantage of the capacity of the still detailed in chapter 5.

Ingredients

4 or 5 boxes of bargain red wine, 4 liters each

Pour the red wine into your still, and distill as usual. Five boxes should yield around 2 liters (about half a gallon) of high-proof weintraube. *Important:* Remember to toss out the first 3 to 5 ounces, since it may contain poisonous methanol.

Beer Schnapps

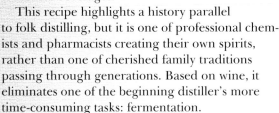

Beer schnapps, or *bierbrandt*, is made the same way as weintraube: you simply distill beer to produce a higher-proof alcohol. The yield with beer is less, however, because the initial ethanol content is lower in beer than in wine.

The next time your guests fail to kill off a keg of beer after a graduation, pig pickin', or other hoedown, drain the remaining beer into your still and distill it as usual. Don't fill the still's boiler more than three-fourths full, because beer tends to foam and spurt into the condenser. If it makes you more comfortable, add a teaspoon of mineral or almond oil, and use moderate heat to keep foaming in check. If you have a particularly hoppy beer, retain a small portion of it to add to the distillate to assure that the hops' aroma comes through clear, in a schnapps that will bear a strong family resemblance to your leftover beer. Avoid stouts, barley wines, and heavy beers, which can turn acrid in a still, and hefeweizens, which easily scorch.

DUMPSTER GRAPPA

Benjamin "Benny Reds" Robling is a mad pow-erhouse of cheese facts and trivia—and of fine foods in general. While attending college in New York's Hudson Valley, Reds became obsessed with the idea of making grappa—a particularly Italian style of brandy made from *pomace*, the skins and seeds of grapes pressed for wine—out of the grape "waste" the area's wineries dumped out as garbage. "We figured that by throwing out the pomace they were throwing out 60 percent of their profits; they regarded a product as a byprod-uct and just didn't know what to do with it."

If you're a winemaker or know one, you can help right this egregious waste by creating your own "dumpster"grappa. The pomace from mak-ing red wine will already be fermented and ready for the still. White-wine makers will need to fer-ment the skins of freshly squeezed grapes first by mixing them with water and yeast and, perhaps, a little sugar, and allowing the yeast to do its work for several days.

A traditional grappa-making method calls for putting the fermented pomace alone in the boiler and gently, gently heating the moist mass until it begins to breathe its ethanol vapors into the con-denser. This requires close monitoring, however, and invites a novice to ruin the batch by scorching the mash.

This recipe for Dumpster Grappa pays homage to Ben's great idea but eliminates at least some of the danger of scorching by adding water to the mix.

Ingredients
20 pounds of fermented grape pomace
4 gallons of water

Combine the fermented pomace and the water in the boiler of your still. Mix gently to break up any clumps, and distill carefully over low heat to prevent burning.

Now That You've Made It: Moonshine-Based Recipes

Drinking 'shine straight requires an heroic constitution. It's almost always tempered with something, even if only a splash of branch water. In the documentary film *Moonshine*, North Carolina moonshiner Jim Tom Hedrick and his buddies are shown wisely alternating swigs of whiskey with more moderate sips of cola. That's one way to do it. Another way is to flavor distillates with sweeteners, herbs, spices, or fruits in a tradition that stretches back as far as distillation itself.

In European monasteries, secret and elaborate recipes evolved that included herbs and spices valued more for their supposed curative powers than for their taste. Old manuscripts and herbals called these concoctions, infusions, and tinctures *cordials* after the Latin word *cor*, meaning "heart." These strongly flavored elixirs were medicines intended to stimulate the heart and revive flagging vigor. Many of today's cocktail bitters, cordials, and schnapps are descended from this tradition, even if we no longer regard them as medicine per se.

The recipes that follow aren't meant to stimulate anything more than appetite and conversation. Enjoy.

> **Mr. Cotton always had quart Mason jars filled with pure, white corn whiskey—not for drinking, as I recall, but for cooking tough turkey, lean squirrel and white meat rabbit.**
>
> Doral Chenoweth, *Corn Whiskey Stew, A Cherished Taste*, 1992

Don't Have Moonshine? You Can Still Make These Recipes

The recipes in this section don't necessarily require "real" moonshine—you can also make them by substituting commercial versions of the spirits indicated.

CHERRY BOUNCE

One end of the bounce continuum puts a little pep in your step. The other end bounces your tail right to the floor. Be careful which end you choose. I put my cherry bounce up in June in the brief period when sour cherries are not only the ripest, but also, since I have no tree and have to buy them, the cheapest.

Ingredients

½ gallon of sweet cherries such as Bing
½ gallon of sour "pie" cherries
1 pint of honey (sourwood, elderflower, clover, or tupelo)
Corn whiskey or bourbon
5 cinnamon sticks, 3 inches long (optional)

Wash and drain the cherries, then lightly crush them in a large bowl. Transfer the juice, pulp, and pits to a wide-mouthed 1-gallon glass jar, and add the honey. Fill the container nearly to the top with whiskey, and add the cinnamon, if you're using it. Close the container securely. Shake the bejesus out of it to dissolve the honey; then put it away in a cool, dark place for at least six months, giving it a shake now and then. Drink the cherry bounce neat or serve it with a few of the cherries in a large shot glass.

Note: You may remove the stems from the cherries or not. Leaving them on allows eaters to snag them by the stem. I trim mine halfway. Why? I don't know. It's just the way I was taught. Maybe it looks better, but this much is certain; the more cherries I eat, the more little handles seem like a good idea.

Cherry Bombs

Throughout the American South, an ersatz cherry bounce is often made from dyed maraschino cherries because fresh cherries aren't affordable year-round. Don't scoff. I like both. After a sufficient rest in grain alcohol (certain New Orleans' bars carry vintages as old as last Tuesday), the fire-engine red cherries are sold three for a dollar. To make your own, empty the light syrup from a jar of cherries and refill with high-proof sugar spirits or grain alcohol. Give them at least a week.

CASSIS

Alice B. Toklas's 1954 autobiographical cookbook served up a scandal in its day for including an ungodly spiced hashish fudge recipe, omitted in some later editions. Some of the recipes in her cookbook are more fun than practical, but here's one I've tweaked and come to like.

Toklas was the secretary and long-time companion of American writer Gertrude Stein. While the two lived in France, she did much of the cooking and snagged a recipe for a black currant aperitif known as cassis. Around Dijon, cassis is poured into a wine glass and topped off with chilled dry white wine to cut the sweetness. Don't get your back up; it's not as fancy as it sounds.

Ingredients

    3 pounds of black currants
    ½ pound of raspberries
    A handful of black currant leaves (optional)
    1 quart of 180-proof sugar spirits
        (or substitute ½ pint of water mixed with
        1½ pints of commercial grain alcohol)
    One recipe of sugar syrup, cooled (see page 149)

Wash, drain, and thoroughly mash the combined berries; then cover and set them aside in a cool place for 24 hours. The next day, add a handful of washed and dried black currant leaves, if you choose, and the alcohol. Put the cover back on. Make the sugar syrup and set it aside. On the third day, pour the entire mass through a sieve and use the back of a spoon to express all the juice into a wide-mouthed gallon jar—or, pour the mass into a muslin or nylon brewer's bag, and squeeze it to extract all the juice.

Add the syrup to the berry juice and alcohol. Allow this to stand covered for several hours, then strain into bottles.

CRANBERRY CORDIAL

One year I straight-up lost my mind and made about five gallons of cranberry cordial. At the time, we were guzzling cosmopolitans that used this concoction instead of cranberry juice. I've backed off the trendy cosmos, but remain pleased with how well the cordial stands up over time. Here's a more reasonable version.

Ingredients

    12 ounces of fresh cranberries, washed and drained
    2 cups of sugar
    4 cloves
    2 cinnamon sticks, 3 inches long
    1 quart of tangerine brandy (see Note)

Grind the cranberries and sugar together in a food processor until they form a gritty pink-and-red-flecked mass. Next, put the mixture into a glass container large enough to hold all the ingredients, and add the remaining items. Cover the container tightly. Shake it once every few days for a month to ensure that all the sugar dissolves. Strain the cordial through a muslin bag, squeezing out as much of the liquid as possible, and funnel it into bottles.

Note: If you don't have tangerine brandy, substitute ½ cup of tangerine or orange peel and 1 quart of 80-proof sugar spirits (such as aguardiente), vodka, or 21st Century Moonshine (see page 136).

CURTIDO Y MISTELA

Curtido y Mistela is a specialty of the southern Mexican state of Chiapas. Traditionally created by steeping fruit in aguardiente, the result is a double treat: *curtido*, the alcohol-infused fruit, is eaten as a dessert; and *mistela*, the fruit-infused alcohol, is enjoyed as a powerful celebratory drink. Curtido y mistela is sold year-round, but is most especially connected to fairs and feast days. The women who make it sell fruit-filled jars to students who take it, along with local cheeses and sausages, back to university.

This version comes from Isabel Moreno Pereyra, a justifiably proud mother who also makes wicked good cheese.

Ingredients

2¼ pounds of fruit (see Note)
1 quart of aguardiente, vodka, or 21st Century Moonshine (see page 136)
2¼ pounds of sugar

Prepare the fruit by puncturing it all over. Put it and the aguardiente in a large container, seal it, and put the mixture in a cool, dark place (not refrigerated) for 15 days. Add approximately 2 cups of water to the sugar in a saucepan, and cook over high heat until it becomes very sticky, like honey. When it is cool, add the syrup (called miel) to the infusion, and let everything rest another month in a cool, dark place.

Note: The tropical fruits *jocote* and *nance* are common additions in Chiapas, but can be difficult to track down in the United States. If you live in a community with a large Latino population, check the produce sections of Latin grocery stores. Jocote is also called cashew apple, *jocote rojo*, Spanish plum, and *acaju*. Nances are known under various close spellings throughout Latin America, but you may also see these small, yellowish fruits called *tapal*. Pears, apples, plums, and peaches are all also acceptably authentic ingredients.

FIGGADEEN

Italian and Sicilian immigrants brought deeply rooted wine- and cordial-making traditions to the United States during the nineteenth and early twentieth centuries. Homemade wine, and *figgadeen* in particular, remain popular today where those communities remain strong. What? You've never heard of figgadeen? How about prickly pears? Cactus pears? Las tunas? Barbary figs? Indian figs? Along with figgadeen, they are all names for the same thing: the fruit of a North American cactus (*Opuntia ficus-indica*) that is now naturalized in many places, including along the Mediterranean. The south Philadelphia Italian dialect that gave us *brushoot* for *prosciutto* and *looga-dell* for *locatelli* would have us all render the Italian *fico d'India* as the more blue-collar figgadeen.

Ingredients

3½ pounds of prickly pears (cactus pears)
1 quart of 180-proof grappa (or substitute ½ pint of water mixed with 1½ pints of commercial grain alcohol—or, in a pinch, use vodka)
One recipe of sugar syrup, cooled (see page 149)

Wearing heavy rubber gloves and using a sharp paring knife and due caution (the small spines in each indentation can be difficult to remove and exquisitely painful), skin and slice the cactus pears: First, slice the top and bottom ends off each fruit. Then cut through the skin along one side and turn the knife's blade under the skin. Cut the skin away from the red flesh and discard it. Finally, cut each fruit crosswise into rounds and drop the pieces into a large jar. Discard the skins.

Next, add the grappa, cover the container tightly, and allow the mixture to macerate for two to four weeks. Strain the mixture through a muslin or nylon brewer's bag, squeezing the fruits well. Stir in the cooled syrup. Bottle and age the figgadeen for three months.

Note: This recipe makes a very sweet, but authentic, south Philadelphia figgadeen. I prefer mine much less sugary and would use maybe half the amount of syrup called for here and cut it with a bit more water. But, then, I'm not Italian.

Simple Sugar Syrup
◖●◖●◖●◖

Sugar syrup is great to have around the kitchen and is essential for the bar. It can be flavored with citrus zest, herbs, or spices for drizzling over cakes, adding to iced tea (no more gritty, crunchy beverage), or added to cordials and cocktails. In the summer, I stash a one-liter bottle in the fridge, cooked up with a big double handful of fresh mint for tea and unorthodox juleps.

6 cups (about 3 pounds) of granulated
   table sugar
3 cups of water
Herbs or spices (optional)

Heat the sugar and water (plus the herbs or spices, if you're using them) in a pot to boiling. Lower the heat, gently simmer the liquid for five minutes, and then set it aside and allow it to cool completely. Strain away any herbs or spices. Bottle the syrup. Nineteenth century saloon "professors" sometimes added a raw egg white while heating their simple syrup, to clear it of impurities. After skimming away the cooked white and its adhering particulates, they were rewarded with an especially clear and limpid product.

THE STUFF
(AKA NANCY'S BRANDIED FRUIT)

When I was very young, a butter churn in a dark corner of my parents' basement was an irresistible draw, despite my general unease about dark places (and basements in particular). In the churn lurked a mass of peaches and cherries that my mother had blessed with sugar and brandy: the makings of The Stuff, which my mother distributed as gifts around Christmas. Given its ragged and swarthy appearance, she recently mused, some folks may have thought she was giving them a jar of something she had scraped off the basement floor, and decided not to taste it. Poor them! Our German cousins would have known better and called it *rumtopf*.

Use a combination of two to four varieties of fresh fruits such as peaches, wild grapes, apricots, red currants, cherries, blueberries, or raspberries (avoid apples and citrus) as they come in season. In a pinch, use dried fruits such as peaches or figs, or a mix of fresh and dried.

Ingredients
   2 parts of mixed fresh or dried fruits,
      free of blemishes, washed
   1 part of sugar
   Brandy or rum

Cut the fruit into spoon-size pieces. Scrub a crock, large glass container, or butter churn until it's "really, really clean." Put the fruit in the container, add the sugar on top of the fruit, and pour in enough alcohol to cover everything. Using a clean plate that fits inside the container, weigh the fruit down so that no part floats above the liquid level. Make the container airtight by covering it with rubber-band-secured plastic wrap (fruit flies love The Stuff). Stir gently every four to five days, and top off with more alcohol as necessary to keep the fruit submerged.

The Stuff might be ready in as soon as six weeks or take from May to December to macerate. When it's sufficiently heady, serve the fruit pieces as a side dish with poultry or pork and cornbread dressing, spoon them over ice cream or toasted pound cake, or simply top them with whipped cream. The remaining fruit-infused alcohol makes good sippin' stuff.

SASSAFRAS NIP

Sassafras (*Sassafras albidum*) is a perennial tree that ranges throughout eastern North America. It's also called ague tree, cinnamon tree, and smelling-stick, and has been used to flavor root beer, toothpaste, and even chewing gum. Some dote on its flavor while others gag at the thought of it. Generations of children have chewed its twigs as a treat or as a primitive toothbrush. Its dried leaves are pounded and sifted to yield filé, an essential thickening agent for making gumbo filé, a South Louisiana soupy stew that regularly graces my table. This recipe, from my friend Chef Fritz Blank, relies on the fresh oblong berries to impart that classically sassy flavor to plain alcohol. You'll have to gather the berries yourself; they're just not available commercially. Look for clusters of the little dark-blue berries, each supported by a tiny red cup, in summer.

Ingredients

- 1 quart of light whiskey, vodka, or 21st Century Moonshine (see page 136)
- 2 cups of fresh sassafras berries (whole or lightly crushed)
- 1 cup of sugar syrup (see page 149)

Place all of the ingredients in a glass container, cover it, and shake everything gently. Allow the nip to slumber undisturbed in a cool, dark place for six weeks until the liquor takes on a clear mahogany hue. Add more sugar syrup to taste, if you like. Strain, discard the berries, and serve.

Note: Before going hog-wild and making gallons of sassafras nip, be aware that safrole, a component of sassafras oil, is used to make the illicit drug ecstasy; large doses may have unintended narcotic effects. Used in moderation, sassafras has no such effects. Sassafras tea, for instance, remains a popular spring tonic among folks who would never dream of rollin' on X with go-go boys and club kids beyond sunup. If you have concerns about its use, consult your physician.

FISH HOUSE PUNCH

An apocryphal tale about George Washington relates that the first American president (who was a distillery owner) was once a guest at an exclusive Philadelphia social club called the State in Schuylkill, also known as the Fish House, where this punch originated. His diary for the three days following is rumored to be inexplicably blank. General Washington's crippling hangover may be only the stuff of legend (bourbon, for one, wasn't around in the eighteenth century), but I can attest that the punch is sly and potent. For this version, as for so many things, I am indebted to the late Gretchen Worden, director of Philadelphia's Mütter Museum until her egregiously early death in 2004. Slainte, Gretchen!

Ingredients

- 1 quart of fresh lemon juice (about 4 dozen lemons, squeezed)
- 1½ pounds of sugar
- 1 pint of curaçao, tangerine brandy, or orange-flavored liquor
- 1 pint of dark rum
- 1 pint of Benedictine
- 1 quart of peach brandy
- 1 gallon of bourbon
- 1 pint of strong cold tea

In Gretchen's precise words: "Put the above gutrot in a three-gallon jug, and shake the hell out of it. Place the jug in a cool place, and shake it once a day for at least three weeks; two months is better. Do not cork it tightly, and keep it cool or chilled or else the lemon juice will cause the whole thing to go off. Serve chilled, not over ice." I might add: serve it in small cups.

Neither Unlettered nor Men

When the U.S. Commissioner for Internal Revenue declared in his 1876 to 1877 report that moonshiners were "unlettered men of desperate character," he was leaving out a great many moonshiners: women.

Despite the celebrated "moonshine kings" of this or that county, we should never forget that distillation has long been regarded as women's work. Men inarguably fill the ranks of distillers who make moonshine for sale, in part because whiskey making in volume is hard, backbreaking, dangerous labor. The home distilling scene today remains skewed toward men, but with smaller volumes of raw materials and no pressure to sell goods, women are taking up the hobby in larger numbers. Not surprisingly, women historically have never proven shy about running off moonshine in stillrooms, kitchens, and backyards.

In the nineteenth and early twentieth centuries, small *coffin stills* (*coffin* is an old word for a container and says nothing about the quality of its output), or later *alky cookers* that sat atop stoves, were often

> **One of my great-grandmothers said she made several runs of whiskey. When the moonshine was ready to be sold, she would place it in a fruit jar that had been painted white. This way when anyone saw the jars that were being peddled, they would think that the contents were milk.**
>
> Ruby Allen
> "Moonshining as a Fine Art on a Kentucky Creek," 1975

wholly the domain of women. The tradition of the home still dates at least to seventeenth century England, when women who kept stillroom keys used alembics to distill rosewater, brandies, and cordials.

With such expertise at their fingertips and an outright duty to manage household finances, it is foolish to think that women have avoided the market entirely. In the lore of whiskey making, one American stands out for her legendary stature and excellent moonshine: Mahala "Aunt Mahaley" Mullins (circa 1824 to 1898) of Hancock County, Tennessee. Mullins, who was mother to many children and who grew to be a very large woman, directed production of corn whiskey and apple brandy from her cabin home and sold it openly. Unlike fleet-footed moonshiners who bounded away at the merest suggestion of unexpected visitors to their stills, she was easily caught, but could not be brought to court because of her immense size (estimates range from 300 to 700 pounds). In fact, a young buck lawman is said to have once served her a warrant, but returned to town without his quarry. Stymied by her girth, he declared her "ketchable but not fetchable."

Women's work. When this guide to housekeeping was published in the eighteenth century, distilling was as much a part of female domestic duties as cooking and cleaning.

ENGLISH HOUSE-KEEPER. 351
, and keep it for ufe. N. B. You may
ll bean-flowers the fame way.

To diftill PENNY-ROYAL WATER.
GET your penny-royal when it is full grown,
d before it is in bloffom, then fill your cold
ll with it, and put it half full of water, make
moderate fire under it, and diftill it off cold,
hen put it into bottles, and cork it in two or
three days time, and keep it for ufe.

To diftill LAVENDER WATER.
TO every twelve pounds of lavender-neps,
put one quart of water, put them into a cold
ftill, and make a flow fire under it, and diftill it
off very flow, and put it into a pot till you have
diftilled all your water, then clean your ftill well
out, and put your lavender water into it, and
diftill it off as flow as before, then put it into
bottles, and cork it well.

To diftill SPIRITS of WINE.
TAKE the bottoms of ftrong beer, and any
kind of wines, put them into a hot ftill about
three parts full, then make a very flow fire under it, and if you don't take great care to keep
it moderate, it will boil over, for the body is fo
ftrong, that it will rife to the top of the ftill;
the flower you diftill it the ftronger your fpirit
will be, put it into an earthen pot till you have
done diftilling, then clean your ftill well out,
and put the fpirit into it and diftill it flow a
before, and make it as ftrong as to burn in y
lamp, then bottle it, and cork it well, and kee
it for ufe.   A cor-

ICE CARAWAY

During America's national Prohibition against alcohol, recipes for simulating liquors made with a neutral spirit base abounded (bathtub gin, anyone?). Philadelphia chef Fritz Blank recently gave me one manuscript of such recipes, a handwritten book like none I'd ever seen, filled with formulas for beading oils, bourbon mash, corn whiskey, flavorings, essences, and a few dozen absinthes. The recipes, in English and German, are the work of a professional, but as-yet anonymous, pharmacist.

Admittedly, I haven't tried this one. It's such an elegant recipe, though, that keeping it to myself would constitute a shameful lack of grace:

"Boil 50 pounds of hard crystallized sugar with 2 gallons of water to a syrup, filter through flannel and, while still hot, add 6 gallons of strong alcohol and 10 ounces of Russian caraway essence. Filter hot and as quickly as possible and fill into white glass bottles to three-fourths of their content. The bottles are stoppered and placed in a vat filled with crushed ice mixed with some table salt. While cooling, the sugar crystallizes slowly, and the more slowly the more beautiful are the crystals. The bottles are finally filled with any desired caraway liquor of high alcohol content."

Looking ahead to the inevitable day when I'll give this recipe a try, I've calculated the amounts of basic ingredients for a smaller experimental batch:

Ingredients

- 3¼ pounds of granulated table sugar
- 2 cups of water
- 1½ quarts of 190-proof alcohol (or substitute commercial grain alcohol)

I'm not a big fan of caraway liquors, so I'd probably replace the caraway essence with a smaller amount of cinnamon or juniper oil, or use candy red-hots in place of all the sugar, and top off the bottles with vodka, Dutch genever, or 21st Century Moonshine (see page 136). Who's with me?

Miscellaneous Concoctions

Homemade alcohol is a useful ingredient all on its own, for making the likes of cough syrup or flavorings such as the ones described below. Remember, too, that in a pinch you can always substitute store-bought liquor for the homemade spirits specified in these recipes.

COUGH SYRUP

In frontier America, where formally trained doctors were few and far between, whiskey was not just a cost-effective way to get crops to market. It was bartering tender, a reliable antiseptic for midwives, a way to keep warm through bitter winters, a medium in which to preserve fruits, and medicine. Here, honey and corn whiskey combine in a bracing syrup that has helped countless coughing children slumber over the last 300 years.

Ingredients

- 1 part of corn whiskey, rye, or bourbon
- 1 part of strong-flavored honey (or horehound candies)

Mix the whiskey (or substitute your favorite brandy) and honey together. Set the mixture aside in a cool, dark place, and gently swirl the liquid now and then to ensure a thorough mixing. If horehound candy is your preference, substitute an equal volume of the hard candies for the honey, and shake gently once or twice a day until they dissolve completely.

VANILLA EXTRACT

Vanilla extract is a favored nip among down-on-their-heels drinkers, not for its homey aroma but because the easily shopliftable flavoring hovers around 80 proof, even if it does leave a perfumed high. This one is for baking, not drinking. We trust that you will not stumble into work late, wearing last night's clothes and reeking of cake …

Ingredients

    4 vanilla beans (Mexican or Bourbon beans,
        if possible)
    8 ounces of the whiskey of your choice, vodka,
        or 21st Century Moonshine (see page 136)

Using a paring knife, slice down the long center of each bean and open it like a book. Cut each one into ½-inch sections and put them—and all the tiny black specks of seeds—into a half-pint bottle. Add the alcohol, cover tightly, and shake gently. Store the bottle in a cool, dark place, and shake now and then. When the flavor seems strong and good to you, use it. Six months is more than enough. Topping off the bottle with more alcohol is perfectly acceptable. Use your homemade extract just as you would regular vanilla extract.

ORANGE BITTERS

I have lived in, and am undoubtedly destined for, unspeakably hot places. As a prophylactic against sweltering summer heats, I have taken to doctoring my drinking water with cocktail bitters. Though they bear a family resemblance to mountain tonics made of whiskey and medicinal plants such as ginseng and snakeroot, bitters are a little more urban. These old-fashioned concoctions are not especially pleasant on their own, but as a minor ingredient (a dash or two) in mixed drinks or even cupcake frostings, they allow other flavors to shine through.

Ingredients

    4 ounces of Seville orange peel, dried
    ¾ ounce of European gentian root (*Gentiana lutea*),
        dried and cut
    1 cinnamon stick, 3 inches long
    ¼ ounce of anise seed
    ¼ ounce of coriander seed
    ¼ ounce of black cardamom seeds
    2 cups of 180-proof alcohol (or substitute ½ pint
        of water mixed with 1½ pints of commercial grain
        alcohol—or, in a pinch, use vodka)

Bruise and crush the spices in a large mortar or bowl. Do not pulverize them. Transfer them to a 1-quart glass jar, add the alcohol, and seal and shake. Vigorously shake the container once or twice a day for 14 days, then strain the liquid into a different bottle. Add the dregs to a nonreactive pot (such as one of copper or stainless steel), cover with pure water and bring to a boil. Reduce the heat and simmer five to eight minutes. Allow to cool and then strain this new mixture through a muslin or nylon bag into the alcohol base, squeezing strongly to extract as much flavor as possible from the solids. Mix gently and thoroughly, then strain once more into bottles. The bitters are ready to use without further aging.

Note: Well-stocked herb or health food stores that deal in bulk spices are good places to begin looking for the Seville (bitter) orange peel or gentian.

Appendix

HYDROMETER CORRECTION TABLE
(see page 112)

Degrees Fahrenheit	Proof Hydrometer Reading		
	0-24	25-49	50 +
	Adjustment		
100	-14	-12	-16
95	-12	-10.5	-14
90	-10	-9	-12
85	-8.5	-7.5	-10
80	-7	-6	-8
75	-5	-4.5	-6
70	-3	-3	-4
65	-1.5	-1.5	-2
60	0	0	0
55	1.5	1.5	2
50	3.5	3	4
45	5	4.5	6
40	7	6	8
35	9	8	10
30	10.5	9	12
25	12	10.5	14
20	14	12	16
15	16	13.5	18
10	18	15	20
5	19	16.5	22
0	21	18	24

To use the table, determine the temperature of your spirit. Take a reading and compare that with the correction table. For temperatures below 60°F, add the indicated value to the observed hydrometer reading. For temperatures above 60°F, adjust the observed reading by the indicated amount.

Readings at 60°F need no adjustments. For example, a spirit at 70°F that reads 75 proof should be adjusted by -4 to give an adjusted reading of 71 proof. Likewise, an observed reading of 49 proof at 20°F yields an adjusted reading of 61 proof.

Note that hydrometers often come with manufacturer's correction tables. If your does, refer to that.

METRIC CONVERSION CHART

To convert from U.S. units to metric, multiply by the number given in the middle column, then round the resulting number up or down. Example: To convert 10.1 gallons to liters, multiply by 3.785412; the answer is 38.232661, which can be rounded to 38.2. To convert from metric units to the U.S. system, divide rather than multiply.

U.S. "Inch-Pound" System	Multiply By	To Determine Metric Equivalent
LENGTH		
Inch	25.4	Millimeter
Inch	2.54	Centimeter
Foot	0.3048	Meter
Yard	0.9144	Meter
AREA		
Square inch	645.16	Square millimeter
Square foot	0.09290304	Square meter
Square yard	0.8361274	Square meter
MASS		
Ounce	28.34952	Gram
Ounce	0.02834952	Kilogram
Pound	0.45359237	Kilogram

U.S. "Inch-Pound" System	Multiply By	To Determine Metric Equivalent
VOLUME		
Fluid ounce	29.57353	Milliliter
Gallon	3.785412	Liter
Cubic inch	16.387064	Cubic millimeter
Cubic foot	0.02831685	Cubic meter
Cubic yard	0.7645549	Cubic meter
TEMPERATURE		
Formula: Degrees Fahrenheit	Subtract 32, multiply by 5, then divide by 9	Degrees Celsius

Resources

If this book has done its job and whetted your appetite for learning more about the history, current status, and how-to of distillation, you're in luck: A cadre of good, solid books and other publications on the subject stand as reliable references for would-be home distillers. In addition, the Internet has become extraordinarily fertile ground for those wishing to explore the subject and related issues in detail, and to share questions, know-how, opinions, and advice with like-minded others. Magazines, associations, and a variety of other helpful information sources are available to you, too. Likewise, you should have no trouble locating sources for the equipment, ingredients, and materials involved in distilling.

No listing of resources can be truly complete, but those mentioned here will help point the curious to more detailed discussions of the craft and business of distilling, how to get legal, and where to find supplies. You'll find a wealth of additional information by tracking down the sources you'll find cited in the Bibliography starting on page 164.

BOOKS

History and Lore

Joseph Earl Dabney, *Mountain Spirits* (Asheville, N.C.: Bright Mountain Books, 1974). The cornerstones of any American distiller's library, Joseph Earl Dabney's books trace—through historical research and oral history interviews—the origins and decline of American moonshining through the 1970s.

Joseph Earl Dabney, *More Mountain Spirits* (Asheville, N.C.: Bright Mountain Books, 1980).

David W. Maurer, *Kentucky Moonshine* (Lexington, Ky.: The University Press of Kentucky, 1974). A scholarly but easily readable account of folk distilling traditions, including sections on moonshiners' lingo and material culture.

John McGuffin, *In Praise of Poteen* (Belfast: Appletree Press, 1999) and *Aidan Manning's Donegal Poitin: A History* (Letterkenny: Donegal Printing Company, 2002). Accounts of illicit whiskey-making, law-evading, ether-drinking (!), and song in western Ireland. Lots of insight into folk distilling traditions that parallel and inform America's.

Stuart McHardy, *Tales of Whisky and Smuggling*. (Argyll, Scotland: House of Lochar, 2002). Rousting historic tales of Gaelic bravado among the peatreek distillers and excise men in the Scottish Highlands, whose descendants filled the ranks of Appalachian distillers.

Paul Spapens en Piet Horsten, *Tappen uit een geheim vaatje: De geschiedenis van de illegale alcoholstokerijen in Nederland*. (Hapert, Netherlands: De Kempenpers, 1990). Dutch distillers have ridden the white mule for centuries. Here's a look at illicit distilling in Holland over the last hundred years. In Dutch.

Eliot Wigginton (editor), *The Foxfire Book* (Garden City, N.J.: Anchor Books, 1974). A classic of American oral histories, backwoods lore, hog butchering, mountain living...and whiskey making. On a sentimental note, my first moonshining book, which I pored over in front of my parents' fireplace before I was old enough to bend copper.

How-To

M. La Fayette Byrn, *The Complete Practical Distiller*. Raudins Publishing (2002). Original edition, Philadelphia, PA: Henry Carey Baird (1875).

Joseph Earl Dabney, *The Corn Whiskey Recipe Book* (Atlanta: Sassafrass Press, 1977).

Leon W. Kania, *The Alaskan Bootlegger's Bible* (Wasilla, Alaska: Happy Mountain Publications, 2000). Still building, recipes, and tall tales from the Far Northwest.

Bettina Malle and Helge Schmickl, *Schnapsbrennen als Hobby*. (Göttingen, Germany: Verlag die Werkstatt, 2003). Home distilling with information on brandies, essential oils, and using aromatics to steam-flavor distillates. In German.

Samuel M'Harry, *The Practical Distiller*. Raudins Publishing (2004). Original edition, Harrisburgh [sic], PA: John Wyeth (1809).

Michael Nixon and Michael McCaw, *The Compleat Distiller* (Auckland, New Zealand: Amphora Society, 2004). The definitive modern guide for serious home distillers. If you want to pursue this hobby and become more experienced in the distilling arts, give this tome an earnest read. You'll find the answers to most of your physics and chemistry questions here.

Josef Pischl, *Schnapsbrennen*. (Graz, Austria: Leopold Stockler Verlag, 2001). Leaning toward more professional small-batch operations than home distilling, still an excellent resource for technical information for the serious student. In German.

Ian Smiley, *Making Pure Corn Whiskey* (Auckland, New Zealand: Amphora Society, 2003). Another grand-slam from the Amphora Society, this book gives detailed information on techniques, recipes, and reflux still construction and use.

MAGAZINES

Malt Advocate (www.maltadvocate.com)

Modern Drunkard Magazine (www.moderndrunkardmagazine.com)

Zymurgy (www.beertown.org/homebrewing/zymurgy.html)

INTERNET RESOURCES

Discussion Sites and Groups

Home Brew Digest (www.hbd.org).

Home Distillation of Alcohol (www.homedistiller.org). Webmaster Tony Ackland's definitive home distilling site.

Yahoo Experienced Distillers' Group (http://groups.yahoo.com/group/Distillers/). This group is for advanced distillers.

Yahoo New Distillers' Group (http://groups.yahoo.com/group/new_distillers). This discussion group is for beginning distillers.

Information Sites

The Alchemy Website (www.alchemywebsite.com). Alchemists were among the earliest distillers, so why not check out a comprehensive discussion of their field of inquiry?

The Alcohol Library (http://distillers.tastylime.net/library).

American Distilling Institute (www.distilling.com). "The American Distilling Institute is the collective voice of the new generation of progressive beverage, medical, and aromatic distillers, and is dedicated to the mission of disseminating professional information on the distilling process." Publisher of American Distiller.

The American Society of Brewing Chemists (www.asbcnet.org).

The Brewers Association (www.beertown.org). The official website of this large organization, formed in 2005 by a merger of the Association of Brewers and the Brewers' Association of America. Also affiliated with the American Homebrewers Association.

The Brewery (http://brewery.org). Wide-ranging discussion of fermentation concerns, including recipe calculators, databases, and supplier contact information.

The Institute of Brewing and Distilling (www.ibd.org.uk). A professional international organization of brewers and distillers, publishers of The Brewer & Distiller and The Journal of the Institute of Brewing.

Raudins Publishing (www.raudins.com). Publisher of the *Classic Brewing and Distilling Series*, reprinting of seminal books on American brewing and distilling.

Schnapsbrennen als Hobby (www.schnapsbrennen.at). If you are in or intend to visit Austria, you might contact the authors for a seminar in authentic Austrian-style schnapps.

The Virtual Absinthe Museum (www.oxygenee.com). David Nathan-Maister's most excellent site, including links to vintage posters, recipes, and original, sealed vintage bottles of spirits for sale.

GOVERNMENT ALCOHOL REGULATION SITES

United States

Alcohol and Tobacco Tax and Trade Bureau (TTB)
www.ttb.gov/spirits/index.shtml

Canada

Canada Revenue Agency
www.cra-arc.gc.ca/tax/technical/exciseduty-e.html

DISTILLING SUPPLIES

The Amphora Society (www.amphora-society.com). Mike Nixon and Mike McCaw's site (authors of The Compleat Distiller and purveyors of the PDA-1 reflux still)

Brewhaus (America) Inc. (www.brewhaus.com). Comprehensive source for distilling ingredients and hardware activated carbon, pH adjusters, chemicals, oak kegs, flavorings, proof hydrometers, etc.

Brewhaus (Canada) Inc. (www.brewhaus.ca).

Carolina Biological Supply Company (www.carolina.com). pH testing materials, thermometers, and general lab equipment.

Gert Strand AB (www.partyman.se). Swedish source for turbo yeasts, flavoring essences, many other supplies.

Gray Kangaroo (www.liquorfilter.com). Maker of pour-through liquor filters.

Kentucky Barrels (www.kentuckybarrels.com). Suppliers of vintage whiskey barrels.

NORIT Activated Carbon (www.norit-ac.com/activatedcarbon.asp).

Outterson, LLC; Brewery, Winery and Distiller Equipment (www.fermentationbiz.com). Gear for professional distillers.

Promash Software (www.promash.com). For the computer-minded brewer and distiller.

Smiley's Home Distilling (www.home-distilling.com).

Still Spirits (www.stillspirits.com). Yeasts, equipment, flavor essences, newsletter, etc.

Homebrew Supplies

Crosby & Baker Ltd. (www.crosby-baker.com). Wholesale vendor of grains, yeasts, and brewing/distilling ingredients.

Northern Brewer (www.northernbrewer.com). Retail vendor of brewing ingredients.

The World of Zymico (www.zymico.com). Home of a variety of mashing and fermenting devices.

General Kitchen Gear

Fante's
www.fantes.com

Sur La Table
www.surlatable.com

Williams-Sonoma
www.williams-sonoma.com

Zabar's
www.zabars.com

Yeast Companies

Brewsters Yeast
www.brewstersyeast.com

Gert Strand
www.distillersyeast.com or www.turboyeast.com

Lallemand
www.lallemand.com

Red Star Yeast Company
www.redstaryeast.net

White Labs, Inc.
www.whitelabs.com

Wyeast
www.wyeastlab.com

Glossary

Alcohol: Any of a series of hydroxyl compounds, the simplest of which are derived from saturated hydrocarbons such as ethanol and methanol that have the general formula $C_nH_{2n}+1OH$.

Alembic: An early still of various designs, derived from alchemical equipment. Also lambic, lambeek, and lambyk.

Abv: Abbreviation for alcohol by volume. The ethanol content of a spirit expressed as a proportion of the total volume of liquid at 20°C. Sometimes expressed as "% abv."

Backins: Weak whiskey left in a thump keg (or boiler at the end of a second run) after most usable alcohol has been extracted.

Bardy grease: See fusel alcohol.

Bead: Air bubbles that form along the meniscus of shaken liquor. The size, duration, and position on the surface are indicative of proof. Contrary to popular belief, a whiskey's ability to hold a bead is not an infallible gauge of its wholesomeness or degree of adulteration.

Beading oil: An oil used by unscrupulous moonshiners and bootleggers to create a false bead in low-proof whiskey that has been watered down and/or adulterated. Not a tool of a true craftsman.

Beer: For distillers, the precursor to whiskey or brandy. Fermented grain or fruit mash (e.g., "peach beer") ready for distilling. Also distiller's beer or wort (pronounced wert).

Boiler: The body of a still that is charged with beer or fermented mash and is heated.

Boiling chips: Small, insoluble, porous stones made of calcium carbonate or silicon carbide used to create an even and smooth boil in heated liquids.

Blind tiger: A place for purchasing illicit alcohol, sometimes where the buyer does not see the seller. A buyer could place cash in a certain location, leave, and come back to find the cash gone and whiskey in its place. Also blind pig.

Blockader: A venerable term for both moonshiner and hauler that predates modern division of labor. Attributed to Appalachian distillers who "ran a blockade" of revenuers and to revolutionary-era smugglers. It may also refer to one who merely transports moonshine.

Bootleg bonnet: A felt hat used as a strainer to filter moonshine as it emerges from the condenser.

Bootlegger: One who sells moonshine or legal alcohol under illegal circumstances.

Bothy: A small structure that serves as a shelter. Especially in Scotland, it may refer to a small enclosed building used as a stillhouse.

Cap: A removable still component, jammed and possibly luted or tied into place, that seals the top of a pot still. The charged boiler is brought to a boil before the cap is sealed into place. May also refer to a more substantial head of a still.

Cap arm: A pipe extending from the head of the still that conveys alcoholic vapors to the thump keg or directly to the condenser.

Cape: The area just below the collar of a pot still that forms the sloping "shoulders" of the still.

Charge: To fill a boiler or thumper with the desired volume of beer, backins, low wines, or feints. On a pot still, usually around 75 to 80% of its capacity.

Condenser: A metal device, in contact with cool water, inside which alcohol vapors revert to liquid. Because of their lead content, auto and truck radiators are wholly unsuited as condensers. See worm.

Curcubit: An obsolete term for a boiler.

Cut: To reduce the alcohol concentration in a distilled spirit by blending it with water, beer, or low wines. The lowest of scoundrels may cut with antifreeze, rubbing alcohol, or methanol as well as water to keep a kick. Also refers to the various stages of a distillation run, differentiated by the proof and composition of the distillate.

Doubled and twisted: High-proof whiskey that has been run through a pot still twice. Also high wines.

Doubler: See thump keg.

Excise: A governmental tax on distilled spirits.

Feints: The leftover liquid in a thump keg after a run, or in a boiler after second or subsequent runs. Sometimes referred to as "thumper tails." These are withdrawn after a run and replaced with fresh beer or backings, to provide alcohol for the thumper's doubling effect.

Fermenter: See mash tub.

Filter: The strainer through which fresh distillate passes when it emerges from the condenser. A filter may be as simple as a felt hat, or a commercial apparatus containing activated charcoal. Filtering removes particulates and unwanted congeners.

Flake stand: A watertight container that holds a copper worm, the end of which emerges from the bottom of the container. It may be a keg, a large tin, an olive barrel, a pickle bucket, etc. In modern setups, cool water enters from the bottom and exits the top of the container through hoses. Flake-stand water never comes in direct contact with the spirits.

Foreshots: The first sputters of poisonous liquid that emerge from the condenser at the beginning of a run, high in fusel alcohols and undesirable congeners such as methanol. Must be discarded.

Fusel alcohol: Bitter, oily liquid, composed of amyl- and butyl-alcohols as well as other undesirable substances, found in whiskey which has not been distilled thoroughly or to a sufficiently high proof. Commonly called fusel oil, though modern distillers regard this as an inaccurate and archaic term.

Gauger: An obsolete British term for a collector of taxes on distilled beverages. So called because he measured, or gauged, the capacity and output of a still for tax assessment. Also exciser.

Hauler: An employee of a wholesale bootlegger who transports moonshine from distillers to market. Also runner or tripper.

Hausgemacht: A German word meaning "homemade."

 Lute: To seal a still's connections with a paste made of flour (or ashes) and water or mud/clay and grass.

Luting: The compound paste used to seal a pot still's connections to prevent vapors from escaping.

Malt: Sprouted, dried, and ground grain. Traditionally barley or corn, but also rye and nearly any other grain that contains diastase, an enzyme that converts nonfermentable carbohydrates into fermentable sugar.

Mash: A mixture of ground grains or meal, water, malt, and wild or cultivated yeast. Mash, wash, beer, wort, and wine are all terms used by folk distillers to refer to a fermented or fermenting mixture, which may or may not be strained of solids. The terms may also, to the consternation of professional distillers, be used to refer to fruit- and sugar-based mixtures.

Mash hound: A derogatory term for a person who drinks beer from mash tubs, sometimes in preference to moonshine, often to excess.

Mash tub: Tubs, barrels, carboys, boxes, or vats in which mash is fermented.

Middlings: Coarsely ground, intermediate-grade mill products such as wheat, rye, barley, or oats.

Moonshine: Illicitly produced, nontax-paid distilled spirits. "A matter or mouthful of moonshine; a trifle, nothing. The white brandy smuggled on the coasts of Kent and Sussex, and the gin in the north of Yorkshire, are also called moonshine." (*Grose's Dictionary of the Vulgar Tongue*, 1785)

Peatreek: Illicit Scotch whisky, so named for the smell of smoldering peat used to dry malted barley.

Poitin: Literally "little pot" and pronounced "puh-cheen." Illicit, untaxed Irish moonshine. Though most famously made from potatoes, it is commonly made from sugar, molasses and/or grains.

Pot-tail: The mash left after a distillation, dipped out and "slopped back" into the mash barrels and mixed with subsequent batches to be fermented. The result is sour mash whiskey. In groundhog and pan stills, the pot-tail is left in the bottom, and sugar and meal are added for fermentation for subsequent distillations.

Proof: The proportion of alcohol in distilled spirits. By American reckoning, proof is exactly twice the ethanol content at 60°F. Under the British system "proof" is abv x 1.75.

Proof vial: A small glass tube used to estimate proof by beading. A vial partially filled with whiskey is shaken, and its resulting bead is read to determine proof.

Revenuer: An agent, originally empowered by Congress, to "protect the revenue" of the United States by hunting and seizing or destroying wildcat stills. Also revenooer.

Rig: A distillery setup. Sometimes merely a still, but may also include mash tubs, condenser, flake stand, and all the appliances and utensils necessary to run a load of whiskey.

Run: One distilling cycle.

Runner: See hauler.

Ship stuff: A low-grade mill product composed of the husks of grains separated from flour during milling. Sometimes used as a mash component.

Singlings: The first run of whiskey distilled in a pot still. Also low wines.

Slop: See pot-tail.

Slopping back: Using hot pot-tails from a previous run as the base for a new batch of mash to create sour mash whiskey.

Still: Any common form of distilling device. A still may consist of merely a boiler and head or may include a furnace, flake stand, and condenser.

Stillhouse: A small structure containing a still. Also shed, shack, or bothy.

Swab stick: A wooden stick with one end splayed out into fine ends like a brush. Used to stir heating mash in a boiler and to scrub the interior walls of a large still to keep mash from sticking before it boils. Also stick or stir stick.

Temp(er)ing tub: Tub used to blend whiskeys of varying proof either from a single run or multiple runs to achieve a uniform proof.

Thump keg: An airtight container sometimes placed between a boiler and condenser of a pot still that increases the proof of a single run, eliminating the need to do a double run. The thump keg is charged with beer, feints, or backins. Hot vapors from the boiler enter under the beer's surface, heat it, and produce higher-proof vapors that exit to the condenser. Also known as doubler, thumper, or thump barrel.

Tun: Among brewers and distillers, any large vessel that holds liquid. A mash tun is designed to hold mash at a particular temperature; a lauter tun allows liquids to drain from spent grains. A hybrid tun can be used for both purposes.

Wildcat: A wildcat sale is a purchase of questionable moonshine from an irregular or undesirable source. Wildcat may refer simply to an unregistered still. Wildcatter refers to moonshiners who operate such stills. The latter two imply merely "illicit" and do not carry the negative undertones of wildcat sale.

Worm: A copper condensing coil submerged in cold running water inside a flake stand. Hot ethanol vapors revert to liquid on contact with the cool copper and exit as a liquid.

Bibliography

BOOKS

Allison, Thomas R., *Moonshine Memories*. Montgomery, Ala.: New South Books, 2001.

Argo, William Vincent, *No Place for Revenuers: The True Story of Present-Day Bootlegging*. New York: Vantage, 1962.

Atkinson, George, *After the Moonshiners*. Wheeling, W.Va.: Frew & Campbell, 1881.

Bilger, Burkhard, *Noodling for Flatheads: Moonshine, Monster Catfish and Other Southern Comforts*. New York: Scribner, 2000.

Burrison, John A., *Brothers in Clay: The Story of Georgia Folk Pottery*. Athens, Ga.: University of Georgia Press, 1995.

Byrn, M. La Fayette, *The Complete Practical Distiller*. Raudins Publishing (2002). Original edition, Philadelphia, PA: Henry Carey Baird (1875).

Carr, Jess, *The Second Oldest Profession: An Informal History of Moonshining in America*. Radford, Va.: Commonwealth Press, 1972.

Carson, Gerald, *The Social History of Bourbon*. New York: Dodd, Mead & Co., 1963.

Carter, Joseph E., *Damn the Allegators*. Tabor City, N.C.: Atlantic Publishing Company, 1989.

Carter, Forrest (Asa), *The Education of Little Tree*. 1976. Reprint, Albuquerque: University of New Mexico Press, 1986.

Caudill, Harry M., *Night Comes to the Cumberlands: A Biography of a Depressed Area*. Boston: Atlantic Monthly Press, 1962.

Cobb, Irvin S., *Red Likker*. New York: Cosmopolitan Book Corporation, 1929.

Cobb, R. A., *The True Life of Maj. Redmond, the Notorious Outlaw and Moonshiner*. Raleigh, N.C., Edwards, Broughton & Co., 1882.

Cooper, A. (Ambrose), *The Complete Distiller*. London, 1762.

Dabney, Joseph Earl, *The Corn Whiskey Recipe Book*. Atlanta: Sassafrass Press, 1977.

——— *Mountain Spirits*. Asheville, N.C.: Bright Mountain Books, 1974.

——— *More Mountain Spirits*. Asheville, N.C.: Bright Mountain Books, 1980.

Davis, Hassoldt, *Bonjour, Hangover!* New York: Duell, Sloan and Pearce, 1958.

Egerton, John (ed), *Cornbread Nation 1: The Best of Southern Food Writing*. Chapel Hill: University of North Carolina Press, 2002.

Erdoes, Richard, *Saloons of the Old West*. New York: Gramercy Books, 1979.

Gabbard, Alex, *Return to Thunder Road: The Story Behind the Legend*. 2nd edition. Lenoir City, Tenn.: Gabbard Publications, 2000.

Gielow, Martha S., *Old Andy the Moonshiner*. New York: Fleming H. Revel Company, 1909.

Glasse, Hannah, *The Art of Cookery Made Plain and Easy*. London, 1747.

Hall, Wade, *Waters of Life from the Conecuh Ridge: The Clyde May Story*. Montgomery, Ala.: NewSouth Books, 2003.

Howard, Kathleen and Howard Gibat, *The Lore of Still Building*. Fostoria, Ohio: Noguska Press, 1999.

Huffman, Barry G., *Catawba Clay: Contemporary Southern Face Jug Makers*. Hickory, N.C.: A.W. Huffman, 1997.

Kania, Leon W., *The Alaskan Bootlegger's Bible*. Wasilla, Alaska: Happy Mountain Publications, 2000.

Kellner, Esther, *Moonshine: Its History and Folklore*. New York: Weathervane Books, 1971.

Krohn, James C., *The Good Booze Recipe and Cookbook*. Boulder, Colo.: Paladin Press, 1988.

Kephart, Horace, *Our Southern Highlanders*. New York: The Macmillin Company, 1913.

LaBan, Craig, "The Legendary Coe Dupuis, Moonshiner." In *Cornbread Nation 1: The Best of Southern Food Writing*. Chapel Hill: University of North Carolina Press, 2002.

Licensed Beverage Industries, *Operation Moonshine 1958: A Comprehensive Survey of the Trend in Illegal Distilling Activities*. New York: LBI, 1959.

———— *Moonshine: Formula for Fraud…and Death*. New York: LBI, 1974.

Logsdon, Gene, *Good Spirits: A New Look at Ol' Demon Alcohol*. White River Junction, Vt.: Chelsea Green Publishing Company, 1991.

Manning, Aidan, *Donegal Poitin, a History*. Letterkenny: Donegal Printing Company, 2002.

Maurer, David W., *Kentucky Moonshine*. Lexington: The University Press of Kentucky, 1974.

May, Robert, *The Accomplisht Cook: or the Art and Mystery of Cookery*. London, 1678.

McCulloch-Williams, Martha, *Dishes and Beverages of the Old South*. 1913. Facsimile, edited by John Egerton, Knoxville: The University of Tennessee Press, 1988.

McCusker, John J. and Kenneth Morgan (eds), *The Early Modern Atlantic Economy*. Cambridge: Cambridge University Press, 2000.

McGuffin, John, *In Praise of Poteen*. Belfast: Appletree Press Ltd., 2000.

McHardy, Stuart, *Tales of Whisky and Smuggling*. Argyll, Scotland: House of Lochar, 2002.

McMullen, W. George, *Twenty-Eight Years a 'T-Man'*. 1986.

Merriman, Stony, *Midnight Moonshine Rendezvous: Secrets of Luke Alexander Denny's Moonshine Running Adventures (1930's – 1960's)*. Smithville, Tenn.: M. Stone Publishing, 1990.

M'Harry, Samuel, *The Practical Distiller*. Raudins Publishing (2004). Original edition, Harrisburgh [sic], PA: John Wyeth (1809).

Miller, Wilbur R., *Revenuers and Moonshiners: Enforcing Federal Liquor Law in the Mountain South, 1865-1900*. Chapel Hill: University of North Carolina Press, 1991.

Moore, Bernard Francis, *The Moonshiner's Daughter: A Play of Mountain Life in Three Acts*. Boston: Walter H. Baker & Co., 1889.

Morrell, Bebe, *Fred's Formula for North Carolina Moonshine*. Asheville, N.C.: Biltmore Press, Inc., 1987.

Nelson, Derek, *Moonshiners, Bootleggers and Rum-runners*. Osceola, Wisc.: Motorbooks International, 1995.

Nelson, Ray, *Memoirs of an Oregon Moonshiner*. Caldwell, Idaho: The Caxton Printers, 1976.

Nye, Bill (Edgar W.), *Remarks*. Chicago: Thompson and Foutz, 1891.

Nixon, Michael and Michael McCaw, *The Compleat Distiller*. Auckland, New Zealand: Amphora Society, 2001.

North Carolina State Board of Alcoholic Control, *First Annual Report*. Raleigh, N.C., 1938.

Oertel, J. F., *Moonshine*. Macon, Ga.: The J.W. Burke Company, 1926.

Pischl, Josef, *Schnapsbrennen (mit Anhang "Kornbrand" von Peter Jäger)*. Graz, Austria: Leopold Stockler Verlag, 2001.

Plat, Sir Hugh, *Delightes for Ladies*. London, 1627.

Raffald, Elizabeth, *The Experienced English House-Keeper*. London, 1784.

Raine, James W., *The Land of Saddlebags: A Study of the Mountain People of Appalachia*. New York: The Council of Women for Home Missions and Missionary Education Movement of the United States and Canada, 1924.

Spapens, Paul en Piet Horsten, *Tappen uit een geheim vaatje: De geschiedenis van de illegale alcoholstokerijen in Nederland*. Hapert, Netherlands: De Kempenpers, 1990.

Smiley, Ian, *Making Pure Corn Whiskey*. Auckland, New Zealand: Amphora Society, 2003.

Smith, Gavin D., *The Secret Still: Scotland's Clandestine Whisky Makers*. Edinburgh: Birlinn Limited. 2002.

Soberg, Ralph, *Confessions of an Alaska Bootlegger*. Walnut Creek, Calif.: Hardscratch Press, 1990.

Stapleton, Isaac, *Moonshiners in Arkansas*. Independence, Mo.: Zion's Printing and Publishing Company, 1948.

Starr, John, *The Purveyor: The Shocking Story of Today's Illicit Liquor Empire*. New York: Holt, Rinehart and Winston, 1961.

Stephenson, Frank, *Carolina Moonshine Raiders*. Murfreesboro, N.C.: Meherrin River Press, 2001.

Toklas, Alice B., *The Alice B. Toklas Cook Book*. New York: Harper & Brothers, 1954.

Twain, Mark, *Roughing It*. Hartford, Conn.: The American Publishing Co., 1872.

White, M. L., *A History of the Life of Amos Owens, the Noted Blockader, of Cherry Mountain, N.C.* Shelby, N.C.: Cleveland Star Job Print, 1901.

Wigginton, Eliot (ed), *The Foxfire Book*. Garden City: Anchor Books, 1972.

Wilkinson, Alec, *Moonshine: A Life in Pursuit of White Liquor*. New York: Alfred A. Knopf, 1985.

Y-Worth, William, *The Compleat Distiller: or the Whole Art of Distillation Practically Stated*. London, 1705.

JOURNALS, NEWSPAPERS, MAGAZINES, AND NEWSLETTERS

Allen, Ruby. "Moonshining as a Fine Art on a Kentucky Creek." *Kentucky Folklore Record* 21 (2): 34-40 (April-June 1975).

Bailey, Jody and Robert S. McPherson. "'Practically Free from the Taint of the Bootlegger': A Closer Look at Prohibition in Southeastern Utah." *Utah Historical Quarterly* 57 (2): 151-164 (Spring 1989).

Barrick, Mac E. "Memories of a Moonshiner" *Pennsylvania Folklife Fall*; XXVI (1): 18-24 (1976).

Cook, John Esten, "Moonshiners," *Harper's Weekly*, February 1879, 380-390.

Blaine, Donald A. "Among the Moonshiners." *Dixie* I: 9-14 (1885).

Ellis, T. and R Lacy. "Illicit Alcohol (Moonshine) Consumption in West Alabama Revisited." *Southern Medical Journal* 91 (9): 858-60 (September 1998).

Frost, William Goodell, "Our Contemporary Ancestors in the Southern Mountains," *Atlantic Monthly*, March 1899, 311-319.

Gaskins, Avery F. "The Copper Rig: Guineas as Moonshiners." *Tennessee Folklore Society Bulletin* XLII (2): 55-64 (March 1976).

Gerhardt R. E. et al. "Trace Element Content of Moonshine." *Archives of Environmental Health* 35 (6):332-4 (November/December 1980)

Holmes, William. "Moonshining and Collective Violence: Georgia, 1889-1895." *Journal of American History* 67: (1980).

——— "Moonshiners and Whitecaps in Alabama, 1893." *The Alabama Review* XXXIV(1): 31-49 (1981)

Holstege, Christopher et al. "Analysis of Moonshine for Contaminants." *Journal of Toxicology: Clinical Toxicology* 42 (5): (2004).

Hubbard, Leonidas, "The Moonshiner at Home," *Atlantic Monthly*, 1902, 234-241.

Ivey, Saundra Keyes. "Aunt Mahala Mullins in Folklore, Fakelore and Literature." *Tennessee Folklore Society Bulletin* XLI (1): 1-8 (March 1975).

Martin, Edward, "Liquid Assets," *Business North Carolina*, May 2002, 38-46.

Montgomery, Richard and Ryan Finkenbine. "A Brief Review of Moonshine Use." *Psychiatric Services* 50: 1088 (1999).

Page, Ron. "Mimic Cask Aging with Wood Chips." *Zymurgy* 17 (4): 104-6 (1994).

Pederson, Lee. "The Randy Sons of Nancy Whisky." *American Speech* 52 (1-2): 112-121 (1977).

Rayburn, Otto Ernest. "Moonshine in Arkansas." *The Arkansas Historical Quarterly* XVI (2): 169-173 (1957).

Shaner, Richard H. "Distillation and Distilleries Among the Dutch." *Pennsylvania Folklife* 13 (3): 39-42 (1963).

Stewart, Bruce E. 'When Darkness Reigns Then is the Hour to Strike: Moonshining, Federal Liquor Taxation, and Klan Violence in Western North Carolina, 1868-1872." *The North Carolina Historical Review* vol LXXX (4): 453-474 (2003).

Williams, Cratis. "Moonshining in the Mountains." *North Carolina Folklore* XV (1): 11-17 (May 1967).

OTHER MEDIA

Wright, Dave, "The Moonshiners: Moonshining in North Carolina…A Story of Big-Time Crime!" Script of June 1, 1961, Channel Two broadcast of same name. Greensboro, N.C.

Potter, Gary W., *The Antecedents of Southern Organized Crime*, http://www.policestudies.eku.edu/POTTER/International/Southhistory.htm

Acknowledgments

Well, Timothy Furnish: Looks like I went on a whiskey diet and lost three years. Thanks, as always, for being there when I came up for air.

When all I wanted to do with my evenings was go to bed before midnight, Ronni Lundy appeared like some Appalachian Lady of the Lake, holding aloft a triple-X jug of moonshine, and convinced me that I'd been dying to write a book on homemade likker. Ronni's like that. Thank you, dear.

Among the non-moonshiners who helped along and inspired this book, I continue to labor under debt to Chef Fritz Blank, whose generosity knows no bounds. Joe Dabney not only inspired this book, but gave me encouragement, leads and continuing insight. Bob Mielke, master of late-night filibusters, and David Williams supplemented my education in unexpected ways. Thanks to my sister Moira, whose moonshine tales are unfit to print; to my sister Molly, who got me in where I never would have gotten alone; and to my mother, who unwittingly brought me to my first still site in the New Jersey Pine Barrens when I was a toddler. I think she's still mortified.

Among library and archives staffs, first thanks must go out to Michael Ryan and John Pollack of the Rare Books and Manuscripts Department of the University of Pennsylvania's Van Pelt-Dietrich Library. I am indebted also to the staff of Tulane University's Howard-Tilton Memorial Library; Pack Memorial Library in Asheville, North Carolina; the University of Mississippi; the Library of Congress; the San Diego Public Library; the Free Library of Philadelphia; the Kansas City Public Library; Kathryn Staley and the rest of the archival staff at Appalachian State University in Boone, North Carolina; Don Veasey at the Birmingham Public Library; Stephen Catlett at the Greensboro Historical Museum; Dennis Pogue at Mount Vernon; at the University of North Carolina, Stephen Fletcher of the North Carolina Collection, as well as Bill Ferris and Tim West; at the University of Missouri in Kansas City, Chuck Haddix and Todd Hannah gave me invaluable musical insights.

My thanks go as well to all those who fed me, housed me, soused me, or just plain pointed me down hidden paths. Jim Myers at the *Nashville Tennessean*, Allan Benton, Jason and Mark Smereczinski, John Fleer, Tom Head, Sarah Fritschner, Brian Stapleton, Bill Smith, Jerry Slater, Brooks Hamaker and Dean McComb of eGullet.org, Sarah Labensky, Tim Patterson, Judy Faye of The Book and The Cook, Nick and Coach of *Modern Drunkard* magazine, Bill Owens at *American Distiller*, and Jon Alonge all put their stamp on this work.

John T. Edge traded tales of peach brandy for songs of absinthe. Joe York, plugged into so many things, confirmed a notion or two of Mississippi 'shine, while John Currence, who has nothing to do with white mule, nonetheless fed me feloniously well on the moonshine trail at Oxford's City Grocery. John Egerton, Robin Kline, and Bill Summers inspire me nearly every week; I'm glad I could offer some inspiration in return. Thanks also to Robin Tama of Flying Fish Brewing Company, Mike Gerhart of Dogfish Head, Lance Winters at St. George Spirits, Chris Morris at Woodford Reserve, David Reis, and to Rick Morris at Brewhaus USA, as well as Carroll Leggett, Bonnie Slotnick, Darren Vella, David White, Doug Zullo, Jim Ezell, Kip Finch, and William Woys Weaver (Will, it turns out that an eleven-foot pole did the trick).

On the trail of *poitín* in Ireland, I am indebted to Corinne Dunne and Andy Donaghy. Seamus and Gertrude Mallon were grand hosts. Larry Nugent, in between birthing calves, poured a comforting drop of spirits and, while we never covered last names, Andy, Brian, Des, Alan, Cait, and Pat demonstrated that there's nothing dead or dying about moonshine out west.

A world away, Pedro Colonel, Reyes Castillo, Noe Espinosa, and Edward Mesa gave invaluable pointers into Latin American potables. *Gracias por todo, mis amigos.* Thanks also to Baldur Stulgies, Christa Quint, Isabel Moreno Pereyra, and the late Gretchen Worden.

The staff of the original DiBruno Bros. kept me fed on the road; but I am particularly indebted to Emilio "MeeMee" Mignucci, Ben Robling, Anthony Screnci, Hunter and Tyler (the Brothers Fike); to Ezekiel J. Ferguson, whose musical memory put me onto a delicious blend of the forgotten and the new; to Mark Monaco; to Mike Ferraiola; and to all the *pinche mamis* at the House of Cheese.

Kudos to the missionary-like work of Tony Ackland, Harry Jackson, and Volodimir Jakovlev. Hats off, gentlemen.

Barry, Eric, Erin, Gabriel, Ken, Leena, Sang-Mi, Shawn, and Vince: I'll never look at saline drips the same again, you reprobates.

At Lark Books, my most sincere thanks go to Terry Krautwurst, my eternally questioning and deeply insightful editor. Paige Gilchrist and Carol Taylor got the project under way, the inestimable Rebecca Guthrie and Nathalie Mornu kept it on track behind the scenes, and Kristi Pfeffer brought the copy to life with her art direction. Ya'll rock.

For all the first-names, no-names, and flat-out false names who have put your stamps on this work, thank you all.

If I've overlooked anyone, please forgive me. For all those who continue to bring and send me bottles and jars of handtooled liquor, bless your hearts. I hope I've been able to give you something in return. Now, I'm off for a few gallons of Gatorade, a plate of huevos, and some ibuprofen…

Matthew Rowley is a former museum curator and board member of the Southern Foodways Alliance. He lives in San Diego, California, and is not now, nor has he ever been, a revenuer. His website is www.matthew-rowley.com

FOR MY FAMILY:

Joe and Nancy, the kids, and Tim

Credits

Photo on back cover from the North Carolina Collection, University of North Carolina Library at Chapel Hill, Kearing Collection.

Page 2, top, courtesy of Greensboro Historical Museum, Greensboro, NC.

Page 2, bottom, from the Earl Palmer Photograph Collection (ep311), Digital Library and Archives, University Libraries, Virginia Polytechnic Institute and State University.

CHAPTER 1

Imagery

Page 10, engraving "Illicit Distillation of Liquors— Southern Mode of Making Whiskey," reproduced from the collections of the Library of Congress.

Page 14, reproduced from the collections of the Library of Congress.

Page 22, courtesy of Greensboro Historical Museum, Greensboro, NC.

Page 24, reproduced from the collections of the Library of Congress.

Lyrics

Page 10, *Mountain Dew* by Bascom Lamar Lunsford/Lulu Belle and Scott Wiseman © 1973 Sony/ ATV Songs LLC & Publisher(s) Unknown. All rights on behalf of Sony/ATV Songs LLC administered by Sony/ATV Music Publishing, 8 Music Sq. W., Nashville, TN 37203. All rights reserved. Used with permission.

Page 17, *White Lightning*. Words and music by J.P. Richardson. © 1959 Glad Music Co. Copyright renewed and assigned to Fort Knox Music Inc., Trio Music Company, and Glad Music Co. International copyright secured. All rights reserved. Used with permission.

Page 22, *The Jake Walk Blues* by Austin Allen and Lee Allen © 1931 by Peer International Corporation. Copyright renewed. International copyright secured. Used by permission. All rights reserved.

Page 25, *Okolehao*. Words and music by Ralph Rainger, Leo Robin, and Don Hartman © 1936 (Renewed 1964) by Famous Music Corporation. International copyright secured. All rights reserved.

Quotations

Page 9, Campbell, John C. *The Southern Highlander and His Homeland*. © 1921 Russell Sage Foundation, 112 East 64th Street, New York, NY 10021. Reprinted with permission.

Page 16, from *Good Spirits* by Gene Logsdon. © 1999 by Gene Logsdon. Used by permission of Chelsea Green Publishing Company, www.chelseagreen.com.

CHAPTER 2

Imagery

Page 27, *Nova Anglia, Novum Belgium, et Virginia* hand-colored map, 1639, from the Lionel Pincus and Princess Firyal Map Division, The New York Public Library, Astor, Lenox, and Tilden Foundations.

Page 29, *Country Gauger's Vade Mecum*. Annenberg Rare Book & Manuscript Library, Van Pelt-Dietrich Library Center, University of Pennsylvania Library.

Page 30, reproduced from the collections of the Library of Congress.

Page 31, *Harpers Monthly*, December 1867, from the Annenberg Rare Book & Manuscript Library, Van Pelt-Dietrich Library Center, University of Pennsylvania Library.

Page 32, courtesy of the Florida Department of State, Division of Library and Information Services.

Page 33, top right, cover of *Harper's Weekly*, November 2, 1878, reproduced from the collections of the Library of Congress.

Page 33, bottom left, from *After the Moonshiners: A Book of Thrilling, Yet Truthful Narratives*, 1881.

Page 34, © Bettmann/CORBIS.

Page 35, reproduced with permission of the West Virginia State Police Department.

Page 36, both courtesy of the Florida Department of State, Division of Library and Information Services.

Page 37, from the John T. Shepherd Papers (217), reprinted with permission of Appalachian State University Special Collections.
Page 38, reproduced from the collections of the Library of Congress.
Page 39, © CORBIS.
Page 41, both courtesy of the Florida Department of State, Division of Library and Information Services.
Page 42, courtesy of the Florida Department of State, Division of Library and Information Services.

Lyrics

Page 33, *Revenooer Man* by Johnny Paycheck © 1959 (Renewed) Sony/ATV Songs LLC. All rights administered by Sony/ATV Music Publishing, 8 Music Sq. W., Nashville, TN 37203. All rights reserved. Used with permission.
Page 43, *The Ballad of Thunder Road* by Robert Mitchum, Don Raye © 1958 by MCA Music Publishing. All rights administered by Universal Music Corp./ASCAP. Used with permission. All rights reserved.

Quotations

Page 40, excerpted from "Saloon Culture" from *Low Life* by Luc Sante. © 1991 by Luc Sante. Reprinted by permission of Farrar, Straus and Giroux, LLC.

CHAPTER 3

Imagery

Page 45, reproduced from the collections of the Library of Congress.
Page 46, reproduced from the collections of the Library of Congress.
Page 48, from the Earl Palmer Photograph Collection (ep311), Digital Library and Archives, University Libraries, Virginia Polytechnic Institute and State University.
Page 52, from the North Carolina Collection, University of North Carolina Library at Chapel Hill, Kearing Collection.

Quotations

Page 47, © 1975, Asheville, NC *Citizen-Times*/ www.citizentimes.com. Reprinted with permission.
Page 48, from *The Foxfire Book* by Eliot Wigginton, published by Doubleday and Random House, Inc. Reprinted with permission.
Page 49, From *Kentucky Moonshine* by David Maurer © 1979. Reprinted with permission of The University Press of Kentucky, www.kentuckypress.com.

CHAPTER 4

Quotations

Page 59, © 1989, Asheville, NC *Citizen-Times*/ www.citizentimes.com. Reprinted with permission.
Page 76, from *North Carolina Folklore Journal* article by Cratis Williams © 1967. Reprinted with permission.

CHAPTER 5

Imagery

Page 79, from the collection of the U.S. National Archives and Records Administration.
Page 80, from the Earl Palmer Photograph Collection (ep560), Digital Library and Archives, University Libraries, Virginia Polytechnic Institute and State University.
Page 82, © CORBIS.

CHAPTER 6

Imagery

Page 115, courtesy of Greensboro Historical Museum, Greensboro, NC.
Page 119, *The Art of Cookery Made Plain and Easy*, by Hannah Glasse, collection of Chef Fritz Blank.

Lyrics

Page 109, lyrics from *Brown-Eyed Woman* by Robert Hunter, copyright Ice Nine Publishing Company. Used with permission.

Quotations

Page 115, from *All Over But the Shoutin'* by Rick Bragg, published by Random House, Inc. Reprinted with permission.

Page 125, from *Pennsylvania Folklife* (Fall XXVI) article by Mac E. Barrick © Ursinus College. Reprinted with permission.

CHAPTER 7

Imagery

Page 151, *The Experienced English House-Keeper*, by Elizabeth Raffald, collection of Chef Fritz Blank.

Lyrics

Page 130, *Alligator Wine*, words and music by Jerry Leiber and Mike Stoller © 1958 (renewed) Jerry Leiber Music and Mike Stoller Music. All rights reserved.

Page 137, *Mountain Dew* by Bascom Lamar Lunsford/Lulu Belle and Scott Wiseman © 1973 Sony/ATV Songs LLC & Publisher(s) Unknown. All rights on behalf of Sony/ATV Songs LLC administered by Sony/ATV Music Publishing, 8 Music Sq. W., Nashville, TN 37203. All rights reserved. Used with permission.

Quotations

Page 145, from *Columbus Dispatch* article by Doral Chenoweth © 1992. Reprinted with permission.

Page 151, from *Kentucky Folklore Record* article by Ruby Allen © 1975. Reprinted with permission of The University Press of Kentucky, www.kentuckypress.com.

Index